THE GROTESQUE IN ENGLISH LITERATURE

Oxford University Press, Amen House, London E.C.4

GLASGOW   NEW YORK   TORONTO   MELBOURNE   WELLINGTON
BOMBAY   CALCUTTA   MADRAS   KARACHI   LAHORE   DACCA
CAPE TOWN   SALISBURY   NAIROBI   IBADAN
KUALA LUMPUR   HONG KONG

THE GROTESQUE IN ENGLISH LITERATURE

Arthur Clayborough

CLARENDON PRESS · OXFORD

1965

PRINTED IN GREAT BRITAIN BY

W. & J. Mackay & Co. Ltd., Chatham, Kent

TO MY MOTHER
EDITH CLAYBOROUGH

PREFACE

In the following work I have attempted to show that a significant relationship can be traced between the various types of grotesque art by considering such art as a product of the interaction of two contrasting sides of human nature; the practical, rational side, and the sense of the eternal; and also to show that such an approach to grotesque art helps to throw light on the work of writers as different as Swift, Coleridge, and Dickens.

I should like to express my gratitude to Professor A. N. Jeffares for his advice and help throughout the writing of this work; to Mr. D. W. Jefferson and Mr. P. Mann for their constructive criticism of the chapters on Swift and Coleridge; to Miss Audrey C. Stead for her generous assistance; and to the Clarendon Press for undertaking the publication.

CONTENTS

ARGUMENT

I

THE WORD 'GROTESQUE'

1. A definition of the word 'grotesque' in its substantival and adjectival uses, of the various cognate forms (grotesquerie, grotesquely, &c.), and of the phrase 'the grotesque', is a natural preliminary feature of the following examination, and this chapter will therefore be devoted to a history of the word and an attempt to establish a generally acceptable definition.

The senses in which a word is employed in various contexts, often a matter of conjecture and sometimes of controversy, especially in the case of a critical term, give us at best only random indications of the word's full symbolic value for a particular writer or generation. One might perhaps compare such examples of usage as those which follow with the visible parts of an iceberg or of a coral island (the latter image suggests the gradual accretion of meaning better), from which certain inferences can be drawn about the part which remains invisible, i.e. the residual nuances of the word for the individual or his generation which, though unrecorded or undiscovered, nevertheless exert an influence upon semantic change. In the nature of things, the following analysis cannot be an exhaustive one.

2. Of the various kinds of semantic development, the development of the word grotesque has been primarily an example of association or transference in its substantival uses, but the adjective has undergone considerable generalization. The noun has also acquired a more general sense, especially the substantival form 'the grotesque', deriving from the adjective.

It is generally accepted that the word grotesque originated as a term descriptive of the fanciful murals, in which human and animal motifs were combined with foliage and floral decoration,[1] found in the chambers ('grotte') of Roman buildings excavated about 1500,[2] particularly in the Domus Aurea of Nero.[3]

---

[1] See note i, p. 19.

[2] This etymology appears first in H. Victor's *Trésor des trois langues fr. it. et esp.* (1606). cf. P. Knaak, *Über den Gebrauch des Wortes 'grotesque'* (Griefswald, 1913), p. 10, also Aglionby, *Painting Illustr.* (1686) (see Appendix).

[3] *Enciclopedia Italiana* (1933), Grottesche; see note ii, p. 20.

The original forms are thus Italian (*la grottesca, grottesco* (occasionally with initial c and/or single t), &c.), forms deriving from *grotta* (ultimately from Gr. κρύπτη, a vault (cf. Gr. κρύπτειν, to hide)).[1]

The word first occurs in French in the form *crotesque* (*crottesque*, &c.) by assimilation to O. Fr. *crote* (from It. *grotta*).[2] The form with a single t occurs already in French as early as 1532, and continues as the prevailing form, in combination with initial c, until the late seventeenth century (Molière and his contemporaries employ the form *crotesque*), when it is displaced by the form *grotesque*, modelled on the original Italian forms, which is occasionally found before 1600. Both forms, *crotesque* and *grotesque*, are given in Duez's French-Italian Dictionary (1660), but Pomey (1676) gives only the latter form, and later dictionaries follow his example.[3] The form *grotesque* occurs first in English about 1640, superseding earlier forms derived from the French (the *O.E.D.*[4] gives *crotescque* as the first recorded English form (1561)) or directly from the Italian (*crotesco, grotesco* (-a) &c.). It thus became the prevailing form in English before it became the standard French form.

SEMANTIC DEVELOPMENT

3. The 'grotesque' murals brought to light by the excavation of the Domus Aurea of Nero, the Palace of Titus, &c., quickly became an object of imitation. In 1502 the artist Pinturicchio was instructed by Cardinal Todeschini Piccolomini to decorate the ceiling-vaults of the library of the Cathedral of Siena in the style 'che oggi chiamano grottesche'.[5] Raphael's decorations in the Vatican—comparatively subdued examples of the new fashion—date from 1515; Luca Signorelli's decoration of Orvieto Cathedral (1499–1504) is of a much more extravagant nature.

During the sixteenth century the new style of ornamentation became immensely popular in Europe, appearing in murals, architec-

---

[1] *grotta* probably derives from L. Latin *crupta* (*grupta*) (cf. 'crypt'). cf. *Encyclop. Brit.*, 11th ed., 1910; also Knaak, op. cit., p. 10 (*crypticus).
[2] cf. *O.E.D.* (see Appendix).
[3] cf. Knaak, op. cit., p. 9.
[4] See Appendix.
[5] cf. W. Kayser, *Das Groteske; seine Gestaltung in Malerei und Dichtung*; Gerhard Stalling Verlag, Oldenburg (Olb) und Hamburg Gesamtherstellung (1957), ch. 1, for an account of the more important artists and 'grotesque' styles in the sixteenth century. Still earlier evidence of 'grotesque' influence may be found, e.g. the frieze in Carlo Crivelli's 'Annunciation' (1486) in the National Gallery. For earlier examples of grotesque art, cf. Ruskin's *The Stones of Venice* (1851–3).

ture, engravings, book-decoration, &c., and ramifying into several distinctive styles. The Arabesque and Moorish styles of decoration were associated with the grotesque style by some sixteenth-century writers on art.[1]

Without settled patterns or positive conventions, the new style of decoration is characterized by its rejection of the 'natural conditions of organisation'[2] and the combining of heterogeneous forms. Natural physical wholes are disintegrated and the parts fantastically redistributed to suit the taste of the artist. Cotgrave's *A Dictionnairie of the French and English Tongues* (London, 1611) describes 'grotesques' as 'Pictures wherein (as please the Painter) all kinds of odde things are represented without anie peculiar sence, or meaning, but only to feed the eye'.[3]

This imitation of the murals excavated in Rome and other parts of Italy brings about the first semantic change in the word grotesque which is extended to describe the imitations as well as the antique originals. It is in this extended sense (Sense 2) of 'fanciful decoration' that the word is first recorded in English:

(1561) Item, twa paintit broddis the ane of the muses and the uther of crotescque or conceptis. (*Inv. R. Wardrobe* (1815), 130.) (*O.E.D.*)

Until late in the seventeenth century, the recorded uses of the word in English are references to the style of art. Sir Thomas Browne observes that 'there are no Grotesques in nature'.[4] In France, however, the application of the word to literature and even to people is already fairly common in the early seventeenth century. Rabelais employs the phrase 'Couillon crotesque' in *Gargantua et Pantagruel* (1535).[5]

In his essay 'On Friendship', Montaigne compares himself to a painter in a passage which shows explicitly how the word grotesque comes to be applied to literature:

Considerant la conduite de la besongne d'un peintre que j'ay, il m'a pris envie de l'ensuivre il choisit le plus noble endroit et milieu de chaque paroy pour y loger un tableau élabouré de toute sa suffisance; et le vuide tout au tour, il le remplit de crotesques, qui sont peintures fantasques n'ayant grace qu'en la variété et estrangeté. Que sont-ce icy aussi à la

---

[1] cf. Kayser, op. cit., pp. 22–23.

[2] cf. G. Santayana, *The Sense of Beauty* (London, 1896); Analysis of grotesque art, pp. 256–8 (see pp. 16–17).

[3] It is interesting to note that Cotgrave's dictionary glosses 'grotesque' as 'A grot, caue, denne, cauerne, hole (under the ground)'.

[4] cf. *Religio Medici*, I. §15 (see Appendix).

[5] cf. Knaak, op. cit., p. 11.

verité, que crotesques et corps monstrueux, rappiecez de divers membres, sans certaine figure, n'ayants ordre, suite, ny proportion que fortuite? (*Essais*, 1580).[1]

Malherbe employs the word in the sense of 'absurdities' or 'monstrosities' in the following passage:

Pour ce qui est de l'histoire, je l'ai suivie exactement . . . mais je n'ais pas voulu faire les grotesques qu'il est impossible d'éviter quand on se restreint dans la servitude de traduire de mot à mot. (*Lettres à Peiresc*, 10. VIII.) (1615)[2]

In *Les Jeux de l'Inconnu* (1630), ascribed to the Comte de Cramail, occurs the phrase 'Un courtisan crotesque'.[3]

The French dictionaries of the late seventeenth century clearly show how wide the application of the word has become, especially in its adjectival form. Richelet's *Dictionnaire français* (Amsterdam, 1680) contains the following interpretation:

Grotesque adj. Plaisant, qui a quelque chose de plaisamment ridicule. Homme grotesque. Fille grotesque. Air grotesque. Visage grotesque. Action grotesque.

Richelet adds a cautionary note to the effect that the figurative use of the word is current only in 'le stile le plus simple, comme dans les vaudevilles, les rondeaux, les épigrammes, et les ouvrages comiques',[4] but in 1694 the wider application of the adjective receives the sanction of the Academy. The *Dictionnaire de l'Académy françoise* describes the word as follows:

Il signifie fig. Ridicule, bizarre, extravagant. Un habit grotesque, ce discours est bien grotesque, mine grotesque.—Grotesquement. adv. D'une manière ridicule et extravagante. Vestu grotesquement, danser grotesquement.—Bizarre, fantasque, extravagant, capricieux.[5]

This definition is repeated in subsequent editions of the *Dictionnaire de l'Académy* during the eighteenth century (1718, 1740, 1742).

[1] cf. Dryden, *Paral. Poet and Paint*, 26. 'A farce is that in poetry which grotesque is in a picture; the persons and actions of a farce are all unnatural, and the manners false—that is, inconsisting with the manners of mankind. Grotesque painting is the just resemblance of this.'
[2] and [3] cf. Knaak, op. cit., sect. 1 for these and many other examples of French usage, chiefly derived from Livet's *Lexique de la langue de Molière* (Paris, 1896), vol. 2, pp. 508 ff., and Littré, *Dictionnaire de la langue française* (Paris, 1863).
[4] cf. Knaak, op. cit., pp. 14, 15.
[5] ibid.

There is little evidence of the use of the adjective in this wider sense of 'bizarre, extravagant, fantastic, ridiculous' in English before the Restoration, though the *O.E.D.* supplies one example (1653):

They . . . ought to bee accounted one of those Grotesco Maximes . . . that doe so disfigure and misguide the life of man. (J. Hall, *Paradoxes*, 45.)

The *O.E.D.* also supplies a single example, prior to the Restoration, of the figurative use of the noun:

(1644–7) A strange Grottesco this, the Church and States. (Cleveland, *Char. Lond. Diurn.*, 28.)

Milton's use of the word (*Paradise Lost*, IV. 136 (1667)):

> . . . a steep wilderness, whose hairie sides
> With thicket overgrow, grottesque and wilde,
> Access deni'd;

suggests that the poet had in mind the fantastic foliage of 'grotesque' decorations.[1] His spelling (-tt-) is Italianate.

As a simple *terminus technicus*, the word grotesque has no emotional coloration, though it may appear in approbatory or disapprobatory contexts, e.g.

(1603) Antike Boscage or Crotesko[2] works, which are fantastical pictures, having no grace, but in the variety and strangenes of them. (Florio's transl. of Montaigne, I. XXVII. 89.)
(1645) The foliage and grotesque about some of the compartments are admirable. (Evelyn, *Mem.* (1857), I. 143.)
(1646) As for Sea-horses . . . they are but Crotesco delineations. (Sir T. Browne, *Pseud. Ep.*, III. XXIV. 170.)

The pejorative tone of the last of these passages derives, of course, from the word *but*. Burke, too, in the following passage, is obliged to supply extraneous pejoratives:

(1756) All the designs I have chanced to meet of the temptations of St. Anthony were rather a sort of odd, wild grotesques, than anything capable of producing a serious passion.

---

[1] The *O.E.D.* interprets Milton's use of the word in the sense of 'romantic, picturesquely irregular'. (cf. Dodsley (1764): The more pleasing parts of this grotesque and hilly country (see App.). In such references to landscape, the stronger pejorative nuances of the word—'unnatural', 'abnormal', etc.—are inapplicable.
[2] So also ed. 1613; ed. 1632 has Grotesko (*O.E.D.* note). cf. pp. 3, 4 (French forms).

When the word is applied to other things than decorative art, however, or deliberate caricature, it becomes possible to use it to express disapproval. Dryden's figurative use of the word in 'The Hind and the Panther' (III. 1044) (1687), is an interesting example:

> An hideous figure of their foes they drew,
> Nor lines, nor lookes, nor shades, nor colours true;
> And this grotesque design expos'd to public view.

The 'grotesque design' stands condemned as a perversion of truth—here, of religious truth—where truth matters.

The word grotesque thus comes to be applied in a more general fashion in English during the Age of Reason—and of Neo-Classicism—when the characteristics of the grotesque style of art—extravagance, fantasy, individual taste, and the rejection of 'the natural conditions of organization'—are the object of ridicule and disapproval. The more general sense (Sense 3) which it has developed by the early eighteenth century is therefore that of 'ridiculous, distorted, unnatural' (adj.); 'an absurdity, a distortion of nature' (noun). Side by side with the simple descriptive application of the word grotesque in its accepted technical sense (or senses, for the type of art to which it is applied, in eighteenth-century use, is not exclusively decorative; Hogarth, for example, in speaking of 'that intermediate species of subject which may be placed between the sublime and the grotesque'[1] clearly has caricature in mind) occur passages like Steele's 'This indeed is Ambition in Grotesque',[2] which employ the word to castigate the socially reprehensible, the excessive, the preposterous. Lady Mary Wortley Montagu's remark: 'These grotesque daubers give me a still higher esteem of . . . natural charms' (Letter to Lady Rich, 10 Oct. 1718) makes a neatly ambiguous use of both the technical and the extended senses of the word.[3]

This third, pejorative, sense of the word grotesque is, of course,

---

[1] 'I therefore turned my thoughts to a still more novel mode, viz., painting and engraving modern moral subjects, a field not broken up in any country and any age. The reasons which induced me to adopt this mode of designing were, that I thought both writers and painters had, in the historical style, totally overlooked that intermediate species of subject which may be placed between the sublime and the grotesque.' (MS publ. posthumously in Ireland's *Hogarth Illustrated* (cf. Goldwater and Treves: *Artists on Art* (Kegan Paul, London, 1947).

[2] cf. *The Tatler*, No. 202. §2 (1710).

[3] This remark may be contrasted with a passage from Shaftesbury: "'Tis the perfection of certain grotesque-painters, to keep as far from nature as possible' (*Characters* (1737), III. 6). Note the importance of the hyphen.

not only extant in such familiar phrases as 'a grotesque blunder', 'a grotesque idea', and so on, but in ordinary colloquial English it is by far the most usual sense of the word, at least in the case of the adjective. It is unnecessary to multiply instances,[1] but one or two examples from the nineteenth century may be given:

(1849) These peculiarities appeared far more grotesque in a faction which ruled a great empire. (Macaulay, *History of Eng.*, II. I. 163.)

(1870) The grotesque doctrine that it is good for trade (R. W. Dale, *Week-day Sermons*, XII. 246.)

(1871) (Noun.) Some men of true genius seem only to make sure of fame by straining themselves into grotesques. (Morley, *Voltaire*, III (1872). 120.)

In considering the next stage in the semantic development of the word, we must return to the use of both noun and adjective in a simple descriptive sense. When it is used with reference to an *accepted* genre the word grotesque has no intrinsically pejorative force, though it may, of course, occur in disapprobatory contexts. Pope uses the word—in its technical sense—as part of a highly 'poetical' description, in retelling the story of the town mouse and the country mouse:

> Behold the place, where if a Poet
> Shin'd in Description, he might show it;
> Tell how the Moon-beam trembling falls,
> And tips with Silver all the walls;
> Palladian walls, Venetian doors,
> Grotesco roofs and Stucco floors:
>   (*Hor. Sat.*, II. VI. 192 (1744).)

As long as they remain in their allotted place, the fantastic and the unnatural need not be condemned and may even be commended:

1715 The Chambers . . . are all . . . painted in grotesque of a very fine Invention. (Leoni, *Palladio's Archit.* (1742), I. 59.)

As Shaftesbury observes, the very excellence of grotesque art, a generally accepted style of decoration, lies in its rejection of nature.

The next stage in the semantic development of the word grotesque is the extension of the word to other things than decorative art as a purely descriptive term. We may conveniently distinguish two aspects of such usage: (*a*) Application to natural objects, and (*b*) Application to other forms of art, particularly to literature.

[1] See Appendix, especially Section B3.

(*a*) The word grotesque, with its artistic connotation of 'unnatural', would seem at first sight to be by definition inapplicable to natural phenomena. Sir Thomas Browne states flatly, 'There are no Grotesques in nature'. The pejorative extension of the word is made with a more limited idea of the natural in mind than Sir Thomas Browne's, just as we speak of the 'unnatural' behaviour of Lear's daughters, implying that though daughters may behave in such a fashion they ought not to do so. In references to dress, manners, and so on, as 'grotesque', the word is used hyperbolically to reprove that which is not consonant with the orthodox ideas of what is right and proper.

(1747) A woman with her head peeping out of a sack, could hardly . . . make a more Grotesque figure. (*Gentl. Mag.*, 347.)

(1862) Where so much is beautiful, the occasional anomalies and grotesqueries[1] of taste fail to offend you. (B. Taylor, *Home and Abr.*, Ser. II. II. 339.)

It is, of course, possible to use the word to describe the physically disagreeable:

(1826) His face, with all its grotesqueness,[1] was infinitely pleasanter to look at than his figure. (Miss Mitford, *Village*, Ser. II (1863). 329.)

In the three passages above the word grotesque and its cognate forms denote an objectionable[2] strangeness. In the third passage, however, there is no *moral* disapproval. The word 'unnatural' might be employed (hyperbolically) in interpreting the sense of 'grotesqueness', but not the word 'ridiculous'.

In references to landscape, the word grotesque may express distaste, but landscape can scarcely be described as unnatural, however hyperbolically, or as ridiculous. We have already remarked the sense in which the *O.E.D.* glosses the word in such references: 'Romantic,

---

[1] The fact that cognate forms are employed in these passages does not affect the point in question.

[2] One may, like Elizabeth Bennet, enjoy the strangeness: 'Follies and nonsense, whims and inconsistencies *do* divert me, I own, and I laugh at them whenever I can.' (*Pride and Pr.*, ch. XI.) (cf. Richelet, op. cit. (see p. 6), 'Grotesque adj. Plaisant, qui a quelque chose de plaisamment ridicule'.) Here we are concerned with the *unintentionally ridiculous*. The laughter it arouses invariably implies reproof; Elizabeth 'never ridicules what is wise or good'. The unintentionally odd or eccentric (it is of great importance to note that ideas of socially 'correct' behaviour grow more liberal throughout the eighteenth century) and the deliberately ridiculous or odd are discussed below (see pp. 10 ff. and Ch. 8, pp. 216 ff.).

picturesquely irregular',[1] and while this interpretation of the word may be a little too appreciatory for such a context as:

(*c.* 1764) The more pleasing parts of this grotesque and hilly country (R. Dodsley, *Leasowes* in *Shenstone's Wks.*, II (1777). 296)

the pejorative force is either very weak or altogether lacking. In such references to natural objects it is only rarely that one can rule out the possibility of a pejorative nuance altogether.[2] It may, for example, be present in the passage above. Similarly, it may be argued that in the companion passage from Milton (see note 1, p. 5, and Appendix) the word is used to emphasize the contrast between the displeasing tangle of vegetation outside the wall of Paradise and the pleasing order within. It is nevertheless clear that in both passages the word grotesque is primarily used in a descriptive sense (i.e. the 'technical' sense, necessarily somewhat modified when extended to natural objects), while the presence or absence of a pejorative nuance is debatable. The same may be said of the following passage:

(1728) Matters of so peregrine and grotesk a Nature as this [History] (Morgan, *Algiers*, I, Pref. 25).

Here 'grotesk' is best interpreted as meaning 'bizarre' or 'outlandish', words which suit well with 'peregrine' (i.e. 'foreign' or 'exotic').

(*b*) The chief way, however, in which the word grotesque acquires an extended descriptive sense without a pejorative tone is by association with other kinds of art than the decorative genre with which it is traditionally connected.

In French, the word grotesque was applied in the early seventeenth century (1620; Monet, *Le parallèle et le Dict. fr.-lat.*)[3] to the work of Jacques Callot (1592–1635), not a decorative painter, but a caricaturist whose pictures have much in common with those of Goya. There are many later references to his work as grotesque. In the eighteenth century Diderot, speaking of the Commedia dell'Arte, describes it as 'Farce excellente . . . Elle suppose une gaieté originale;

---

[1] See note 1, p. 5, and Appendix.
[2] Mention may be made here of the typographical use of the word grotesque: (1875) Southward, *Dict. Typogr.*, Grotesque, the name of a peculiar fancy jobbing type (cf. also: L. Scarfe, *Alphabets* (Batsford, London, 1954) (Grotesque No. 9, &c.)). In this technical sense of a square-cut letter without serifs (i.e. an 'unusual' letter) the word grotesque is purely descriptive.
[3] cf. Knaak, op. cit., p. 13.

les caractères en sont comme les grotesques de Calot, où les princi-
paux de la figure humaine sont conservés.'[1]

The extension of the word to caricature in English in the eighteenth century has already been remarked (see p. 9). In references to
deliberately comic art, of course, the word grotesque is purely descriptive. It is the nature of caricature to be grotesque, as it is also
the nature of farce like the Commedia dell' Arte, or burlesque, like
'Mac Flecknoe' or the 'Dunciad'; one cannot rebuke a clown by
describing his antics as ridiculous. There is obvious approval in the
use of the word grotesque in the following passages:

(1822) Found there Beresford . . . a grotesque-minded person, very
amusing. (Moore, *Mem.* (1853), III. 347.)

(1864) The great grotesque himself will be in the grave. (Sala in *Daily
Tel.*, Nov. 18.)

Burlesque, the literary equivalent of caricature in visual art, employing the grotesque for purposes of ridicule, provided the writers of
the Neoclassical period with a socially acceptable outlet for fantasy.
Like caricature, however, burlesque was considered to be a low form
of art. Steele contrasts the *grotesque* and the *sublime* styles in his
remark:

(1709) You have employed your self more in Grotesque figures than in
Beauties. (*Tatler*, No. 118. §6.)

Burke, too, in a passage already quoted (see p. 5) contrasts 'odd, wild
grotesques' in visual art (he uses the word in a technical, but slightly
extended sense) with 'anything capable of producing a serious passion'.

In flat opposition to both Steele and Burke, as also to Montaigne's
description of grotesque painting as 'n'ayant grace qu' en la variété et
estrangété' (see p. 3), is Horace Walpole's approval of the grotesque
style of art:

(1762–71) Don Julio Clovio, the celebrated limner, whose neatness and
taste in grotesque were exquisite. (*Vertue's Anecd. Paint.* (1786), I. 260.)

This view of grotesque design as a genre capable of revealing exquisite taste is what we should naturally have expected of the author
of *The Castle of Otranto*. He employs the adjective, significantly, in
referring to Gothic architecture:

(1762–5) Those Grotesque monsters . . . with which the spouts . . . of
ancient buildings are decorated. (*Vertue's Anecd. Paint.* (ed. 2), I. 118.)

[1] cf. Kayser, op. cit.

and makes use of the cognate adverb in a semi-technical sense in a 'Gothic' context:

(1740) The wearied arms grotesquely deck the wall. (*Ep. Florence*, 285, in Dodsley, *Coll. Poems*. (1755), III. 80.)

In the last two passages Walpole is obviously thinking of grotesque decoration (the adjective Grotesque is written with a capital letter to avoid ambiguity). The importance of these passages lies in the association of the word grotesque with the Gothic and its 'emancipatory' atmosphere. Together with Walpole's view of grotesque decoration as a style capable of exhibiting exquisite taste, this association points to an increasingly serious conception of grotesque art:

(1856) A fine grotesque is the expression, in a moment, by a series of symbols thrown together in bold and fearless connection, of truths which it would have taken a long time to express in any verbal way. (Ruskin, *Mod. Paint.*, III. IV. VIII. §4.)

In the Romantic period the word grotesque, like the word Gothic, is applied to literature. In Romantic literature its chief senses are 'highly fanciful', 'fantastic', and 'exceedingly strange', without a pejorative coloration.

(1809) He preferred the stately, or rather the grotesque in writing. (Malkin, *Gil Blas*, XI. V (Rtldg.). 404.)
(1820) Our literature . . . is Gothic and grotesque. (Hazlitt, *Lect. Dram. Lit.*, 36.)

By way of extension to phenomena which cannot conceivably be described as 'unnatural' or 'ridiculous', and its application to literature at a time when the extraordinary and the fantastic, far from being ridiculed, are considered to be highly desirable features of serious literature, the word comes to be used, then, in the nineteenth century, descriptively, without a depreciatory nuance, as in Edgar Allan Poe's title: *Tales of the Grotesque and Arabesque* (1840).

It is this fourth type of usage with which we shall be especially concerned in the following chapters. Before attempting a short definition of the word in its present critical sense, it will be necessary to distinguish between what may conveniently be termed the substantival (or primary) and the attributive (or secondary) qualities of the word.

Clearly, in references to other things than the specific style of decoration with which it is etymologically associated, or styles of art (painting, literature, &c.) which are considered to correspond to it (i.e. as other than a *terminus technicus*), the word grotesque, both as noun and adjective, is used to describe that which is not congruous with ordinary experience. It derives from its association with a form of art characterized by its rejection of natural order not merely the sense of 'strange' but that of 'abidingly strange'. The use of the word as a pejorative[1] is, of course, an indication of the attitude of the user which does not affect the fundamental sense.

The semantic development of the phrase 'the grotesque'[2] clearly shows the important change which takes place with the extension of the word grotesque beyond the sphere of decorative art.

Grotesque decoration was considered to be the antithesis of reality, being related to the natural world solely by contrast.[3] In its application to such work as the illustrations of Jacques Callot the word 'grotesque' implied that Callot's figures were a distortion of physical reality.

Already, however, in Hogarth's reference to 'that intermediate species of subject which may be placed between the sublime and the grotesque' (see note 1, p. 6) a more positive conception of the relation between grotesque art and real life, as a source of inspiration, is indicated. As there are sublime subjects, for Hogarth, worthy of sublime treatment, so too there are grotesque subjects which require grotesque treatment (i.e. caricature).

The two connected senses of the phrase 'the grotesque' (as of 'the sublime') implied in the above passage—that of a style of art and that of a subject suited to that style—occur both separately and together in later contexts. In the following passages the phrase 'the grotesque' refers simply to artistic style:

(1809) He preferred the stately, or rather the grotesque in writing. (Malkin, *Gil Blas*, XI. V (Rtldg.). 404.)

(1827) In fact, the grotesque in his compositions partly resembles the arabesque in painting, in which is introduced the most strange and complicated monsters, resembling centaurs, griffins, sphinxes, chimeras, rocs, and all other creatures of romantic imagination, dazzling the beholder as it were by the unbounded fertility of the author's imagination, and sating

---

[1] cf. Johnson's definition of the word (*Dictionary*, 1755): 'Distorted of figure; unnatural; wildly formed.'

[2] This abstract substantive derives from the adjective, which naturally lends itself more readily to semantic development than the corresponding noun.

[3] Ruskin describes the grotesque style of ornamentation as 'an elaborate and luscious form of nonsense' (cf. *The Stones of Venice*, III. III. §XXXIX).

it by the rich contrast of all the varieties of shape and colouring, while there is in reality nothing to satisfy the understanding or inform the judgment. (Scott, The Novels of E. T. Hoffmann; *For. Rev.*, 1827.)

(1888) The grotesque is a branch of the fantastic. (*Pall Mall G.*, Apr. 4. 11/1.)

In these passages there is no suggestion that grotesque art derives its inspiration from a grotesque reality; indeed, the whole tenour of the passage from Scott is contrary to such a supposition.

Poe's title, *Tales of the Grotesque and Arabesque*, which seemingly objectifies the grotesque, must be considered in relation to his explanation in the preface that the adjectives grotesque and arabesque are intended to describe the prevailing tone of the stories which follow. The phrase 'the Grotesque', in Poe's title, is therefore primarily associated with literary style.

In nineteenth-century French literature the phrase 'the grotesque' acquires revolutionary overtones; it is associated with artistic freedom and the overthrow of cramping conventions. It is frequently used both of real life and of artistic style:

(1827) Tout dans la création n'est pas humainement beau—le laid y existe à côté du beau, le difforme près du gracieux, le grotesque au revers du sublime, le mal avec le bien, l'ombre avec la lumière. (Hugo, *La Préface de Cromwell*, p. 8.)

(1853) Le burlesque ou, si vous aimez mieux, le grotesque at toujours existé dans l'art et dans la nature. (Gautier, *Les Grotesques*, p. 353.)

A detailed consideration of nineteenth-century French theories of the grotesque is scarcely to our purpose here.[1] It is, however, important to note that these theories were developed on the basis of a conviction that the grotesque in art corresponded to an objective reality.

Ruskin does not recognize the existence of a grotesque element in nature. His famous distinction between the 'true' and the 'false or ignoble' grotesque[2] is based on the psychology of the artist. 'The workman of the ignoble grotesque can feel and understand nothing, and mocks at all things with the laughter of the idiot and the cretin.'[3] For the style of decoration 'which first developed itself among the enervated Romans'[4] he has nothing but disdain. The 'true' grotesque

[1] See pp. 45 ff.
[2] cf. *The Stones of Venice* (1851–3), III. III (Grotesque Renaissance).
[3] ibid., §XLV.
[4] ibid., §XXXIX.

is a distortion of nature caused by emotion, the spirit of play or fear, but not a rejection of it:

It is not as the creating, but as the *seeing* man, that we are here contemplating the master of the true grotesques. It is because the dreadfulness of the universe around him weighs upon his heart, that his work is wild; and therefore through the whole of it we shall find the evidence of deep insight into nature. His beasts and birds, however monstrous, will have profound relations with the true. He may be an ignorant man, and little acquainted with the laws of nature; he is certainly a busy man, and has not much time to watch nature; but he never saw a serpent cross his path, nor a bird flit across the sky, nor a lizard bask upon a stone, without learning so much of the sublimity and inner nature of each as will not suffer him henceforth to conceive them coldly. He may not be able to carve plumes or scales well; but his creatures will bite and fly, for all that. The ignoble workman is the very reverse of this. He never felt, never looked at nature; [&c.][1]

In spite of the fact that Ruskin understands the phrase 'the grotesque' as applicable exclusively to art, and though he makes it plain that in his opinion the grotesque, at best, has no place in 'the higher walks of art',[2] the overall effect of his analysis of the grotesque is to establish it as a respectable artistic genre, associated in literature with such names as Dante, Spenser, and Bunyan,[3] and to connect that genre with nature in a positive way.

It must be remarked here that in Romantic usage, largely through its relationship with the 'Gothic'—in the widest sense of that term— the word grotesque develops a nuance already latent in Johnson's definition: 'Distorted of figure; unnatural; wildly formed'; the nuance of 'fearful, terrible'. It is with this connotation, which immeasurably enriches the emotive force of the word grotesque—and in particular the suggestiveness of the phrase 'the grotesque'—from the Romantic period onwards, that Poe employs the phrase in his title: *Tales of the Grotesque and Arabesque.*[4] Ruskin insists that in the

---

[1] ibid., §XLVIII.
[2] ibid., III. III. §XXXIII.   [3] ibid., LIII.
[4] The cognate form *grotesquerie*, in particular, is often found in nineteenth-century usage in contexts suggestive of terror: 1877, grim grotesquerie (De Quincey); 1878, wild grotesquerie (Bayne); 1880, brutal grotesquerie (Howells), &c. (see Appendix: Grotesquerie). Poe's use of the word in a striking passage: 'a *grotesquerie* in horror absolutely alien from humanity' (cf. 'The Murders in the Rue Morgue' in *Tales of Mystery and Imagination*, Nelson ed. (1909), p. 198) may have had an influence on this association. Baudelaire, who translated Poe's story into French, employs the word *grotesquerie* elsewhere in association with the terrible. cf. Knaak, op. cit., p. 31.

grotesque (i.e. the 'true' grotesque) a ludicrous and a terrible element are almost invariably found together:

First, then, it seems to me that the grotesque is, in almost all cases, composed of two elements, one ludicrous, the other fearful; that, as one or the other of these elements prevails the grotesque falls into two branches, sportive grotesque, and terrible grotesque; but that we cannot legitimately consider it under these two aspects, because there are hardly any examples which do not in some degree combine both elements; there are few grotesques so utterly playful as to be overcast with no shade of fearfulness, and few so fearful as absolutely to exclude all idea of jest. (*The Stones of Venice*, III. III. §XXIII.)

The idea of a grotesque element in real life is one which many later English writers on the grotesque, unlike Ruskin, are prepared to accept. Walter Bagehot, indeed, accepts the reality of 'grotesque objects', but objects to their being introduced into poetry:

Mr. Browning possibly, and some of the worst of Mr. Browning's admirers certainly, will say that these grotesque objects exist in real life, and therefore they ought to be, at least may be, described in art. But, though pleasure is not the end of poetry, pleasing is a condition of poetry. An exceptional monstrosity of horrid ugliness cannot be made pleasing, except it be made to suggest—to recall—the perfection, the beauty, from which it is a deviation. Perhaps in extreme cases no art is equal to this; but then such self-imposed problems should not be worked by the artist; these out-of-the-way and detestable subjects should be let alone by him.[1]

John Addington Symonds employs the phrase 'the grotesque' at least once in a manner which resembles Hugo's use of it in the preface to his *Cromwell* (1827), where the two senses of a style of art and of an objective reality occur together:

Without ceasing to be Italian in his attention to harmony and grace, he [Tintoretto] far exceeded the masters of his nation in the power of suggesting what is weird, mysterious, upon the borderland of the grotesque.[2]

G. K. Chesterton, in his study of Browning, affirms the objective reality of the grotesque, and emphasizes its 'revolutionary' quality:

. . . the element of the grotesque in art, like the element of the grotesque in nature, means, in the main, energy, the energy which takes its own forms

---

[1] cf. *Wordsworth, Tennyson and Browning; or, Pure, Ornate and Grotesque Art in English Poetry* (1864), ed. Longmans Green and Co: *Literary Studies*, vol. II (1895), New ed., p. 374.

[2] cf. *A Venetian Medley*, IV (Selected Engl. Essays, ed. Peacock, O.U.P. (1943), p. 498).

and goes its own way. Browning's verse, in so far as it is grotesque, is not complex or artificial; it is natural and in the legitimate tradition of nature . . . Energy which disregards the standard of classical art is in nature as it is in Browning. (*Robert Browning* (Macm. 1903), pp. 149–50.)

The word grotesque, originating as a technical term designating a Late Roman style of decoration, thus becomes applicable to whatever is incongruous with the accepted norm, in life or art. In ordinary colloquial use it is commonly associated as a pejorative with the unintentionally ridiculous or the monstrous. In critical use, it may be employed to describe any style of art which deviates from conventional patterns. As has already been seen, the primary sense in both these extended uses of the word, whether as noun or adjective, is that of incongruity with the real or the normal.

This historical examination of the word may appropriately be concluded with Santayana's analysis of the grotesque in art. It will be noted that Santayana, in contrast to Gautier ('. . . le grotesque a toujours existé dans l'art et dans la nature'),[1] stresses the subjective nature of grotesqueness:

Something analogous to humour can appear in plastic forms, when we call it the grotesque. This is an interesting effect produced by such a transformation of an ideal type as exaggerates one of its elements or combines it with other types. The real excellence of this, like that of all fiction, consists in recreation; in the formation of a thing which nature has not, but might conceivably have offered. We call these inventions comic and grotesque when we are considering their divergence from the natural rather than their inward possibility. But the latter constitutes their real charm; and the more we study and develop them, the better we understand it. The incongruity with the conventional type then disappears, and what was impossible and ridiculous at first takes its place among recognised ideals. The centaur and the satyr are no longer grotesque; the type is accepted. And the grotesqueness of an individual has essentially the same nature. If we like the inward harmony, the characteristic balance of his features, we are able to disengage this individual from the class into which we were trying to force him; we can forget the expectation which he was going to disappoint. The ugliness then disappears, and only the reassertion of the old habit and demand can make us regard him as in any way extravagant.

What appears as grotesque may be intrinsically inferior or superior to the normal. That is a question of its abstract material and form. But until the new object impresses its form on our imagination, so that we can grasp its unity and proportion, it appears to us as a jumble and distortion

[1] See p. 13.

of other forms. If this confusion is absolute, the object is simply null; it does not exist aesthetically, except by virtue of materials. But if the confusion is not absolute, and we have an inkling of the unity and character in the midst of the strangeness of the form, then we have the grotesque. It is the half-formed, the perplexed, and the suggestively monstrous.

The analogy to the comic is very close, as we can readily conceive that it should be. In the comic we have this same juxtaposition of a new and an old idea, and if the new is not futile and really inconceivable, it may in time establish itself in the mind, and cease to be ludicrous. Good wit is novel truth, as the good grotesque is novel beauty. But there are natural conditions of organisation, and we must not mistake every mutilation for the creation of a new form. (*The Sense of Beauty* (London, 1896), pp. 256–8.)

Santayana's cautious attitude towards aesthetic innovations, his depreciatory use of the adjective grotesque, and his equation of grotesqueness with ugliness, have the effect of showing all the more clearly by contrast how firmly the phrase 'the grotesque' has become established by the end of the nineteenth century as a serious critical term. Santayana's succinct definition of the grotesque in art as 'the suggestively monstrous' could scarcely be bettered.

The principal senses of the word grotesque distinguished above may be summarized for convenience as follows:

(i) *Noun:* A Late Roman style of decoration; work in this style. (Obs.)

(ii) *Noun:* The imitation of this style from the late fifteenth century onwards; work in imitation of the above style.
Adjective: Belonging to this derived style.

(iii) *Noun:* An absurdity; a displeasing or ridiculous distortion of nature.
Adjective: Ridiculous, distorted; unusually ugly.

(iv) *Noun:* (A) A distortion of nature, especially in art.
(B) (The grotesque).
(*a*) The ludicrous and/or terrible element in life; in general, the persistently strange and incongruous.
(*b*) A style of art associated with the ludicrous and/or terrible; art of which the form or content is incongruous with accepted ideas of the normal or real.
Adjective: Irregular,[1] wild, bizarre; queer, droll, fantastic,

[1] Obs. as applied to landscape (*O.E.D.*) (see Appendix).

highly fanciful; strangely terrible, incongruous,[1] belonging to the grotesque.

In the following chapters, senses iv (A) and iv (B) will be employed as working definitions of the noun. The adjective will be used chiefly in the sense of 'belonging to the grotesque'.

CONNECTED FORMS

4. It remains to comment briefly on the three cognate forms *grotesquely*, *grotesqueness*, and *grotesquerie*.

(*a*) The adverbial form may be defined on the authority of the *O.E.D.* as meaning simply 'in a grotesque manner'; the other glosses given by the *O.E.D.*: 'with incongruous absurdity, fantastically, whimsically' show that the sense of the adverb in context varies in accordance with the several definitions of the adjective grotesque given above. In Walpole's line of verse

(1740) The wearied arms grotesquely deck the wall[2]

the adverb has the sense of 'in the manner of grotesque decoration'. Lytton uses it in the sense of 'strangely and ludicrously':

(1829) A man of about the middle age, very grotesquely attired. (*Devereaux*, II. ii.)

In Prof. Wilson Knight's essay, 'Lear and the Comedy of the Grotesque', it also occurs in the sense of 'strangely and ludicrously', but with overtones of terror:

(1930) We watch humanity grotesquely tormented. (*The Wheel of Fire* (1941), p. 189.)

(*b*) The word grotesqueness, defined by the *O.E.D.* as 'the quality of being grotesque', shows the same variations of sense, from the strongly pejorative[3] to the simply descriptive. The nonce use of the word, in the sense of 'grotesque objects',

(1883) I sauntered about the studio, taking note of the various beauties, grotesquenesses, and curiosities that it contained. (J. Hawthorne in *Harper's Mag.*, Nov., 926/1.)

---

[1] Certain examples of usage, e.g. 'Cromwell est grotesque' (Hugo, *La Préface de Cromwell*, p. 38, cf. Knaak, op. cit., p. 42), or Ruskin's chapter heading 'Grotesque Renaissance' (*The Stones of Venice*, III. III) are scarcely amenable to such summary treatment.

[2] See p. 11.

[3] See Appendix (Grotesqueness).

may be noted as an example of descriptive use without a pejorative nuance.

(c) The form grotesquerie, the oldest of the three, occurs first in the sense of 'objects in the grotesque style of decoration':

(1654–66) In a large Compartment composed of Groteskery were seen Sphynxes, Harpyes, the Claws of Lyons and Tygers, to evidence that within inhabited Mysteries and Riddles. (Lord Orrerey, *Parthenissa* (1676), 517.)

The remaining examples given by the *O.E.D.* all date from the nineteenth century. Apart from one example in which the word is used loosely in the sense of 'grotesqueness':

(1877) Casting a 'jet' of gentle humour over the grim grotesqueries of the situation. ('H. A. Page', *De Quincey*, I. V. 92.)

the examples of nineteenth-century usage have the sense of 'grotesque activity' or 'a manifestation of grotesqueness'. As with 'grotesquely' and 'grotesqueness', the word is found both in pejorative use, usually with the nuance of 'terrible':[1]

(1880) She showed her sense of degradation in the brutal grotesquery. (Howells, *Undisc. Country*, XIII. 197.)

and as a purely descriptive term:

(1885) The inventive grotesquerie of his [Doré's] later work. (*Manch. Exam.*, 22 July, 3/2.)

NOTES TO CHAPTER I

(i) In his book *Die Wandmalerei Pompejis* (1929), L. Curtius maintains that the 'grotesque' murals excavated in the late fifteenth century were not indigenous to Rome, but were examples of a late style of decoration probably introduced from Asia Minor. He quotes an interesting passage deploring the new style from the *De Architectura* of Marcus Vitruvius Pollio, a contemporary of Augustus:

... all those motifs which are based on reality, have now been forsaken for an injudicious fashion. For monstrosities are painted on the walls rather than clear pictures of real things. Instead of columns, fluted stems are painted; instead of gables (fastigia), panels with curling leaves and volutes. Candelabra likewise support painted edifices (aediculae). On their gables frail flowers, on which random little figures sit, grow in tendrils

[1] See note 4, p. 14.

from their roots. And the slight stems actually bear half-figures, some with human heads, others with the heads of beasts. Such things however, do not exist, never will and never have existed, either.

. . . For, in point of fact, how can a stalk support a roof, or a candelabrum bear the ornaments suitable to a gable? How can such a weak and flimsy tendril support a figure sitting on it, and how can flowers and half-figures grow piecemeal out of roots and tendrils? (cf. W. Kayser, op. cit., p. 20. cf. *De Archit.* VII. V. 3, 4.)

(ii) GROTTESCHE. Con questo nome si designà una determinata specie di decorazione parietale derivante da quella trovata a Roma nei resti sotterranei della *Domus aurea* di Nerone (le cosiddette 'grotte'). Essa è costituita da un leggiero e fantastico disporsi di forme vegetali miste a figurette umane, ad animali stravaganti, a scenette narrative, &c. (cf. *Enciclopedia Italiana* (1933).)

2

WRITERS ON THE GROTESQUE (A)

METHODS OF DEFINITION. POST-NEOCLASSICAL TREATISES

5. In a positivistically-inclined period like the present, when such evaluative terms as 'grotesque', 'sublime'. 'ugly', and such abstractions as 'the grotesque', 'the sublime', 'the ugly', are rightly regarded with suspicion and subjected to rigorous analysis, a study of the aesthetic treatises of the late eighteenth and nineteenth centuries leaves one with a general impression of incautious generalization. Wolfgang Kayser observes with reference to attempts at defining the grotesque during this period: 'The definitions of aesthetic writers comprehended too little of the actual content of the grotesque as it appeared in works of art.'[1] This remark raises an important question. Vitruvius's criticism of the new, fantastic fashion in mural painting[2] contains a detailed description of the style to which he objects, a merit which the following criticism of grotesque art cannot lay claim to:

The free, large, bold, perhaps impudent impulse (*Zug*) which runs through the grotesque creates an impression of entry into the sublime, the extraordinary, the grand. At the same instant, however, this monstrous pretension bursts into an equally grandiose nothing. What lies behind is bottomless nonsense, absolute madness, the most thorough dissoluteness, the most trivial meanness, frantic perversity or any other kind of monstrous nothingness.[3]

This passage is, admittedly, an extract; but its nebulousness is obviously in large measure due to the vastly increased number of phenomena which by the early twentieth century had been verbally united by the term 'grotesque', or to which the semantic development of the term had made it applicable; phenomena including, in the sphere of art alone, the centaur and the satyr, Raphael's decorations in the Vatican, the work of Rabelais, sketches by Callot and Goya, Gothic gargoyles, the Commedia dell'Arte, the Tales of Hoffmann,

[1] cf. Kayser, op. cit., p. 111.
[2] See p. 19.
[3] cf. J. Volkelt: *System der Ästhetik* (Munich, 1905), vol. 2, p. 414 (cf. Beate Krudewig: 'Das Groteske in der Ästhetik seit Kant' (Inaugural Dissertation, Univ. Bonn, 1934), p. 10.)

humorous poems by Wilhelm Busch and horror stories by Edgar Allan Poe, the style of Browning, and the music of Berlioz.[1]

The characteristic forms described and criticized by Vitruvius, who was not encumbered with the verbal difficulties which beset modern critics of grotesque art, could scarcely be drawn from a group of phenomena which ramified into all the media of art. The following are the chief methods employed by modern writers on the grotesque in the attempt to overcome this difficulty:

(i) The grotesque is defined in terms of the attitude of the artist, his deliberate intentions and his involuntary reactions to circumstances: in terms of its *Schaffensvorgang*, the conditions of its creation.

(ii) The effect or impression created upon the reader or spectator is used as a basis for definition.

(iii) The grotesque is defined by stating its relationship with other categories, the sublime, the ugly, the fantastic, the comic, caricature, &c. The multiplication of categories has, of course, the advantage of enabling the writer to reject or to reclassify 'intractable' material.

(iv) The characteristic features of a limited but 'representative' group of works are used as the criteria for a definition of the grotesque.

None of these methods necessarily excludes the others; but in most examinations one method tends to predominate over the others.

Kant's reference to the grotesque in the *Critique of Judgment* (1790)[2] may be quoted as an example of the first of these four methods:

But where for mere purposes of entertainment the free play of the imagination (*Vorstellungskräfte*) is desired, in pleasure gardens, the decoration of rooms, in every kind of embellishment of household effects and things of that sort, regularity, which makes its presence felt as a restraint, will be avoided as much as possible. Thus, indeed, the English taste in gardens, the baroque taste in furniture, rather urges the power of imagination (*Einbildungskraft*) to something approaching the grotesque, and supposes that it is in this very separation from all constraint of rules that taste can reveal its greatest perfection in the projection of the imagination (*Einbildungskraft*).

Scott's description of the 'fantastic' mode of writing in his essay on Hoffmann,[3] 'in which the most wild and unbounded license is given

---

[1] *Grotesques de la Musique* (1859).

[2] *Kritik der Urteilskraft*, §22 (72). cf. Krudewig, op. cit., pp. 3–4.

[3] 'The Novels of Ernest Theodore Hoffmann', *Foreign Review* (1827); see below, pp. 32 ff.

to an irregular fancy, and all species of combination, however ludicrous, or however shocking, are attempted and executed without scruple', is also primarily a description of the artist's attitude.

Volkelt's diatribe against the grotesque is an excellent example of the second type of approach, the description of the effect of grotesque art upon its audience. Edgar Allan Poe's description of the masqueraders in 'The Masque of the Red Death' (1842), according to Dr. Kayser 'perhaps the completest and most appropriate definition which the word grotesque has ever been given by an artist',[1] is also of this kind:

> Be sure they were grotesque. There were much glare and glitter and piquancy and phantasm—much of what has been since seen in 'Hernani'. There were arabesque figures with unsuited limbs and appointments. There were delirious fancies such as the madman fashions. There were much of the beautiful, much of the wanton, much of the *bizarre*, something of the terrible, and not a little of that which might have excited disgust. To and fro in the seven chambers there stalked, in fact, a multitude of dreams. And these—the dreams—writhed in and about, taking hue from the rooms, and causing the wild music of the orchestra to seem as the echo of their steps.[2]

The following quotations, examples of the third of these methods, show the general disagreement regarding the precise relationship of the grotesque with other aesthetic categories:

(1827) The grotesque in his (Hoffmann's) compositions partly resembles the arabesque in painting. (Scott.)[3]

(1851–3) Those grotesques or arabesques of the Vatican. (Ruskin.)[4]

(1896) The good grotesque is novel beauty. (G. Santayana.)[5]

(1897) Dans la littérature, le grotesque est le laid comique. (M. Souriau).[6]

The morally or aesthetically ugly—where it does not amount to frightening proportions—can only be utilised in art, *in specie* poetry, when the artist reflects it in the mirror of humour, when it is born again, as it were, through humour. It is in this way that what we call the 'grotesque' arises. (Th. Storm.)[7]

---

[1] cf. Kayser, op. cit., pp. 83–84.
[2] cf. *Selected Tales*, Penguin Books, 1956, pp. 194–5.
[3] cf. Scott, op. cit.: see below, note 1, p. 32.
[4] cf. *The Stones of Venice*, III. III. XLVIII.
[5] cf. *The Sense of Beauty* (London, 1896), p. 258.
[6] cf. *La Préface de Cromwell*, ed. Maurice Souriau (Paris, 1897), p. 136 (cf. Knaak, op. cit., p. 74).
[7] Letter to Erich Schmidt (*Works of Th. Storm*, ed. A. Köster, vol. 8, p. 273). cf. Kayser, op. cit., p. 217 (notes).

(1888–91) We are not to look for real ugliness in the sublime, the humorous, or the grotesque. (B. Bosanquet.)[1]

(1895) The grotesque is a special kind of caricature. (H. Schneegans.)[2]

(1934) The grotesque, far more [than caricature] conceals a valuable idea behind the distortion which mounts into the fantastic. (B. Krudewig.)[3]

As regards the fourth method, clearly, only by demonstrating that all the works of art which have ever been described as grotesque had certain concrete features in common could one establish general criteria of a simple factual kind. The selection of 'representative' works and of 'characteristic' forms necessarily impairs the general validity of the ensuing definition. This fourth method is employed (by Ruskin, for example, in his contrast of Gothic grotesque work with the grotesque art of Renaissance Venice,[4] and by Wolfgang Kayser, who devotes the best part of three pages in the final chapter of his book[5] to a list of forms favoured in grotesque art) in association with one or more of the three previous methods. The simple descriptive history of Thomas Wright,[6] primarily a history of caricature and satire, makes no attempt at establishing general criteria; indeed, Wright declares at the outset: 'It is not my intention . . . to enter into the philosophy of the subject; I design only to trace the history of its outward development, the various forms it has assumed, and its social influence.'[7] He does, however, commence his history with a few remarks on the psychological origin of caricature and the grotesque which are, in fact, an example of the first of the above methods.

6. In an amusingly cavalier dismissal of Kant's *Observations on the Feeling of the Sublime and the Beautiful* (1764), which draws heavily upon Burke's *Essay on the Sublime and the Beautiful* (1756), Bertrand Russell writes: 'Like everybody else at that time, he wrote a treatise on the sublime and the beautiful. Night is sublime, day is beautiful; the sea is sublime, the land is beautiful; man is sublime, woman is beautiful; and so on.'[8]

The interminable discussion of the relationships of various arbi-

---

[1] cf. 'The Aesthetic Theory of Ugliness' (*Proceedings Arist. Soc.* 1888–91, p. 47). cf. L. B. Campbell, 'The Grotesque in the Poetry of Rbt. Browning', *Bulletin Univ. Texas*, no. 92 (1907), p. 9.

[2] cf. Introduction, *History of Grotesque Satire*, cf. Kayser, op. cit., p. 112.

[3] cf. Krudewig, op. cit., p. 31.

[4] cf. *The Stones of Venice*, III. III (Grotesque Renaissance).

[5] op. cit., pp. 195–8.

[6] cf. *A History of Caricature and Grotesque in Literature and Art* (Virtue Brothers and Co., London, 1865).

[7] op. cit., p. 1.

[8] cf. *History of Western Philosophy* (Allen and Unwin, 1946), p. 732.

trary categories with which late eighteenth- and early nineteenth-century aesthetic treatises so largely concern themselves, often merely 'ringing the changes upon technical terms of aesthetic',[1] strikes the present-day reader as unprofitable, chiefly because of our more critical attitude towards the abstractions involved. The Procrustean Neoclassical attitude did at least lead to the examination of actual bodies, however much it may have mutilated them. The aesthetic treatises which succeeded Neoclassicism seem rarely to put their ideal beds to the test of supporting a body at all.

The really valuable element in such treatises is the expanding sense of artistic *possibility*, the feeling that the classification of the forms of art, and the criticism of art, no less than its production, ought not to be restricted to, or by, previous work, but should explore the periphery of the conceivable; the feeling that

> There is . . .
> At best, only a limited value
> In the knowledge derived from experience.
> The knowledge imposes a pattern, and falsifies,
> For the pattern is new in every moment
> And every moment is a new and shocking
> Valuation of all we have been.[2]

Ultimately, the new attitude was to lead to the realization that every new work of art 'offers to anyone who wishes to examine it the principles necessary to form a judgment of it'.[3] In the intermediate stage represented by the late eighteenth- and early nineteenth-century treatises, such thoroughgoing relativity was not systematic enough to be generally acceptable; but from the late eighteenth century onwards a less normative spirit prevails, classification rather than criticism is the aim of aesthetic writers, and if these treatises lose something through dissociation from actual works of art, much is gained through the examination of the human mind.

The remainder of this chapter will be devoted to an examination of opinions which are germane to the subject of the grotesque in the late eighteenth and early nineteenth centuries.[4]

---

[1] cf. B. Bosanquet, *A History of Aesthetic* (Allen and Unwin, 2nd ed., 1956), p. 399.

[2] cf. T. S. Eliot, *East Coker* (*Four Quartets*), II. ll. 81–87.

[3] Manzoni, Preface to *Il Conte di Carmagnola*. cf. Lascelles Abercrombie, *Principles of Literary Criticism*, 'An Outline of Modern Knowledge' Series (Gollancz, 1931), p. 905.

[4] Hugo's theory of the grotesque in *La Préface du Cromwell* (1827) is considered in ch. 3 (see pp. 45–49).

IMMANUEL KANT, EDMUND BURKE

7. Little more is to be gained from a detailed analysis of Kant's aesthetic writing, regarding his specific views on the grotesque, than is evident in the passage quoted above (see p. 22) from the *Critique of Judgment* (1790). He associates the grotesque, in eighteenth-century fashion, with kinds of decorative art. It is the product of extreme subjective fantasy. Kant connects it by implication ('for mere purposes of entertainment') with the pleasant rather than the beautiful. He distinguishes sharply between the beautiful and the pleasant—the former has 'subjective universality' (*subjectives Allgemeingültigkeit*)[1]— and between 'free' and 'dependent' beauty, the latter being that which approximates most closely to the objective world of 'things in themselves'. The more the sense of purpose is in evidence in a beautiful thing, the less 'free' and subjective it is.[2] He regards decorative art as 'free' 'because it is not bound to represent any object conditioned by a positive idea', and it is undoubtedly in this way that he regards the grotesque. The question of the grotesque in nature does not therefore arise for Kant at all.

The chief point of interest in his passing mention of the grotesque is his concern with the psychology of the decorative artist who believes that the less he is bound by the need to observe rules, to imitate 'regular' forms, the better he is able to demonstrate his 'taste'.

Apart from this brief reference to the grotesque, however, there is one other aspect of Kant's aesthetic—a far more important one for Kant himself—which may be mentioned as having a considerable influence on ideas about the grotesque: his view of the sublime. The distinction between the sublime and the beautiful was a major preoccupation of aesthetic treatises from the late eighteenth century onwards, until Rosenkranz[3] eventually ranked the sublime as a species of the beautiful, this being in Bosanquet's opinion 'a great advance on the theory of Kant'.[4]

If we read Burke's observations on the nature of the sublime (which he clearly regards as being superior to the merely beautiful), bearing in mind Santayana's description of the grotesque as 'the half-formed, the suggestively monstrous',[5] it is obvious that there are certain affinities between the two. A critical attitude is emerging

[1] cf. Bosanquet, op. cit., pp. 263–4.
[2] ibid., pp. 270–1.
[3] *Ästhetik des Hässlichen* (Königsberg, 1853), p. 167.
[4] Bosanquet, op. cit., p. 402.
[5] See p. 17.

which is propitious to the development of an obscure and fantastic form of art. Needless to say, Burke would have denied any similarity between the sublime and the grotesque; for him, as for Hogarth, they were antithetical kinds.[1] For Burke, strength and magnitude are essential qualities of the sublime, while the grotesque—or rather, grotesque art—is characterized by triviality.[2] In view of later ideas concerning the grotesque, however, there is obvious significance in such statements in Burke's *Inquiry* as 'a clear idea is another name for a little idea',[3] that formlessness and ugliness are elements of the sublime,[4] and that the intellectual, symbolic quality of words is less important than their power of suggestion.[5]

Lascelles Abercrombie's remark '. . . obscurity, like ideas of boundlessness and infinitude, sets the mind free to expand its inner powers unconditioned by the outer actuality of things'[6] suggests the link between Burke's insistence on the aesthetic importance of obscurity or formlessness, and Kant's comment on the rejection of 'regularity' by kinds of art which tend towards the grotesque.[7] Burke's views assume that the beautiful and the sublime exert their influence upon a surrendering, receptive mind. Kant introduces a more dynamic conception of aesthetic pleasure. Pleasure in the sublime, in his view, is the pleasure we derive from overcoming the assault of the power of nature upon our senses and from proving to ourselves our spiritual superiority to this power: '[Kant] seems to think that the pleasure in the sublime consists in the mind's recovery from the imminent overwhelming force of natural grandeur'.[8] He agrees, however, with Burke, that the sublime, unlike the beautiful, has no necessary connexion with form: '[It] may depend on "Unform", a useful idiom which may cover both formlessness and deformity.'[9]

GEORG WILHELM FRIEDRICH HEGEL

8. It will be most convenient to consider next the references to the grotesque made by Hegel in his posthumously published *Lectures on*

[1] See p. 6.
[2] See p. 5.
[3] cf. Edmund Burke, *A Philosophical Enquiry into the Origin of our Ideas of the Sublime and Beautiful*, ed. J. T. Boulton (Routledge & Kegan Paul Ltd., London, 1958), p. 63.
[4] ibid., p. 119.
[5] cf. Legouis and Cazamian, *Hist. Eng. Lit.* (Dent, 1930, repr. 1945), p. 950.
[6] cf. Abercrombie, ibid.
[7] See p. 22.
[8] cf. Abercrombie, op. cit., p. 904.
[9] cf. Bosanquet, op. cit., p. 276.

Aesthetic (1835),[1] and those general ideas in his work which are necessary to a full understanding of these references.

Briefly, Hegel distinguishes three chief kinds of art, the symbolic, the classical, and the romantic. Hegel considers this to be both the correct historical order and the ascending order of aesthetic value. He associates grotesqueness with both the symbolic and the romantic kinds of art, for reasons which a short account of his description of each kind will make clear; but it is primarily associated with symbolic art.

Each of the three kinds arises from an attempt to express the spiritual in concrete terms.

(i) Symbolic art, which is closely associated with the primitive attribution of spiritual (divine) characteristics to natural objects, attempts to represent the spiritual in distorted shapes, to express, as it were, the *super*natural by the *un*natural. Architecture, which attempts to provide a sensuous vessel for the spiritual—in the temple or church—is the fundamental type of symbolic art.

(ii) Only one shape is really 'appropriate to concrete mind',[2] namely the human form, and 'physiology ought to have made it one of its axioms that life had necessarily in its evolution to attain to the human shape, as the sole sensuous phenomenon that is appropriate to mind.'[2] In sculpture, the fundamental type of classical art, mind finds a satisfactory vehicle; there is a harmony of form and content. Perfect as this agreement is, however, classical ar tonly expresses a special form of the spiritual:

> This condition has the effect that Mind is by it at once specified as a particular case of mind, the human mind, and not as simply absolute and eternal, inasmuch as mind in this latter sense is incapable of proclaiming itself otherwise than as intellectual being.[3]

In other words, classical art can express the human mind, but not Mind, the universal and divine spirit. This is entirely suitable for the depiction of Greek gods, which are anthropomorphic: 'The Greek god is the object of naïve intuition and sensuous imagination. His shape is, therefore, the bodily shape of man.'[4]

---

[1] cf. *The Philosophy of Fine Art*, trans. F. P. B. Osmaston (Bell and Sons, London, 1920). cf. also Bosanquet, op. cit., Appendix 1, pp. 471–87 for a translation of vol. 1, pp. 89–114. Quotations are taken chiefly from the latter translation.

[2] cf. Bosanquet, op. cit., p. 477.

[3] ibid.

[4] ibid., p. 478.

Christianity, however, 'brings God before our intelligence as *spirit*, or mind, not as particularized individual spirit, but as absolute, in *spirit* and in truth'.[1]

(iii) Classical art, in fact, goes as far as mere art can go. Romantic art, in attempting to represent universal Mind, in concrete terms, attempts to transcend the limitations of art. It endeavours to do this by extreme subjectivity, by reducing the external element, the medium of expression, to an absolute minimum.

The fundamental types of romantic art are painting, which represents three-dimensional extension in space more intellectually, more subjectively, on a plane surface; music, which also 'treats the sensuous as ideal' and is still more subjective; and poetry: '[Poetry is] the universal art of the mind which has become free in its own nature, and which is not tied to find its realization in external sensuous matter, but expatiates exclusively in the inner space and the inner time of the ideas and feelings.'[2]

It has already been remarked that, according to Hegel, grotesqueness may be associated with both the symbolic and the romantic kinds of art, for somewhat different reasons in each case. In romantic art, grotesque forms have a negative significance. They are evidence of the indifference of the spirit, as it were, to the merely phenomenal world:

The aspect of external existence is committed to contingency, and left at the mercy of freaks of the imagination, whose caprice is no more likely to mirror what is given *as* it is given, than to throw the shapes of the outer world into chance medley, or distort them into grotesqueness.[3]

The grotesque in romantic art, then, if I understand Hegel's view correctly, reveals the presence of the spiritual much as, say, the splashing of walls and the overturning of chairs might reveal the presence of a poltergeist. Romantic art does not so much attempt an incarnation of the spiritual as a demonstration of its existence. The artist frankly despairs of finding any satisfactory concrete equivalent for the spiritual, and it is this which distinguishes the romantic from the symbolic artist.

In symbolic art, the grotesque plays a more positive role. It is also produced by a profound dissatisfaction with natural forms; but the artist still naïvely hopes to find a satisfactory concrete form for the spiritual in an artistic—as distinct from a natural—shape.

[1] ibid., p. 479.
[2] ibid., p. 486.
[3] ibid. (Appendix I).

The initial stage in symbolic representation is the simple charging of 'the meanest objects' with 'absolute import', for example 'when a lion is used to mean strength'.[1] A natural object is taken as a symbol of the divine. But this being obviously unsatisfactory, because of the essential 'foreignness of the Idea to natural phenomena', the spiritual (or the Idea)—working through the artist, of course—has recourse to distortion:

Having no other reality to express it, [it] expatiates in all these shapes, seeks itself in them in all their unrest and proportion, but nevertheless does not find them adequate to itself. Then it proceeds to exaggerate the natural shapes and the phenomena of reality into indefiniteness and disproportion, to intoxicate itself in them, to seethe and ferment in them, to do violence to them, to distort and explode them into unnatural shapes, and strives by the variety, hugeness and splendour of the forms employed to exalt the phenomenon to the level of the Idea.[2]

Before considering Hegel's remarks on Indian art, where he develops his views on the grotesque most fully, it is important to note how fundamental this idea of the distortion of natural forms is, in Hegel's views on art. Thus architecture is contrary to nature (*naturwidrig*) in its smooth columns, straight lines, right-angles, even surfaces, and so on. Such stylization, though necessary and desirable, may, however, in his view only legitimately be applied to inorganic and vegetable nature, which does not contain 'sensitive Individuals' (*empfindende Individuen*).[3]

The forms of Indian art, which are explicitly described by Hegel as grotesque, whilst they are symbolic in so far as they attempt to provide an appropriate concrete embodiment of the spiritual, cannot without qualification be termed symbolic art, in Hegel's opinion, because 'there is no essential connection and relationship in the narrower sense'[4] between form and content, as there is, for example, between strength and the lion:

Particular shapes are drawn out into colossal and grotesque proportions in order that they may, as forms of sense, attain to universality. The particular form of sense, which is taken to express not itself and its own characteristic meaning as a fact of external existence, but a universal significance which lies outside it, fails to satisfy the imagination until it has

[1] cf. Bosanquet, op. cit., pp. 476 ff.
[2] ibid.
[3] cf. Kayser, op. cit., p. 109.
[4] ibid., p. 110.

been torn out of itself into vastness which knows no measure or limit. This is the cause of all that extravagant exaggeration of size, not merely in the case of spatial dimension, but also of measurelessness of time-durations, or the reduplication of particular determinations, as in figures with many heads, arms, and so on, by means of which this art strains to compass the breadth and universality of the significance it assumes.[1]

The term which he applies to such art is 'fantastic symbolism' (*fantastische Symbolik*).

Kayser's comment on Hegel's view of the grotesque, 'Always, however, there belongs to the grotesque the characteristic of reaching beyond itself (*das Übersichhinausweisen*) into a sphere of the higher powers',[2] suggests the purposive and—to employ a somewhat over-worked word—numinous character which Hegel ascribes to grotesque art, in so far as it coincides with 'fantastic symbolism';[3] but it should not be forgotten that, in Hegel's opinion, such art is also futile and wrongheaded.

A certain similarity between the characteristics of the sublime—as described by Burke and Kant—and those of grotesque art has already been noticed. Hegel explicitly recognizes this affinity; such monstrosities as those of Indian art have 'an echo of the sublime':

> The sublime in art is the attempt to express the infinite without finding in the realm of phenomena any object which proves itself fitting for this representation.
> As a case of inadequate expression it is akin to the ugly or at least to the deformed and monstrous of the symbolic . . . phase of art . . . But yet these monstrosities have only 'an echo of the sublime', because they half satisfy, or are taken to satisfy, the need of expression by the very distortion, or magnitude, barbaric splendour and the like . . . which makes them monstrous; whereas, in the true sublime, a sharp consciousness of in-adequacy is required.[4]

In other words, it is not so much the futility of fantastic-symbolic art which Hegel censures as its inability to perceive its futility. In roman-tic art, as we have seen, Hegel finds this sense of the inadequacy of all sensuous means of expression. It is this which gives romantic art its sublimity, its poignancy.

[1] cf. Osmaston (trans.), op. cit., vol. 2, pp. 53–54.
[2] cf. Kayser, op. cit., p. 110.
[3] Hegel employs the term 'arabesque' to describe the 'grotesque' style of ornamentation. cf. Kayser, op. cit., p. 108.
[4] cf. Bosanquet, op. cit., p. 356.

SIR WALTER SCOTT

9. The first detailed consideration of the grotesque in English is Sir Walter Scott's essay on the stories of Hoffmann (1827),[1] which deals, of course, specifically with the grotesque in literature. In a wise and closely written critique which touches upon the problem of accounting for common elements in the folk-tales of different countries, and in which 'the various modes in which the wonderful and supernatural may be introduced into fictitious narrative' are 'slightly traced', Scott censures 'the fantastic mode of writing'[2] exemplified by Hoffmann for its lack of both internal consistency and moral content: 'The reader is led astray by a freakish goblin, who has neither end nor purpose in the gambols which he exhibits, and the oddity of which must constitute their own reward.'[3] Scott is, of course, no enemy of the preternatural as a literary device, and states that old legends and folk-tales have a powerful effect upon him, 'though irreconcileable to sober truth'.[4]

Such stories, generally enjoyed in the dark ages 'when society, however differing in degree and station, was levelled and confounded by one dark cloud of ignorance', lost their universal appeal with the advance of knowledge; nevertheless, though such legends are 'sometimes trite, sometimes tiresome, sometimes childish', they 'form a step in the history of the human race', and possess, moreover, a strange power over the mind. Seemingly deriving from 'a common stock of superstitition', these simple, rude, popular legends 'often possess points of interest, of nature, and of effect, which . . . carry with them something that the mind is not averse to believe, something in short of plausibility, which, let poet or romancer do their very best, they find it impossible to attain to'.[5]

The question of the source of this 'something of plausibility' which Scott finds in the wonders of the folk-tale but not in the tales of Hoffmann—with one significant exception, 'The Entail'—is an important one to which we shall have to return in dealing with Scott's adverse criticism of Hoffmann's 'fantastic mode of writing'.

First, however, we must note that Scott distinguishes this fantastic style from the work of such writers as Count Anthony Hamilton and

---

[1] See note 3, p. 22. References are to *The Misc. Prose Works of Scott* (R. Cadell, Edinburgh; Whittaker and Co., London, 1834–6, vol. 18, Article X.
[2] cf. op. cit., pp. 290–1.
[3] ibid.
[4] ibid., pp. 283–4.
[5] ibid.

Fleur d'Epine, whose stories are burlesque parodies of the folk-tale. He suggests that Ariosto, in certain passages, also has his tongue in his cheek. This distinction runs counter to the view increasingly accepted by later nineteenth-century writers on the grotesque, such as Thomas Wright (1865),[1] J. A. Symonds (1890),[2] H. Schneegans (1894),[3] that the grotesque is closely associated with caricature.

The type of narrative exemplified by the stories of Hoffmann is described by Scott as follows:

> . . . the attachment of the Germans to the mysterious has invented another species of composition, which, perhaps, could hardly have made its way in any other country or language. This may be called the FAN-TASTIC mode of writing,—in which the most wild and unbounded license is given to an irregular fancy, and all species of combination, however ludicrous, or however shocking, are attempted and executed without scruple. In the other modes of treating the supernatural, even that mystic region is subjected to some laws, however slight; and fancy, in wandering through it, is regulated by some probabilities in the wildest flight. Not so in the fantastic style of composition, which has no restraint save that which it may ultimately find in the exhausted imagination of the author. This style bears the same proportion to the more regular romance, whether ludicrous or serious, which Farce, or rather Pantomime, maintains to Tragedy and Comedy. Sudden transformations are introduced of the most extraordinary kind, and wrought by the most inadequate means; no attempt is made to soften their absurdity, or to reconcile their inconsistencies; the reader must be contented to look upon the gambols of the author as he would behold the flying leaps and incongruous transmutations of Harlequin, without seeking to discover either meaning or end further than the surprise of the moment.[1]

The barrenness of the style of writing thus described is contrasted with the fantasy of *Frankenstein* and *Gulliver's Travels*, which 'suppose the existence of the most extravagant fictions, in order to extract from them philosophical reasoning and moral truth'.[4]

What are, in fact, the 'slight laws' to which the mystic region of the folk-tale is subjected, the probabilities which regulate the wandering fancy in, say, Grimm's *Märchen*? They are, of course, primarily ethical. The hero vanquishes the monster, the hero being by definition good and the monster bad; courage, kindness, and loyalty bring their

[1] See note 6, p. 24.
[2] See pp. 51 ff.
[3] Introduction, *Geschichte der grotesken Satire*, Strasbourg, 1894 (see p. 24).
[4] cf. Scott, op. cit., pp. 290–2. cf. Dryden, note 1, p. 4.

inevitable reward, and their opposites inevitable punishment. It is these constant values, gyroscopes in a sea of evils, which enable the reader to enjoy such stories without moral disquietude. The novels of Anne Radcliffe, and of Scott himself, have the same comfortable quality. The 'whodunit' and the Stevenson-Buchan type of adventure story are present-day equivalents.

Hoffmann, too, frequently extols the virtues of courage, kindness, loyalty, &c. Scott warmly praises his story 'The Entail' for its description of the courage of a man faced with the preternatural. 'Fraulein von Scuderi' describes the courage and philanthropy of an old lady who saves an innocent man from execution. Even in 'The Sandman', the story singled out for especial censure by Scott, the loyalty of Klara and her brother Lothar to the unfortunate hero Nathaniel is exemplary. But, as might be expected in a writer of his period (1776–1822), Hoffmann is not content to sunder the inside world from the outside one. This is indeed the case in many of his earlier stories, where grotesque phenomena and occurrences are the work of the devil—an objective evil, parallel to the wickedness of the witches, giants, dragons, &c., of the folk tale—and dreams are the main vehicle of the subjective grotesque. 'The Entail', which so pleased Scott, and 'The Golden Pot' are examples of such stories in which evil is objective.

In later stories, however—'The Sandman' is perhaps the chief example—Hoffmann writes 'psychologically'. Like Poe,[1] but still more like Kafka, he deliberately confounds the subjective and the objective worlds. Much of the interest of his later stories centres upon the peculiar nature of the artist's mind; Cardillac, for example, the villain of 'Fräulein von Scuderi', the greatest goldsmith of his time, fashions masterpieces by day and murders his clients by night to get them back. Nathaniel, in 'The Sandman', suffers from a persecution complex. As a child he identifies a visitor to his father's house with the wicked Sandman—a bogyman he has heard of from his nurse. The Sandman figure dominates his entire life and eventually drives him to madness and suicide. Hoffmann deliberately—and artistically—leaves us in doubt as to whether the various figures whom Nathaniel identifies with the Sandman are, in fact, one and the same person—the original visitor—or not. But the key is certainly provided by a letter written to Nathaniel by Klara: 'Only, I will

---

[1] cf. 'The Tell-Tale Heart'. Apart from writers of narrative, there are close affinities in this respect between Hoffmann and Blake.

avow to you directly that in my opinion, all the frightful and terrible things you speak of only took place in your mind; the real, true outer world had indeed little to do with it."[1] The powers of evil outside us, she tells him, can only take hold upon us if we are willing to allow them to do so.

It is largely this deliberate blurring of the 'facts' which annoys Scott. Overlooking the subjective explanation strongly and continually suggested,[2] Scott sees no point at all in the Sandman's hounding of Nathaniel.

He objects, too, to the absurdity of Nathaniel's passion for Olimpia, whom the hero first sees through a viewing-glass bought from a man half identified with the Sandman. When she turns out to be a mechanical doll Nathaniel goes insane. Hoffmann devotes a page to imaginary criticism and comments, including those of a professor who reproves the literal-minded with the words: 'Highly respected ladies and gentlemen! Cannot you see, then, what the point is? The whole thing is an allegory—an extended metaphor! You understand me—Sapienti sat!'[3]

Hoffmann does not, of course, approve the professor's view any-more than the other 'common-sense' comments. The term 'allegory' is clearly unsuitable. But it is obvious that he is very much alive to the symbolic possibilities of literature.

Apart from Scott's objection to the lack of moral content in Hoffmann's work, we may note a further reason for his disapproval. The wonders of the old legends and folk-tales of which he speaks so warmly, and of the ballads, conform to a traditional pattern which the 'Gothic' writers of the late eighteenth century regarded almost as a sacred ritual. Scott was, of course, a devotee of 'the Gothic' with an exceptional feeling for tradition. Hoffmann, for Scott, was guilty of apostasy in eschewing the traditional atmosphere, in inventing wonders of a highly original kind and placing them for the most part in a comparatively recent setting. It is significant that the story which he singles out for praise, 'The Entail', is a traditionally Gothic tale, set in a bleak ruin, with a ghost, a secret door, and so on.

[1] cf. E. T. A. Hoffmann, *Der Zauberspiegel; Ausgewählte Erzählungen* (Knaur Volksausgabe, Munich, 1952), p. 89.

[2] 'Yes, Nathaniel, you are right! Coppelius [the Sandman] is a wicked, hostile force, He can do dreadful things as a devilish power that enters your life in visible form. But only when you don't shut him out of your mind and thoughts. As long as you believe, he both exists and acts; in your belief alone lies his power' (op. cit., p. 96).

[3] ibid., p. 110.

To summarize, then, Scott's view of the grotesque as it emerges from his essay on Hoffmann: he makes it clear that he has no sympathy with fantastic narrative for its own sake. It ought to have a moral purpose, as it has in *Gulliver's Travels* and *Frankenstein*, or at least point towards the supernatural in the manner of the old legends and folk-tales, which have a traditional atmosphere which disarms criticism. Their wonders are not merely wilful like those of Hoffmann, who ought to know better, but the product of superstitious beliefs which can not only be excused but enjoyed as 'a step in the history of the human race'. 'Modern tales of wonder', whether ludicrously or seriously intended, ought in so far as possible to draw upon this traditional atmosphere. We are told that:

Hoffmann seems to have been a man of excellent disposition, a close observer of nature, and one who, if this sickly and disturbed train of thought had not led him to confound the supernatural with the absurd, would have distinguished himself as a painter of human nature, of which in its realities he was an observer and an admirer.[1]

One is strongly reminded of Hegel's remarks on 'fantastic symbolism', the vain attempt to represent the supernatural through the unnatural. In spite of his remark that the reader must be content to read work of this 'fantastic mode' 'without seeking to discover either meaning or end further than the surprise of the moment', it is clear from the above passage that Scott is not merely censuring Hoffmann for being absurd, but for being seriously and pretentiously absurd.

We have already noticed Scott's comparison of the grotesque in Hoffmann's work to 'the arabesque in painting'.[2] He further associates the grotesque with the horrible: 'The grotesque, also, has a natural alliance with the horrible; for that which is out of nature can be with difficulty reconciled to the beautiful.'[3]

JOHN RUSKIN

10. Ruskin, in his elaborate analysis of the grotesque in *The Stones of Venice*,[4] attributes horror, together with a feeling for nature and 'the true appreciation of beauty', only to 'the noble grotesque'. The 'ignoble grotesque' is never horrible, only disgusting. Like the other

[1] cf. op. cit., p. 307.
[2] See p. 12.
[3] cf. op. cit., p. 324.
[4] See pp. 13 ff. References are to the New Universal Library ed. (Routledge and Sons, 1907), vol. III (The Fall), ch. III (Grotesque Renaissance).

writers on the grotesque whose views have been examined, Ruskin regards the grotesque as a purely artistic phenomenon. The grotesque in architecture, for example, in contradistinction to the picturesque element, is 'not produced by the working of nature and time, but exclusively by the fancy of man'.[1]

Ruskin, rejecting a distinction between the ludicrous and the terrible grotesque on the grounds that all grotesque art contains elements of both the ludicrous and the terrible, bases his theory on two sets of distinctions which cut across each other: the isolation of four psychological types—'the men who play wisely; who play necessarily; who play inordinately; and who play not at all';[2] and of three 'peculiar tempers' in which the 'terrible grotesque'[3] is produced —'sometimes (A) of predetermined or involuntary apathy, sometimes (B) of mockery, sometimes (C) of diseased and ungoverned imaginativeness'.[4]

Of the four degrees of play, the second and third (necessary and inordinate play) are those with which Ruskin is chiefly concerned. All grotesque art, he insists, contains an element of play or sportiveness. There are, generally speaking, two kinds of men in whom the spirit of play is almost entirely lacking, those who are too high-minded for play, and those who are too low-spirited. Of the first he observes: 'It is evident that the idea of any kind of play can only be associated with the idea of an imperfect, childish, and fatigable nature.'[5] A perfect nature would be above play. Men of the highest spiritual type, though necessarily imperfect by nature, play only in the most restrained manner. Such 'wise' playfulness is to be found in Plato and Wordsworth. Grotesque art of a sublime, terrible, and deeply earnest kind may be produced by such men. In the work of Dante, 'the central man of all the world', 'the grotesque reaches at once the most distinct and the most noble development to which it was ever brought in the human mind.'[6]

At the other extreme are those men 'who are so dull and morose as to be incapable of inventing or enjoying jest . . . or else men utterly oppressed with labour, and driven too hard by the necessities of the world to be capable of any species of happy relaxation'.[7] Such

[1] cf. op. cit., p. 149 (§XXXVII).
[2] cf. op. cit., pp. 140–1 (§XXV).
[3] See note 1, p. 38.
[4] cf. op. cit., p. 155 (§XLIV).
[5] ibid., p. 141 (§XXVI).
[6] ibid., p. 175 (§LXVII).
[7] ibid., p. 144 (§XXX).

G.E.L.—D

men 'are little likely to find expression in any trivial form of art, except in bitterness of mockery; and this character at once stamps the work in which it appears, as belonging to the class of terrible, rather than of playful, grotesque'.[1]

Between these extremes lie two further groups in which the spirit of play is much more in evidence:

(i) Those who play necessarily; those, that is, who are obliged to use their energies in work 'incapable of interesting the nobler faculties'. When they do have leisure to gratify their nobler instincts their energies are too depleted for the really intense and disciplined exertion required to do justice to noble ideas. They can only toy with these ideas, fancifully, 'without any determined purpose and under no vigorous restraint'.

> This stretching of the mental limbs as their fetters fall away [Ruskin observes]—this leaping and dancing of the heart and intellect, when they are restored to the fresh air of heaven, yet half paralysed by their captivity, and unable to turn themselves to any earnest purpose—I call necessary play.[2]

Such play produces the noble or true grotesque.[3]

(ii) Those who play inordinately. Those who belong to this group are in general men of higher education, and are better situated than those of the previous group. Their apathy is not the result of temporary exhaustion—indeed, they have the energy to indulge in unnecessary play—but of a weak and sensual temper. 'The art through which this temper is expressed will, in all probability be refined and sensual—therefore, also, assuredly feeble.'[4]

---

[1] ibid., p. 151 (§XL). Earlier (p. 139 (§XXIII)) Ruskin observes that the grotesque cannot legitimately be considered under the two aspects of sportive and terrible grotesque; only a few examples are wholly the one or the other. The term 'terrible grotesque' is therefore to be understood for the most part in the sense of 'work in which the terrible element preponderates over the playful'.

[2] ibid., p. 142 (§XXVII).

[3] Ruskin seems to regard Dante's grotesque art as being different from this in kind, not merely in degree. He does, however, state plainly (ibid., p. 154 (§XLIII)): '. . . there is a Divine beauty, and a terribleness or sublimity coequal with it in rank, which are the subjects of the highest art; and there is an inferior or ornamental beauty, and an inferior terribleness coequal with it in rank, which are the subjects of grotesque art.' (Not, note, the subject of *an inferior type* of grotesque art.) It is clearly implied that even in Dante grotesque art cannot attain to the higher level of 'terribleness or sublimity'.

[4] ibid., p. 149 (§XXXVIII).

The ignoble or false grotesque is the work of such men. The grotesque style of decoration is of this ignoble kind:

Its highest condition is that which first developed itself among the enervated Romans, and which was brought to the highest perfection of which it was capable, by Raphael, in the arabesques of the Vatican.[1] It may be generally described as an elaborate and luscious form of nonsense. Its lower conditions are found in the common upholstery and decorations which, over the whole of civilized Europe, have sprung from this poisonous root; an artistical pottage, composed of nymphs, cupids and satyrs, with shreddings of heads and paws of meek wild beasts, and nondescript vegetables.[2]

The difference between the true and the false grotesque, in brief, is that the true grotesque is 'the expression of the *repose* or play of a *serious* mind', whereas the false grotesque is 'the result of the *full exertion* of a *frivolous* one'.[3] Careful elaboration and attention to detail is thus characteristic of the false grotesque.

The terrible grotesque is the result of the preoccupation of the mind with 'the proper subjects of human fear', namely those associated with sin and death, in three 'peculiar tempers':

(A) Predetermined or involuntary apathy. A man of strong feelings and noble instincts cannot be content to look at the bright side of existence: '[He cannot] confine his thoughts to mere loveliness . . . He sees more in the earth than these—misery and wrath, and discordance, and danger, and all the work of the dragon and his angels; this he sees with too deep feeling ever to forget.'[4] The workman or artist produces the terrible grotesque when working apathetically, in a fanciful, half-serious fashion, because, despite himself, he infuses into such work a sense of the underlying, tragic quality of life: 'The horror . . . comes upon him whether he will or not.'[5] Horror, nature, and mercy show through the joy and fantasy.[6]

The kind of apathy which produces the ignoble grotesque has already been described above; in contrast to the true 'apathetic' grotesque, the false grotesque is produced when 'a man *naturally* apathetic is forcing himself into temporary excitement'.[7] Blind to the tragic

[1] Even Raphael's arabesques are described as 'an unmeaning and monstrous abortion' (ibid., p. 160 (§L)).
[2] ibid., p. 150 (§XXXIX).
[3] ibid., p. 158 (§XLIX).
[4] ibid., p. 156 (§XLV).
[5] ibid., p. 157 (§XLVII).
[6] See p. 14.
[7] Ruskin, op. cit., p. 157 (§XLVII).

quality of life, 'incapable of true imagination', such artists produce forms 'which will be absurd without being fantastic, and monstrous without being terrible'. Instead of horror, nature, and mercy, such work is characterized by grossness,[1] unnaturalness,[2] and malice.[3]

(B) Mockery, or satire.[4] The exercise of satire and humour, especially on the failings of superiors, is one of the keenest pleasures of 'the vulgar mind'. 'All this was formerly thrown into noble art, and became permanently expressed in the sculptures of the cathedral.'

In modern times, this vulgar satire and humour, expressed in language, 'has become the especial study of the group of authors headed by Charles Dickens'. In medieval times, when 'it was generally recognized that folly and sin are, to a certain extent synonymous', workmen were encouraged to represent the various vices 'under the most ridiculous forms'.

The monstrous depiction of devils by the medieval workmen, and by Dante, illustrates the same attitude at different levels of art. Both are to be preferred to Milton's more dignified descriptions: 'Milton makes his fiends too noble, and misses the foulness, inconstancy, and fury of wickedness.'[5]

There is a base condition of the satirical grotesque, as there is of the apathetic grotesque, distinguishable from the noble form by its lack of the three qualities of horror, nature, and mercy.

(C) Diseased and ungoverned imaginativeness. This is by far the most interesting and profoundest of the three categories into which Ruskin divides the 'terrible grotesque'. It is significant that in treating this section in detail, he alters the heading to 'Ungovernableness of the imagination', simply.[6] He makes it abundantly clear[7] that in his view, as in Plato's, 'the madness which is of God is a nobler thing than the wisdom which is of man'.

Ruskin begins by saying that the lowest manifestation of the imagination is in dreams, where there is least discipline and control; but the implication that it is some kind of conscious control which makes the imagination artistically creative is not to his liking. He goes on to speak of the great dreams of the Bible, e.g. Joseph's dream of the fat and the lean kine, which is 'a true grotesque' and a noble one. Almost as an afterthought he observes that with such dreams another type of grotesque appears—the symbolic grotesque (a term which is

[1] ibid., p. 151 (§XXXIX).   [2] ibid., p. 158 (§XLVIII).
[3] ibid., p. 150, (§XXXVIII).   [4] ibid., pp. 161 ff. (§LII ff.).
[5] ibid., p. 162 (§LIII).   [6] ibid., p. 166 (§LIX).
[7] cf. especially his long footnote to sect. LX (pp. 167–8).

applicable to many of the examples of grotesque art of which he has previously spoken). He then dilates upon the symbolic significance of mythological figures, especially in Northern mythology—giants, goblins, kelpies, etc., all of which are produced by man's sense of the mysterious and preternatural. Ruskin speaks of these creations approvingly; they are grotesque and they are noble. Clearly, however, they are not the product of disciplined and systematic art. How then are the noble manifestations of this third 'peculiar temper' to be told from the ignoble ones? How are the wild but noble grotesques of the Teutonic peoples—and of the Egyptians and Assyrians[1]—to be distinguished from the savage and ignoble grotesques of 'the Hindoo and . . . the Sandwich islander'? Ruskin considers the distinction to be of great importance:

I believe that there is no test of greatness in periods, nations, or men, more sure than the development, among them or in them, of a noble grotesque; and no test of comparative smallness or limitation, of one kind or another, more sure than the absence of grotesque invention, or incapability of understanding it.[2]

The criterion he suggests is that in the noble grotesque there is always evidence of 'the true appreciation of beauty.'[3] which is, of course, disappointingly vague. The underlying idea, however, is clear enough. He could not have made his criterion 'evidence of noble instincts' without outright tautology; and in a sphere where noble and ignoble forms alike—the gnome as well as the idol—are non-natural, feeling for nature would scarcely be satisfactory. 'True appreciation of beauty' is obviously meant to denote those feelings of which Ruskin has previously spoken at length—awareness of the things of the spirit and a sense of the tragic predicament of man. The imagination is a means of apprehending spiritual truth, and no creation of the imagination, however strange—or however insignificant—in itself, can be ignoble if it shows spiritual awareness:

It cannot but have been sometimes a subject of wonder with thoughtful men . . . that a calf, a lion, an eagle, and a beast with a man's face, should in all ages have been preferred by the Christian world, as expressive of Evangelistic power and inspiration, to the majesty of human form.[4]

[1] 'I hardly know whether most to admire the winged bulls of Nineveh, or the winged dragons of Verona' (ibid., p. 176 (§LXIX)).
[2] ibid., p. 175 (§LXVII).
[3] ibid., p. 177 (§LXX).
[4] ibid., p. 171 (§LXIII); see p. 11 (Ruskin quotation).

The ignoble grotesque is unbeautiful because it is rooted in vice and sensuality and lacks this spiritual, symbolic quality.

Whilst agreeing with Vitruvius, then, in his censure of the 'grotesque' Roman murals, Ruskin would disagree with the grounds on which the Augustan architect bases his criticism. They are to be censured not because they are unrealistic but because they are evil; because they are weak, sensual, and frivolous. Again, whilst Ruskin agrees with Hegel in assigning a low place to the grotesques of Indian art, he does so because of their sensuality and lack of spiritual, symbolic qualities; not, like Hegel, because they vainly attempt to express the spiritual in concrete form.

Though grotesque art, for Ruskin, is incapable of attaining the highest level of all, it has genuine merits; it may even be great, in the hands of an artist like Dante. The third cause of the terrible grotesque, ungovernableness of the imagination, is spoken of as being due to 'fear [ultimately of sin and death] operating upon strong powers of imagination or by the failure of the human faculties in the endeavour to grasp the highest truths'.[1]

Such fear and such failure of the faculties are not only compatible with a noble nature but 'it is evidently not intended that many men should even reach, far less pass their lives in, that solemn state of thoughtfulness which brings them into the nearest brotherhood with their Divine Master'.[2]

We are still further assured that:

> . . . the fallen human soul, at its best, must be as a diminishing glass, and that a broken one, to the mighty truths of the universe around it; and the wider the scope of its glance, and the vaster the truths into which it obtains an insight, the more fantastic their distortion is likely to be, as the winds and vapours trouble the field of the telescope most when it reaches farthest.[3]

The implication is that all but the very highest art, produced by men of extraordinary spiritual powers, is in some way grotesque, whether nobly or ignobly.

The noble grotesque arises, then, according to Ruskin, from the distortion of man's intuitions of supernatural truths by his physical circumstances. It represents the divine aspirations of 'an imperfect, childish, and fatigable nature'.[4]

[1] ibid., p. 166 (§LIX).   [2] ibid., p. 141 (§XXVI).
[3] ibid., p. 169 (§LXI).   [4] See note 5, p. 37.

3

WRITERS ON THE GROTESQUE (B)

WALTER BAGEHOT

11. With the view of Hegel and Ruskin that the grotesque in art is
produced by the conflict between man's intuitions of the infinite and
his physical limitations, we may compare a striking passage by Walter
Bagehot:

> But taken as a whole, the universe is absurd. There seems an unalter-
> able contradiction between the human mind and its employments. How
> can a *soul* be a merchant? What relation to an immortal being have the
> price of linseed, the fall of butter, the tare on tallow, or the brokerage on
> hemp? Can an undying creature debit 'petty expenses', and charge for
> 'carriage paid'? All the world's a stage;—'the satchel, and the shining
> morning face'—the 'strange oaths';—'the bubble reputation'—the
>
> > Eyes severe and beard of formal cut
> > Full of wise saws and modern instances.
>
> Can these things be real? Surely they are acting. What relation have they
> to the truth as we see it in theory? What connection with our certain hopes,
> 'In respect of itself, it is a good life; but in respect it is a shepherd's life, it
> is nought.' The soul ties its shoe; the mind washes its hands in a basin.
> All is incongruous.[1]

One might perhaps have expected a writer with so deep a feeling for
the oddness of the human predicament to show some sympathy with
the 'numinous' view of the grotesque, to be one of those to whom the
deliberate distortion of the natural order might appear as an attempt
to penetrate into some region of supernatural order. In Bagehot's
explicit remarks on grotesque art, however, this is far from being the
case. The title of his essay, *Wordsworth, Tennyson, and Browning: or,
Pure, Ornate and Grotesque Art in English Poetry* (1864),[2] places both
artists and kinds of art in Bagehot's order of preference, and Browning
and the grotesque are given short shrift.

---

[1] cf. Lord David Cecil's essay on Shakespearean Comedy (*The Fine Art of
Reading*, Constable, 1957), p. 30. cf. Bagehot, 'The First Edinburgh
Reviewers' (1855), *Literary Studies*, vol. I.
[2] References are to *Literary Studies*, vol. II, Longmans Green and Co.,
1895 (new ed.).

Bagehot understands the word grotesque not so much in the sense of 'fantastic' as in the sense of 'ugly, monstrous', and is thus prepared to accept the existence of grotesque objects. His essay is based upon the idea that whereas perfect material should be treated simply, imperfect material requires some kind of artistic camouflage; the following passage suggests a conception of art as a kind of photographic retouching:

> ... ornate art is, within the limits, as legitimate as pure art. It does what pure art could not do. The very excellence of pure art confines its employment. Precisely because it gives the best things by themselves and exactly as they are, it fails when it is necessary to describe inferior things among other things, with a list of enhancements and a crowd of accompaniments that in reality do not belong to it. Illusion, half belief, unpleasant types, imperfect types, are as much the proper sphere of ornate art, as an inferior landscape is the proper sphere for the true efficacy of moonlight. A really great landscape needs sun and bears sunlight; but moonlight is an equaliser of beauties; it gives a romantic unreality to what will not stand the bare truth. And just so does romantic art.[1]

One is reminded of Mark Twain's remark that one should never tell the naked truth in the presence of ladies.

Some faces, however, are beyond retouching:

> An exceptional monstrosity of horrid ugliness cannot be made pleasing, except it be made to suggest—to recall—the perfection, the beauty, from which it is a deviation. Perhaps in extreme cases no art is equal to this; but then such self-imposed problems should not be worked by the artist; these out-of-the-way and detestable subjects should be let alone by him.[2]

The introduction of ugly objects into art cannot simply be justified on the grounds that 'these grotesque objects exist in real life'.[1] They must be made indirectly pleasing by being used to heighten our appreciation of beauty and perfection—obviously, by contrast. 'Perfection' here means natural perfection, Santayana's 'natural conditions of organisation',[3] rather than supernatural perfection. For Ruskin, whose standard is the latter one, grotesque art has a far more positive character. The Apocalyptic beasts are an attempt to suggest perfection, but not by force of contrast; indeed, as symbols, they have been accepted as a sublime representation of supernatural truth.[4]

[1] cf. Bagehot, op. cit., p. 365.
[2] cf. Bagehot, op. cit., p. 374 (see p. 15).
[3] See p. 17.
[4] See p. 41.

The chief points of interest in Bagehot's remarks on the grotesque are his tacit admission that grotesque objects exist in real life, and his somewhat reluctant approval of the use of such objects in art for purposes of contrast.

VICTOR HUGO

12. The idea of contrast between the grotesque and the sublime as an artistic device is to be found also in Hugo's *La Préface du Cromwell*,[1] where he sets forth his views on the grotesque at length:

> . . . la même impression, toujours répétée, peut fatiguer à la longue. Le sublime sur le sublime produit malaisément un contraste, et l'on a besoin de se reposer de tout, même du beau. Il semble, au contraire, que le grotesque soit un temps d'arrêt, un terme de comparaison, un point de départ d'où l'on s'élève vers le beau avec une perception plus fraîche et plus excitée.[2]

Primarily, however, Hugo regards the grotesque not merely as a useful source of contrast but as a necessary complement without which the sublime and the beautiful must remain imperfect.

In Hegelian fashion, Hugo emphasizes the antithetical structure of the world. The world has always been composed of opposites, but pre-Christian art preferred on the whole to ignore the fact and to deal with the sublime aspects of existence, suppressing those antithetical aspects which Hugo calls 'the grotesque': 'All that stands in opposition to the serious, the sublime, the good and the beautiful in the world, in nature and in man, Victor Hugo terms the grotesque.'[3] Grotesques are, of course, to be found in the art of antiquity: 'Rien ne vient sans racine; la seconde époque est toujours en germe dans la première.'[4] The tritons, satyrs, Cyclops are grotesque; the sirens, the Furies, the Parcae, the harpies are grotesque; Polyphemus is a terrible grotesque, Silenus is a comic grotesque. But it is all rather half-hearted:

> Le grotesque antique est timide et cherche toujours à se cacher. On voit qu'il n'est pas sur son terrain, parce qu'il n'est pas dans sa nature. Il se dissimule le plus qu'il peut. Les satyres, les tritons, les sirènes sont à peine difformes. Les parques, les harpies, sont plutôt hideuses par leurs attributs que par leurs traits; les furies sont belles, et on les appelle

---

[1] References are to *Préface du Cromwell*, ed. Edmond Wahl (Clarendon Press, Oxford, 1909).
[2] cf. Hugo, op. cit., pp. 15–16.
[3] cf. Knaak, op. cit., p. 41.
[4] cf. Hugo, op. cit., p. 13.

euménides, c'est-à-dire *douces, bienfaisantes*. Il y a un voile de grandeur ou de divinité sur d'autres grotesques. Polyphème est géant; Midas est roi; Silène est dieu.[1]

It is significant that tragedy rather than comedy is the great dramatic genre of antiquity: 'Près des colosses homériques, Eschyle, Sophocle, Euripide, que sont Aristophane et Plaute?'[2]

Only with the coming of Christianity did men become fully conscious of the antithetical nature of the world: 'Du jour où le christianisme a dit à l'homme:—Tu es double, tu es composé de deux êtres, l'un périssable, l'autre immortel, l'un charnel, l'autre éthéré . . . —de ce jour le drame a été créé.'[3] Drama is, for Hugo, the great modern art form:

. . . le caractère du drame est le réel; le réel résulte de la combinaison toute naturelle de deux types, le sublime et le grotesque, qui se croisent dans la vie et dans la création. Car la poésie vraie, la poésie complète, est dans l'harmonie des contraires.[4]

By making man conscious of his own dual nature Christianity has also made him more deeply aware of the antithetical structure of the external world. This is naturally reflected in art: '. . . car le point de départ de la religion est toujours le point de départ de la poésie. Tout se tient.'[5]

Like the Christian religion, the 'modern muse' sees things in a higher and broader fashion:

Elle sentira que tout dans la création n'est pas beau, le difforme près du gracieux, le grotesque au revers du sublime, le mal avec le bien, l'ombre avec la lumière . . . Elle se mettra à faire comme la nature, à mêler dans ses créations, sans pourtant les confondre, l'ombre à la lumière, le grotesque au sublime, en d'autres termes, le corps à l'âme, la bête à l'esprit.[6]

A new type, the grotesque, and a new art form, comedy, in which it can be developed, thus emerge in modern art; both of them, though not entirely unknown to antiquity, nevertheless alien to the pre-Christian attitude of mind.

It will be clear from the above that Hugo's use of the word grotesque, whilst original and audacious, is rather in the sense of 'ugly' than in the sense of 'fantastic'. Art, if it is to be 'true' and

---

[1] ibid.   [2] ibid.   [3] ibid., p. 23.
[4] ibid., p. 24. I have not thought it necessary to consider Hugo's use of the term *le drame* more fully here.
[5] ibid., p. 12.
[6] ibid., pp. 11–12.

'complete', must reflect the whole of life. It must therefore concern itself with ugly, trivial, and evil things as well as with things which are beautiful, grand, and good. Hugo thus not only separates the word from its connotation of 'unreal' but he applies it to an immensely wide range of natural phenomena—everything, indeed, which is antithetical to a 'sublime' quality. We have already seen that by implication at least, Ruskin considers all but the highest levels of art to be in some way grotesque because of the distorting effects of material circumstances upon the human spirit. Hugo recognizes much the same state of affairs, but his terminology is different. The noble grotesque, for Ruskin, arises from the distortion of the sublime by the trivial. It resides, therefore, in the juxtaposition, the amalgamation of the spiritual and the worldly. Ruskin can thus speak of the grotesque as having a sublime quality.

For Hugo, on the other hand, the phrase 'noble grotesque' would appear at first sight to be a contradiction in terms, since he regards the grotesque as essentially ignoble. We must distinguish, however, between Hugo's view of the grotesque in nature and in art. In a note to a passage of Ruskin's: 'Beauty deprived of its proper foils and adjuncts ceases to be enjoyed as beauty, just as light deprived of all shadow, ceases to be enjoyed as light',[1] Hugo observes:

La division du beau et du laid dans l'art ne symétrise pas avec celle de la nature. Rien n'est beau ou laid dans les arts que par l'exécution. Une chose difforme, horrible, hideuse, transportée avec vérité et poésie dans le domaine de l'art, deviendra belle, admirable, sans rien perdre de sa monstruosité, et, d'une autre part, les plus belles choses du monde, faussement et systématiquement arrangées dans une composition artificielle, seront ridicules, burlesques, hybrides, laides.[2]

In nature the grotesque is the antithesis of everything that is sublime, noble, beautiful; but in art, where it is the treatment which matters, not the material, a grotesque object may be aesthetically sublime. Hugo too, then, may be said to recognize a 'noble grotesque' in this sense. We may also note in passing that this view of art is directly opposed to Bagehot's assertion that the material is of primary importance in a work of art.

Hugo insists on the need for the grotesque in art not in advocacy of a more fantastic but of a more realistic kind of art; he insists that art

[1] cf. *Modern Painters* (1859), III. IV. 3, 12, 15.
[2] cf. *La Préface du Cromwell*, p. 71.

must be more inclusive, broadening and deepening its scope with the ironic confrontations and antitheses of real life. For him the term grotesque, far from having the connotation of 'out of nature', to employ Scott's useful phrase,[1] has strongly physical associations. He sees the grotesque as a kind of Sancho Panza to the sublime: 'Elle [la poésie] se mettra à faire comme la nature, à mêler ses créations, sans pourtant les confondre, l'ombre à la lumière, le grotesque au sublime, en d'autres termes, le corps à l'âme, la bête à l'esprit.'[2]

Whereas Ruskin, in speaking of the 'wild and wonderful images' of Northern mythology—'kelpie and gnome, Lurlei and Harz spirits'—emphasizes their 'numinous' quality (they stand as 'symbols between us and our God'),[3] Hugo contrasts the ugly figures of folk-lore with the beautiful ones: 'le gnome embellit le sylphe.' For Ruskin, grotesqueness always implies distortion. The less grotesque an object of art is the truer it must be either to the world of nature or to the supernatural world:

The reader is always to keep in mind that if the objects of horror, in which the terrible grotesque finds its materials, were contemplated in their true light, and with the entire energy of the soul, they would cease to be grotesque, and become altogether sublime.[4]

For Hugo, the grotesque is associated with truth: '. . . les euménides grecques sont bien moins horribles, et par conséquent, bien moins vraies, que les sorcières de Macbeth.'[5]

Hugo thus sees the grotesque as having an essentially relative value; it rounds out and completes the sublime side of life. Just as the sublime alone gives a one-sided view of life, so, too, 'Ce qui n'est que grotesque, n'est pas complet.'[6]

It is not the contrast, the antithesis, which is grotesque, any more than it is sublime; the antithesis is, simply, real.[7]

Hugo does not, therefore, regard the grotesque in art as a genre which impatiently rejects the forms of the natural world and strives to establish contact with a higher sphere of reality through the bizarre

[1] See p. 36.
[2] cf. Hugo, op. cit., pp. 11–12.
[3] cf. Ruskin, *The Stones of Venice*, III. III. §LXVI.
[4] ibid., III. III. §LIX.
[5] cf. Hugo, op. cit., p. 15.
[6] cf. Knaak, op. cit., p. 60 (Hugo, *Notes de Cromwell*, p. 393).
[7] cf. Hugo, *La Préface de Cromwell*, p. 24. Hugo's view may be contrasted with the following: 'The grotesque is no other than the slender connection of the ugly with the beautiful, to bring out a sharp contrast' (Sleumer, *Die Dramen Victor Hugos* Berlin, 1901). cf. Knaak, op. cit., p. 75.

and the distorted. Nevertheless, the employment of the grotesque—bearing in mind his special sense of the phrase—does, for Hugo, bring art into closer contact with the supernatural, that is, with God: 'Vous savez que Dieu est pour moi le grand faiseur de l'antithèse.'[1] Christianity has made man conscious of his dual nature, and art which emphasizes the dual nature of man and of the world is Christian art. The endeavour to establish contact with supernatural truth does not entail the rejection of the natural world which God made and in which His laws operate. God made ugliness, or what we call ugliness, which is really part of 'un grand ensemble qui nous échappe, et qui s'harmonise, non pas avec l'homme, mais avec la création toute entière.'[2] Ugliness in all its forms—evil, triviality, grotesqueness—is therefore an essential element in serious art, which can best approach God by faithfully portraying His universe.

THOMAS WRIGHT

13. In the later nineteenth century, when the romantic view of grotesque art as possessing a 'numinous', transcendental quality loses ground, a third view of the grotesque becomes current, according to which the grotesque is neither a rejection of reality nor an actual part of it; the view that it is fantasy with a practical aspect—parody, burlesque, mockery, caricature.

The idea is not, of course, entirely novel. Ruskin lists mockery or satire as one of the kinds of grotesque art. Hugo, in the *Préface du Cromwell*, describes Callot[3] as 'le Michel-Ange burlesque', and observes: 'Si du monde idéal [i.e. the world of Dante and of Milton] il [le grotesque] passe au monde réel, il y déroule d'intarissables parodies d'humanité.'[4] For neither of these writers, however, is there any necessary connexion between grotesque art and caricature. Thomas Wright (1865)[5] and John Addington Symonds (1890)[6] regard caricature as an essential part of the grotesque.[7] Something must be said,

---

[1] cf. Hugo, *Le Rhin*, vol. II, p. 201, cf. Knaak, op. cit., pp. 39–40.
[2] cf. Hugo, op. cit., p. 17, cf. Pope:
   All Discord, Harmony not understood;
   All partial Evil, universal Good:
                                   Essay on Man, Epistle I, ll. 291–2.
[3] See p. 9.   [4] cf. Hugo, op. cit., p. 14.
[5] cf. *A History of Caricature and Grotesque in Literature and Art* (see p. 24).
[6] cf. *Essays Speculative and Suggestive* (see p. 51).
[7] cf. Schneegans, op. cit. (see pp. 24, 33): '[The grotesque] is a special kind of caricature . . . caricature stretched to impossibility'; Volkelt, op. cit. (see p. 21): 'All grotesque [art] is caricature in the widest sense.' (cf. Krudewig, op. cit., p. 30.)

however, about the senses in which they understand the word caricature.

Thomas Wright's work, as has already been remarked,[1] is a
simple historical account in which little attempt is made to define
either caricature or the grotesque. In his opening sentence he associates both, by implication, with the comic: 'It is not my intention in the
following pages to discuss the question what constitutes the comic or
the laughable, or in other words, to enter into the philosophy of the
subject.'[2] In the following paragraph he gives his opinions, briefly,
on the origins of caricature and the grotesque as follows:

A tendency to burlesque and caricature appears, indeed, to be a feeling
deeply implanted in human nature, and it is one of the earliest talents dis-
played by people in a rude state of society. An appreciation of, and sensit-
iveness to, ridicule, *and a love of that which is humorous*,[3] are found even
among savages, and enter largely into their relations with their fellow men.
When, before people cultivated either literature or art, the chieftain sat in
his rude hall surrounded by his warriors, they amused themselves by
turning their enemies and opponents into mockery, by laughing at their
weaknesses, joking on their defects, whether physical or mental, and giving
them nicknames in accordance therewith,—in fact, caricaturing them in
words, or by telling stories which were calculated to excite laughter. When
the agricultural slaves (for the tillers of the land were then slaves) were
indulged with a day of relief from their labours, *they spent it in unrestrained
mirth*. And when these same people began to erect permanent buildings,
and to ornament them, the favourite subjects of their ornamentation were
such as presented ludicrous ideas. The warrior, too, who caricatured his
enemy in his speeches over the festive board, soon sought to give a more
permanent form to his ridicule, which he endeavoured to do by rude
delineations on the bare rock, or on any other convenient surface which
presented itself to his hand. Thus originated caricature and the grotesque
in art. In fact, art itself, in its earliest forms, is caricature; for it is only by
that exaggeration of features which belongs to caricature, that unskilful
draughtsmen could make themselves understood.[4]

Although, in the passage above, Wright emphasizes the primitive
love of mockery, he is clearly alive to the fact that ridicule does not
exhaust the possibilities of humour. His insertion of the words which
I have italicized shows his desire to leave room for other kinds of
humour than satire. He is anxious, however, to make the terms

[1] See p. 24.
[2] cf. Wright, op. cit., p. 1.
[3] The italics are mine throughout.
[4] cf. Wright, op. cit., p. 2.

caricature and the grotesque as nearly synonymous as possible, and with this end in view he employs a much wider sense of the word caricature in the last sentence of the passage than in the first, where it clearly implies mockery, or at least intentional humour. The unskilful artist, we are told, was obliged to exaggerate the characteristics of his subject merely in order to make it recognizable, not in order to create a humorous effect.[1]

The question arises how far one can extend the sense of the term caricature without altogether losing sight of its conventional meaning. Here, Wright uses the word without any connotation of ridicule or humour in the sense of 'an exaggerated representation'. A few pages later even this sense is further extended:

> The monstrous is closely allied to the grotesque, and both come within the province of caricature, when we take this term in its widest sense. The Greeks, especially, were partial to representations of monsters, and monstrous forms are continually met with among their ornaments and works of art.[2]

One can scarcely speak of an 'exaggerated representation' of a monster, for there is no natural form to be exaggerated (Wright supplies a cut of the Egyptian god Typhon by way of illustration).[3] The term caricature must thus be understood here simply in the sense of 'a fantastic representation' which is neither satirical or humorous, nor exaggerated.

It is clear from the outset that Wright would have been happier with the thesis that caricature comes within the province of the grotesque. The 'widest sense' in which he is obliged to employ the term caricature robs it of all independent value.

JOHN ADDINGTON SYMONDS

14. In his essay *Caricature, the Fantastic, the Grotesque*,[4] Symonds, like Wright, insists that caricature is invariably present in grotesque art. Unlike Wright, however, he attempts to justify his opinion by

---

[1] Once later (cf. op. cit., p. 59) Wright speaks of such non-humorous exaggeration, due to lack of skill, as 'unintentional caricature'. This qualifying adjective, however, is elsewhere omitted, e.g. '. . . in innumerable cases serious pictures of the gravest and most important subjects are simply and absolutely caricatures. Anglo-Saxon art ran much into this style, and is often very grotesque in character.' (cf. op. cit., p. 57.)

[2] ibid., pp. 8–9.

[3] ibid., p. 9.

[4] cf. *Essays Speculative and Suggestive* (London, 1890). References are to the third edition (Smith, Elder and Co., 1907).

limiting the sense of the phrase 'the grotesque', rather than by extending the sense of the word caricature so as to make it applicable to forms (such as the sphinx and the dragon) which are not intended to provoke ridicule. He is, nevertheless, constrained to extend his initial definition of caricature in dealing with grotesque art.

Symonds defines caricature as 'a distinct species of characterisation, in which the salient features of a person or an object have been emphasized with the view of rendering them ridiculous', an admirable definition which is reinforced by a reference to the etymology (It. *caricare*, to surcharge), an addition which makes his convenient neglect of the etymology of the word grotesque the more culpable.

In his view, grotesque art is art in which 'an element of caricature, whether deliberately intended or imported by the craftsman's spontaneity of humour, forms an ingredient in the thing produced'. He therefore contradicts Wright[1] by asserting: 'What resembles grotesqueness in the archaic stages of Greek sculpture . . . must be ascribed to naïveté and lack of technical skill.'[2] Where there is no spirit of mockery, there is no grotesqueness.

Symonds contends that grotesque art is almost exclusively the work of 'the Teutonic section of the Aryan family'. It is a constant element in medieval Teutonic art, in Gothic cathedrals, in 'Scandinavian poetry of the best period':

> Grotesqueness may be traced in all the fantastic beings of Celtic and Germanic folk-lore—in gnomes inhabiting the mountains, in kelpies of the streams and mermaids of the ocean, in Puck and Robin Goodfellow, in fairies of the heath and woodland, in the princesses of Border ballad-literature fated by magic spells to dree their doom as loathly dragons.[3]

A great part of the section devoted to the grotesque, however, consists of a list of fanciful creatures which are not, in Symonds's view, grotesque:

> Ugly stories about Zeus and Cronos, quaint stories about the metamorphoses of Proteus, and the Phorcydes with their one eye are not grotesque . . . Princesses transformed into parrots, djinns with swarthy faces doting on fair damsels, water-carriers converted by some spell into caliphs, ghouls, animals that talk, immense birds brooding over treasures in the wilderness are not grotesque.[4]

[1] See p. 51.
[2] cf. Symonds, op. cit., p. 158.
[3] ibid., p. 159.
[4] ibid.

Even 'Hindoo idols, Chinese and Japanese bronzes, Aztec bas-reliefs, and such things', though they seem to us grotesque, may not be so; their form may be due to religious symbolism.[1]

It would seem to be somewhat arbitrary to maintain that a princess turned into a dragon is grotesque, but a princess turned into a parrot is not; that Puck is grotesque, but not the Cyclops. The narrow rigidity of Symonds's criterion is still more apparent in the section on the fantastic: '. . . the chimaera of Hellenic sculpture, the horned and hoofed devil of medieval painting, Shakespeare's Caliban, Milton's Death, Goethe's Mephistopheles' are all 'products of fantastic art'. Since they were not created in a spirit of mockery, however, they are not grotesque.[2] Nor are the sphinx and the dragon and so on.

Curiously, Symonds is obliged by this thesis to deny that the works of art which originally gave rise to the term grotesque are grotesque:

. . . arabesques devised by old Italian painters—frescoed patterns upon walls and ceilings, in which tendrils of the vine, acanthus foliage, parts of beasts and men and birds and fabulous creatures are brought into quasi-organic fusion with candelabra, goblets, lyres, and other familiar objects of utility.

—these are the 'merely graceful result' of 'an exercise of the capricious fancy, playing with things which it combines into arbitrary non-existent forms'. Here, etymology is conspicuously lacking.

Agreeing with Wright that there is an essential connexion between caricature and the grotesque, and yet rejecting at the outset Wright's extension of the term caricature to seriously intended art, Symonds's chief difficulty is in justifying the application of the term caricature, as he defines it, to the examples which he supplies of the grotesque. The question arises whether the requirements are met in such examples of the grotesque—which by his definition must contain 'an element of caricature'—as 'gnomes inhabiting the mountains . . . kelpies of the streams and mermaids of the ocean . . . fairies of the heath and woodland.'[3]

---

[1] ibid., p. 160. Kayser (op. cit., pp. 194–5) makes a similar point regarding the possible stylized nature of such art. Symonds's point, however, is not that we do not know such art to be intentionally fantastic but that we do not know it to be intentionally ludicrous.

[2] 'The fantastic lacks that deliberate intention to disparage which lies at the root of caricature' (and, by implication, of the grotesque) (ibid., p. 156).

[3] cf. Symonds, op. cit., p. 159.

Are we to assume that Symonds regards these figures as caricatures of seriously intended gods and tutelary spirits, a kind of vast Teutonic travesty of the mythologies of less sophisticated peoples? Why, then, one asks, are fairies listed with satyrs and nymphs amongst 'examples of the fantastic,'[1] since the fantastic 'lacks that deliberate intention to disparage which lies at the root of caricature'?[2]

In point of fact, Symonds modifies his initial definition of caricature as soon as he begins to define the grotesque: 'The grotesque contains an element of caricature, *whether* deliberately intended *or* imported by the craftsman's spontaneity of humour.'[3] It is suggested that, after all, caricature need not be deliberate or intentional. He adds later that caricature is always 'a conscious or semi-conscious element' in grotesque art.[4]

These qualifying phrases suggest that what Symonds actually sees in the fanciful creatures of Celtic and Teutonic folk-lore is a kind of overflow of playfulness, a taste for humorous absurdity; that he regards them as having closer affinities with, say, the characters of *Alice in Wonderland* than with the monsters and sirens of the *Odyssey*. He takes it for granted that 'the Phorcydes with their one eye' are entirely serious creations. The figures of Teutonic folk-lore are not meant to be taken seriously. But then, neither is 'The Dong with the Luminous Nose', but the term caricature is scarcely applicable to it (though Chesterton remarks that if it had been written in the seventeenth century it would have been taken for a dull satire on Oliver Cromwell).[5]

Symonds's train of thought leads him to conclude:

The Asiatic and Greek minds, however, lacked a quality which was demanded in order to elicit grotesqueness from fantasy. That quality the Teutonic section of the Aryan family possessed in abundance; it was all-pervasive in the products of their genius. We may define it broadly as humour.[6]

As it stands, however, this statement that the grotesque is humorous fantasy is too broad for Symonds's thesis, and he continues: 'I do not deny humour to the Greeks and Orientals; but I contend that Teutons have the merit of applying humour to caricature and the fantastic, so as to educe from both in combination what we call grotesqueness.' Perhaps the term 'burlesque' might have been

---

[1] ibid., p. 157.   [2] ibid., p. 156.   [3] ibid., p. 158.   [4] ibid., p. 159.
[5] See below, note 3, p. 94.
[6] Symonds, op. cit., p. 159.

appropriate to Symonds's conception of the grotesque as a genre midway between caricature and the fantastic—burlesque in the loose sense of 'mock-seriousness',[1] mock-serious, that is, without mocking anything more specific than seriousness itself.[2]

Everything considered, Symonds gives no really valid reason for regarding the grotesque as invariably a combination of fantasy and caricature, an interpretation which runs counter to the etymology and to much of the semantic history of the word grotesque. Nevertheless, the element which he sees in grotesque art, a kind of mocking or defiant humour, a spontaneous 'distortion, degradation of form, burlesque', must be borne in mind in attempting an examination of the grotesque in art.

Symonds's remarks on the origin of the fantastic are much more penetrating than his consideration of the grotesque, anticipating the ideas of modern psychology in notable fashion:

> In the higher manifestations of fantastic art ... real conditions of man's subjective being have taken sensuous shape at the bidding of creative genius. The artist, while giving birth to such fantastic creatures of imagination, resembles a deeply-stirred and dreaming man, whose brain projects impossible shapes to symbolise the perturbations of his spirit. Myth and allegory, the metamorphosis of mortals into plants, fairies, satyrs, nymphs, and tutelary deities of sea or forest, are examples of the fantastic in this sphere of highest poetry ... They are felt to be actual through the force with which their makers felt them, and through their adaptation to the fancies of imaginative minds in general.[3]

The relation of 'unreal' forms to 'real conditions of man's subjective being', the perception of the vital fact that the interior world is no less real than the exterior one, is the only sound starting-point for a consideration of fantastic—and of grotesque—art.

GEORGE SANTAYANA

15. Santayana's views on the grotesque[4] have already been referred to,[5] but they require a more detailed consideration.

Like other late nineteenth-century writers on the grotesque, Santayana considers grotesque art in terms of art rather than in ethical

---

[1] cf. *C.O.D.* (1954).
[2] Symonds does indeed remark: 'The free play of the Northern fancy ran over easily into distortion, degradation of form, burlesque' (op. cit., p. 159).
[3] ibid., pp. 157–8.
[4] cf. *The Sense of Beauty*, part IV (Expression), sect. 64 (The Grotesque), pp. 256–8 (Adam and Charles Black, London, 1896).
[5] See pp. 16–17.

or philosophical terms. Ruskin, the professional art critic, scrutinizes the motives and influences which lead the artist to create grotesque forms, and launches into a profuse account of the spiritual and moral implications of grotesque art. He is prepared to judge whole civilizations by their grotesques.[1] Santayana, the professional philosopher, is content to take it for granted that the artist simply desires to be original,[2] and describes the grotesque, placidly, as 'an interesting effect'.

Santayana considers grotesqueness from the spectator's point of view rather than from the artist's, and his remarks on grotesque art are for the most part applicable to any attempt at artistic originality. Grotesqueness is regarded as an intermediate stage between our initial lack of comprehension of a novel form of art and our ultimate understanding of and familiarity with that form.

What strikes us as being utterly chaotic and meaningless does not seem to us to be grotesque: 'If this confusion is absolute, the object is simply null; it does not exist aesthetically, except by virtue of materials.' Again, forms which have become familiar, however distorted or impossible, physically speaking, are not grotesque: 'The centaur and the satyr are no longer grotesque; the type is accepted.' Only when 'we have an inkling of the unity and character in the midst of the strangeness of the form' does the grotesque occur.

In considering the grotesque in this way, from the stand-point of the audience, Santayana ignores a difference which is vital from the standpoint of the artist—from which, admittedly, we cannot in strict logic consider a work of art—the difference between work which is deliberately obscure or bizarre and work which is not intentionally so. The grotesque, he remarks, is 'the half-formed, the perplexed, and the suggestively monstrous'. But as a description of the reaction of the audience these words are applicable both to work which is intended to remain 'suggestively monstrous'—the work of Kafka, for example, and perhaps the poetry of Dylan Thomas—and to work which appears strange in spite of the artist's intentions simply because of its novelty

[1] See p. 41.
[2] cf. Dr. Tillyard's remarks on 'the nineteenth century cult of originality': 'How powerful this cult is we can see at once by the instinctive welcome we give the word. A headmaster, considering the testimonial of a would-be assistant, little as he would like a man to be odd, would emit approval if he read that the man had a vein of originality. Contrariwise to say of someone that he has no originality is an unmitigatedly adverse criticism. Such a state of affairs did not exist before the nineteenth century' (Poetry and its Background (Chatto and Windus, 1955), p. 84).

and originality, as Wordsworth was attacked for his 'foppish singu-
larity of style'[1] or T. S. Eliot for his obscurity.

It is above all with the latter kind of grotesqueness that Santayana
concerns himself. For him the test of good grotesque art is that on
further acquaintance the grotesqueness disappears:

> We call these inventions comic and grotesque when we are considering
> their divergence from the natural rather than their inward possibility. But
> the latter constitutes their real charm; and the more we study and develop
> them, the better we understand it. The incongruity with the conventional
> type then disappears, and what was impossible and ridiculous at first takes
> its place among recognised ideals. The centaur and the satyr are no longer
> grotesque; the type is accepted.

But, of course, in proportion as the incongruity of the centaur with
'the conventional type' disappears, the figure loses the strangeness
which is an essential part of its appeal. Santayana's attitude towards
the comic shows a similar neglect of artistic intention: 'In the comic
we have this same juxtaposition of a new and an old idea, and if the
new is not futile and really inconceivable, it may in time establish
itself in the mind, and cease to be ludicrous.' He would seem to
regard it as actually desirable that the comic should 'cease to be
ludicrous'.

Santayana's statement that 'good wit is novel truth, as the good
grotesque is novel beauty' is significant of his attitude; he clearly
regards the adjective 'novel', in each case, as dispensable: 'New things
are therefore generally bad because, as has been well said, they are
incapable of becoming old.'

Clearly, in the case of work which is only 'accidentally' grotesque,
i.e. temporarily regarded as grotesque through the lack of understanding of the reader, who later comes to understand and appreciate
it more fully, it is desirable that the type should be accepted. But the
case of deliberately grotesque work is different; unless it continues to
be regarded as 'perplexed, suggestively monstrous', it loses its
raison d'être. It is not the better for being 'no longer grotesque', but
very much the worse. When the 'suggestively monstrous' ceases to be
monstrous—that is, to strike us as monstrous—it ceases to be suggestive.

Assuming that Santayana is correct in saying that work which

---

[1] cf. W. H. Ireland, *Scribbleomania, or, The Printer's Devil's Polichronicon*,
printed for Sherwood, Neely and Jones, Paternoster-Row, London, 1815
(p. 78).

appears to us to be absolutely incoherent is not grotesque, the question arises whether there is any *lasting* intermediate position for a work of art between being 'simply null' and becoming 'a recognised ideal' which is 'no longer grotesque'.

'What was impossible and ridiculous at first takes its place among recognised ideals', Santayana tells us, when we study and develop its 'inward possibility'. But cannot a thing be at once impossible and ridiculous—or at least, ludicrous—*and* a recognized ideal? What was initially regarded as impossible and ridiculous may or may not cease to be so regarded with increasing familiarity. The cosmic theory of Galileo is no longer so regarded. On the other hand, 'The Owl and the Pussy-Cat', even in the process of becoming a 'standard' example of nonsense, can scarcely cease to be regarded as impossible and ridiculous—or ludicrous. To say of such a creation as the centaur or the gargoyle that 'nature might conceivably have offered it', and that its inward possibility rather than its divergence from the natural constitutes its real charm, does not mean that its unnaturalness can be ignored or forgotten. Its grotesqueness rests on a securer basis than mere artistic novelty. It is due to the rejection of those 'natural conditions of organisation' of which Santayana speaks. Art which simply rejects an existing artistic convention may come to lose its ephemeral grotesqueness; but art which rejects the natural order to which we are bound by 'our fixed method of perception' must remain grotesque, however hackneyed it becomes, until men grow eyes in the middle of their foreheads and eat with runcible spoons.

Concentrating as he does on the synthetic, *creative* aspect of grotesque art which 'constitutes its real charm', Santayana tends to ignore the negative side. The grotesque artist not only makes; he unmakes. Santayana does indeed remark that it is in view of this negative side—the divergence from the natural—that we speak of such art as grotesque, but he then dismisses this less-attractive aspect of grotesque art from his examination and considers the grotesque simply in the sense of 'a new form'. However recognized the centaur becomes, it can only become a recognized grotesque.

G. K. CHESTERTON

16. In his book on Browning,[1] Chesterton considers Browning's use of the grotesque from three complementary points of view;[2] as a

---

[1] cf. *Robert Browning* (Macmillan and Co. Ltd., 1903).
[2] cf. ch. VI in particular (Chesterton, op. cit.).

reflection of the actual world,[1] as a deliberate artistic device,[2] and as a temperamental peculiarity.[3]

Nature, Chesterton tells us, 'in the sense of what is ordinarily called the country', contains not only things which are commonly called stately and beautiful, such as stars and lilies, but also 'cows and pigs, and creatures more humorous than can be found in a whole sketch-book of Callot'. We normally think of the grotesque as being man-made (as Ruskin does), but it is ultimately inspired by nature:

The whole world of the fantastic, all things, top-heavy, lop-sided, and nonsensical are conceived as the work of man, gargoyles, German jugs, Chinese pots, political caricatures, burlesque epics, the pictures of Mr Aubrey Beardsley and the puns of Robert Browning. But in truth, a part, and a very large part of the sanity and power of nature lies in the fact that out of her comes all this instinct of caricature.[4]

In producing grotesque art Browning is thus, in the first instance, simply reflecting an objectively real side of nature:

Browning's verse, in so far as it is grotesque, is not complex or artificial; it is natural and in the legitimate tradition of nature. The verse sprawls like the trees, dances like the dust; it is ragged like the thundercloud, it is top-heavy like the toadstool. Energy which disregards the standard of classical art is in nature as it is in Browning. The same sense of the up-roarious force in things which makes Browning dwell on the oddity of a fungus or a jellyfish makes him dwell on the oddity of a philosophical idea.[5]

The grotesque is 'the first thing on which the eye of the poet [i.e. Browning] lights in looking at a landscape'.

Before considering the peculiarity of temper which leads Browning to select the grotesque rather than the stately and beautiful as a subject, Chesterton endeavours to justify the use of the grotesque as 'definitely valuable . . . in all poetry' for the purpose of sharpening the reader's interest in the natural world. The bulk of the hippopotamus, for example, is grotesquely and admirably emphasized in the Book of Job: 'Canst thou play with him as with a bird, canst thou bind him for thy maidens?'[6] Apart from being a reflection of reality, the

---

[1] ibid., pp. 149–51.   [2] ibid., pp. 151–2.   [3] ibid., pp. 152–4.

[4] ibid., p. 149. The term caricature is employed here in an extended sense reminiscent of Thomas Wright's use of the term (see p. 51).

[5] cf. Chesterton, op. cit., pp. 149–50.

[6] ibid., pp. 151–2. In point of fact the verse refers to Leviathan, not to Behemoth (cf. Job xli.5).

grotesque is thus in the second place an artistic device which does not so much serve to draw our attention from the natural world as to make us see the world with new eyes in a way which is not less but more truthful than the usual attitude of casual acceptance. It provokes the sense of wonder we ought always to feel in contemplating a wonderful universe.

Third, in Browning's case it is also the result of something 'perverse and unusual'. His mind was 'like a strong piece of wood with a knot in it', and this gives rise not only to his preference for subjects which are actually grotesque and to his 'serious use of the grotesque' to show the world in a new light, but also to 'horse-play', to the 'frivolous stupidity' of 'Pacchiarotto', and 'an inability to keep a kind of demented ingenuity even out of poems in which it was quite inappropriate'[1] such as 'The Pied Piper of Hamelin'.

The chief point of interest in Chesterton's remarks on the grotesque is the idea that the grotesque may be employed as a means of presenting the world in a new light without falsifying it. As in the fine passage in which Bagehot comments on the 'absurd' nature of the universe,[2] Chesterton is concerned with the strangeness of the world to an immortal being. Conversely, he regards the use of the grotesque which is devoid of this purpose of stimulating interest in 'ordinary' phenomena as mere 'horse-play', though even Browning's 'frivolous stupidity' is 'to a certain extent the mark of a real hilarity', as it is in the 'elephantine ingenuity' of much of Shakespeare's quibble-hunting: 'Energy and joy [are] the father and mother of the grotesque.'[3]

17. For Chesterton the value of grotesque art increases in proportion to its connexion with the natural world; the wilful, subjective grotesque which rejects all natural forms and does not exist to draw attention to them is 'frivolous stupidity', though nonsense may be acceptable when it is meant to be comic. In this respect Chesterton's views on the grotesque are similar to those of other writers dealt with in the present chapter.

We have seen that these later writers on the grotesque, whether or

---

[1] cf. Chesterton, op. cit., p. 153.
[2] See p. 43.
[3] cf. Chesterton, op. cit., p. 148. cf. T. A. Meyer's association of the grotesque with exuberance (*Lebensüberfluss*): 'Here belongs all that teems and gushes and bubbles with life, all in which one sees that the stream of life does not flow feebly nor moderately, but rushes on its way chattering and turbulent.' (*Ästhetik* (Stuttgart, 1923), p. 83; cf. Krudewig, op. cit., p. 11.

not they regard grotesqueness as being objectively real, attempt to explain the grotesque as something other than an endeavour to transcend the limitations of the natural order.[1] They consider it to be of serious aesthetic value when it has an obvious practical purpose; when it is employed as a means of ridicule, when it refreshes our interest in the normal, and so on. Fantasy, subjective art which has a perceptible coherence and intrinsic discipline, is acceptable, even admirable; but 'incoherent' fantasy can only be saved from absolute condemnation on the understanding that we are intended to laugh at it.

Wolfgang Kayser observes:

Aesthetics, in its evaluation of the grotesque, has up to the present day been unable to find its way back to the high place of the definitions between 1770 and 1830; it places [the grotesque] in the low levels of the coarsely comic (*den Niederungen des Grobkomischen*).[2]

So far as actual dissertations specifically concerned with the grotesque are concerned, this generalization is largely justifiable, though even within this restricted field it is not difficult to find exceptions in twentieth-century theses.[3] But in the general field of art and criticism it is scarcely the case. Art which may fairly be described as grotesque in view of the general semantic development of the word[4] is far from being regarded as 'coarsely comic', unless one is prepared to apply this phrase wholesale to the work of Picasso, Klee, Dali, and Henry Moore; of Baudelaire, Gogol, Joyce, Kafka, and Samuel Beckett.

---

[1] cf. the view of T. Tyndall Wildridge (*The Grotesque in Church Art*, Andrews and Co., London, 1899) that grotesque art in church carvings may in part be due to 'the copying of an earlier work with executive ability, with strong perception of its unintentional and latent humour, but without respect to, or without knowledge of, its serious meaning' (p. 8). Tyndall suggests as a parallel the gradual oral distortion of verses into our present nursery-rhymes, e.g. 'Hey Diddle Diddle!' may originally have been 'a satire in derision of the worship of Diana' (cf. op. cit., p. 40). The last line of this verse may originally have read 'Dis ran away with Persephone'! (p. 42.)

[2] cf. Kayser, op. cit., p. 112.

[3] cf. Campbell, op. cit., p. 20: '. . . the great or inevitable grotesque . . . with its conflict of ideal and real, its revolts, its picturing of the incomprehensible, and its revealing of the shams of life'; Krudewig, op. cit., p. 31: 'The grotesque, far more [than caricature] conceals a valuable idea behind the distortion which mounts into the fantastic'; R. Petsch, *Dt. Literaturwissenschaft*, 1940 ('Das Groteske'): 'The grotesque . . . the symbolic realisation of the exaggerated directed towards deeper, background values and above all towards a world of wider margins and greater depths than that which everyday life offers us' (cf. Kayser, op. cit., p. 217).

[4] See p. 17, sect. 4.

Moreover, the critical theories which accompany such art, mani-
festoes, expositions, analyses, profoundly influenced by psychological
theory, largely advocate the rejection, in art, of 'the natural conditions
of organization' in the simple objective sense of the phrase: 'Retour-
nons, mes frères, vers les grandes eaux de l'Inconscient.'[1]

Kayser is naturally aware of this distinction. Indeed, he lists the
modern period as one of the three great ages of grotesque art. But it is
as well to remember how restricted the field in which he speaks of an
aesthetic devaluation of the term grotesque actually is.

[1] cf. Laforgue, *Entretiens* (cf. A. G. Lehmann, *The Symbolist Aesthetic
in France 1885–1895* (Blackwell, Oxford, 1950), p. 116).

4

WRITERS ON THE GROTESQUE (C)

WOLFGANG KAYSER

18. Dr Kayser's book[1] consists chiefly of a detailed history of the grotesque in German literature, with incursions into other literatures principally for comparative purposes. The consideration of visual art is ancillary to that of literature. In both fields Kayser restricts his examination almost entirely to the period subsequent to the appearance of the term grotesque i.e. from the sixteenth to the twentieth century. Criticism is devoted to actual works of art rather than to theories of the grotesque, the latter being briefly described rather than analyzed.

Kayser's own theory of the grotesque, given in his final chapter,[2] commences in inductive fashion as an attempt to define the grotesque by listing the elements which are common to the works previously examined. Strictly speaking, of course, the question arises as to the criteria on which his initial selection of grotesque works of art is based. He does, in fact, observe that not all the things to which the term grotesque has been applied at one time or another are examples of the grotesque, considered in the light of a 'timeless' definition.[3] Here the subjective nature of the assessment is particularly obvious. Waiving this formal objection, it may fairly be allowed that the works dealt with are examples of grotesque art from which common elements may be extracted for the purpose of generalization.

At this point Kayser becomes frankly subjective. The grotesque, we are told, has three aspects, like any other form of art; the conditions of its creation (the artist's state of mind, etc.), the actual work, and the impression it makes on the reader or spectator. It is the latter, Kayser insists, that must be considered of greatest importance in attempting a definition; we can only consider a work according to the impression it makes on us. This is undeniable; though simple factual description of content might reasonably be accepted as objectively valid, without argument. Kayser does, in fact, give some examples of

---

[1] cf. *Das Groteske; Seine Gestaltung in Malerei und Dichtung.*
[2] cf. op. cit., *Zusammenfassung,* pp. 193–203.
[3] ibid., p. 193.

the content of grotesque art. We are told that snakes, owls, toads and spiders, nocturnal animals, reptiles and vermin, are the favourite animals of grotesque artists—above all, the bat; that climbing plants, self-propelled vehicles, puppets, robots, masks, skulls, skeletons, and madness are other typical ingredients.[1] These details of content are, however, given only incidentally. No systematic attempt is made to define the grotesque or to establish criteria by which it may be identified through simple description; the task is, of course, scarcely possible.

The basis of Kayser's definition is thus the impression made upon him by the works of art which he has previously examined, though, in fact, of the four complementary descriptions of the grotesque which he gives, only one is a straightforward description of the effect which grotesque art has upon him:

(i) The grotesque is the alienated world (*die entfremdete Welt*).

(ii) The grotesque is created by an impersonal force associated with the 'id' of psychological theory.

(iii) The creations of the grotesque are a game with the absurd.

(iv) The creation of the grotesque is the attempt to banish and exorcise the demonic element (*das Dämonische*) in the world.

Only the first of these four statements is immediately concerned with the *representative* side of grotesque art. The others are concerned rather with its *expressive* side, i.e. with the artist's point of view; we are told in each case about the attitude of mind, conscious or unconscious, which produces grotesque art.

(i) The grotesque is the alienated world.

Kayser insists that in genuinely grotesque art the everyday world is *suddenly* changed into a strange and unpleasant place, into a world in which we do not wish to live. The grotesque arouses in us not fear of death but anxiety about life (*Lebensangst*). A merely alien world, one which is completely strange to us from the outset, as in the fairy-tale, is not grotesque; it is not a transformation of our own world.

The question arises whether it is possible to conceive of a world other than that of every day which is not a transformation of our own world. Human art must clothe itself from the wardrobe of human experience, whether it does so according to an accepted convention or arbitrarily and fantastically. The world of the fairy-tale is connected by an unbreakable thread to the everyday world. It is only in virtue of this connexion that it is wonderful.

[1] ibid., pp. 195–8.

The important word in Kayser's assertion is the word 'suddenly'. What was trusted and familiar is instantly metamorphosed into the alien and uncanny. By this criterion, *Through the Looking Glass* might be called grotesque, but not 'The Owl and the Pussy-Cat', since in the former we actually see familiar things become strange and dreamlike, whereas in the latter the strangeness is there from the outset and is all of a piece, as it is in the fairy-tale.

The difficulty in accepting this view appears when one considers, say, the 'grotesque' murals, where there is no question of a sudden transformation of the physical world. Kayser would seem to be thinking of the type of grotesque art which introduces the monstrous into real life, as in Kafka's story 'Die Verwandlung', where a commercial traveller unaccountably turns into a cockroach. The grotesqueness is all the greater for its occurrence in everyday life. But it is one thing to agree that this is an especially vivid kind of grotesque art and quite another to deny that two-headed giants are grotesque because they inhabit an alien, not an alienated, world. The two-headed giant and the dragon may, like the centaur, have lost much of their imaginative impact; but that is a different matter entirely.

(ii) The grotesque is the creation of an impersonal force. Kayser speaks of this force as being 'uncanny' (*spukhaft*), and as having affinities with the psychologically impersonal and with the 'cosmic' impersonal suggested in such impersonal verbs as 'it is raining'.

There is no direct identification of this impersonal force with the 'id' of psychological theory. Whereas the quality which is most commonly associated with the unconscious mind is energy, Kayser emphasizes rather the strangeness and the autonomous nature of this impersonal force to which he refers. This emphasis is to be found throughout. The list of characteristic elements which he gives is presented as 'uncanny'—nocturnal animals, reptiles, vermin, &c. Even in describing madness, it is not dementia, insane energy which he stresses, but the strangeness and impersonality of madness: 'It is as though an alien, inhuman spirit had entered the soul.'[1]

The term absurd, Kayser observes, is applicable to tragedy as well as to grotesque art. It is absurd for a mother to kill her children, for a son to slay his mother, for a father to eat the flesh of his sons. The differences are that tragedy is chiefly concerned with single acts, that these acts upset the moral order, and that the tragic is not utterly incomprehensible. We are able to see something that makes sense in

[1] ibid., p. 198.

the prevailing senselessness, in the divine fate of the protagonist and the greatness which he achieves through suffering. The grotesque, on the other hand, does not concern itself with single acts, nor primarily with moral disorder, though the latter may constitute an element in grotesque art. Moreover, the grotesque artist may not and cannot attempt to make sense of his work (*darf und kann keine Sinngebung versuchen*).

Kayser considers the differences between tragic and grotesque art in absolute fashion. There would seem, however, to be no valid reason for limiting grotesque art to works which are entirely, or even predominantly, grotesque. To do so would mean denying that Shakespeare's—or Browning's—Caliban is an example of grotesque art, and that the term grotesque may legitimately be applied to parts of *King Lear* because the work as a whole makes sense.

To contrast tragic art with grotesque art, whilst admitting that tragedy is intimately concerned with the absurd, is to oversimplify the problem. One must make some distinction between 'pure' grotesque art and the use of grotesque figures, ideas, and so on for an artistic purpose which is not itself 'grotesque'.

In considering the relationship between grotesque art and humour, Kayser does indeed distinguish between the satirical and the fantastic grotesque, which suggests the kind of distinction between the 'pure' and 'applied' forms of grotesque art mentioned above. Humour of a scornful, cynical variety is to be found in the caricatures of the satirical grotesque; but Wieland, who isolated in the grotesque the three elements of laughter, horror, and astonishment, found humour in the fantastic grotesque of Brueghel. Was it, Kayser asks, the laughter of desperation that he found? 'Did he mean that laughter with which we involuntarily react to a situation which leaves us as it were no other possibility of release?'[1]

Kayser then proceeds to develop the idea of the grotesque as a kind of Mephistopheles which takes possession of the soul of the artist in his third definition:

(iii) The creations of the grotesque are a game with the absurd. This definition is made with reference to Goethe's lines:

> . . . wer heiter im Absurden spielt
> Den wird auch wohl das Absurde ziemen

—whoever plays merrily with the absurd will become the absurd.

[1] ibid., p. 201.

Kayser's point, then, is that the 'Es', the impersonal, autonomous force of which he has previously spoken, robs the artist of his freedom and gains control of his mind; not, however, invariably. Where the artistic creation succeeds we can still detect a trace of deliberate sportiveness. Still more important is the psychoanalytic or cathartic effect of successful grotesque art. It gives a habitation and a name to our secret fears: 'The obscure is sighted, the uncanny revealed, the incomprehensible called to account.'[1]

Hence Kayser's final definition:

(iv) The creation of the grotesque is the attempt to banish and exorcise the demonic element in the world.

It is not quite clear whether Kayser means that this attempt is conscious and deliberate or not. It is difficult to reconcile the idea of a deliberate attempt to get rid of uncomfortable and uncanny elements with the third definition.

The intangibles which grotesque art tries to depict are regarded here with particular antagonism; it is indeed this which distinguishes Kayser's attitude from Hegel's view of the grotesque as an attempt to express the inexpressible. Moreover, Kayser speaks of 'successful' grotesque art in which these intangibles are in some sense presented in concrete form.

Grotesque art, then, is an attempt to banish demons, or, less poetically, to get rid of our fears of something hidden and unpleasant by dragging it into the light. Two questions arise, first as to what, in Kayser's opinion, this unpleasant thing is, and second, as to what is in fact making the attempt at exorcism, since we have already been told that the grotesque is the creation of the 'Es', an impersonal force.

Kayser remarks:

Amidst all the helplessness and dread of the dark powers (*dunklen Mächte*) which loom in and behind our world, and which can alienate it from us, the genuine artistic creation at the same time acts as a secret liberation. The obscure is sighted, the uncanny revealed, the incomprehensible called to account.[2]

These dark powers, like the 'demonic element' of his fourth definition, with which they are clearly identified, are spoken of as though they are objectively real. But whether one understands these dark powers as a reference to the superstitious and irrational fears associated in psychology with the unconscious (or subconscious) mind, or as having

[1] ibid., p. 202.   [2] ibid., p. 202.

an actual external existence, it seems fairly clear that they have nothing in common with rationalism and systematic thought. The natural
interpretation would appear to be that grotesque art provides a
satisfactory conscious equivalent, a concrete depiction of these demons
of disorder. It is not clear whether the entity which makes this attempt
is the impersonal force—which is itself described as 'uncanny'— or,
as would appear to be more probable, the artist, consciously.

This point has been dealt with at some length because of the apparently conflicting assertion which follows: 'The creations of the
grotesque are the loudest and most remarkable contradiction to all
rationalism and to every kind of systematic thought.'[1] In the latter
statement grotesque art appears not as the banisher of dark powers,
the liberator of the mind from the uncanny and demonic, but as the
opponent of rigid order and system, the liberator of the mind from
the cramping bonds of logic, a reaffirmation that

> There are more things in heaven and earth, Horatio,
> Than are dreamt of in your philosophy.

It may be that one is intended to regard grotesque art in both ways,
as simultaneously an insurrection and a banishment; or that one is
meant to distinguish between the autonomous grotesque which has
run riot and enslaved its master, and the directed or 'applied' grotesque in which the fantastic elements are consciously employed for
the purpose of the artist. In any case, Kayser might well have been
more explicit at this juncture. The idea of grotesque art as a kind of
rebellion against systematic thought suggests an emotional attitude
on the part of the creator which is in contrast to Kayser's view, expressed earlier, that 'the unity of the perspective in grotesque art lay
in the cold view (*in dem kalten Blick*) of worldly affairs as an empty,
senseless puppet-play, a grotesque marionette-theatre'.[2]

The epithet cold, whilst it sorts perfectly with Kayser's description
of the uncanny, impersonal 'Es' which assumes control in grotesque
art, is scarcely warranted by the fact that grotesque art depicts the
world as a cold, mechanical place, supposing this to be the case. It
would seem, on the contrary, that a depiction of the world as cold
and mechanical, especially in satirical grotesque art, suggests rather
a passionate and indignant view of worldly affairs on the part of the
creator.

The most valuable of Kayser's four complementary definitions of

[1] ibid., p. 203.   [2] ibid., p. 200.

the grotesque, in my opinion, is the second: 'The grotesque is the creation of the "Es" ', if the latter term is understood in the sense of 'the unconscious mind'. Unless one is prepared to accept the idea that grotesqueness is objectively real, and that the grotesque in art is a simple reflection of actual phenomena—an idea which might apply to the depiction of 'an exceptional monstrosity of horrid ugliness', but scarcely to the original 'grotesque' murals—there is no practicable alternative to the attempt to find a psychological explanation for grotesque art. To make such an attempt is, after all, only to follow the general trend of the theories with which we have been concerned.

5

AN APPROACH THROUGH PSYCHOLOGY

THE ALIENATED WORLD. PROGRESSION AND REGRESSION

19. In general, it may be said that the chief idea involved in the various senses of the term grotesque is that of incongruity, of a conflict between some phenomenon and an existing conception of what is natural, fitting, &c.

Incongruity does not of itself necessarily produce an effect of grotesqueness; it may be of a purely formal kind. In geometry, for example, the phrase *Quia absurdum est* is used without any of the emotional force which the term absurd possesses in ordinary speech, to indicate purely logical incongruity.

It is, however, worth noticing how readily the *non sequitur* creates an effect of oddness when words, with their greater emotive content, are substituted for mathematical symbols: 'Well is this place called Stony Stratford, for never was I bitten by so many fleas in my life before.'[1] An examination of the emotional effect of the *non sequitur*—usually a humorous effect—sheds light on the nature of our reaction to grotesque art.

Not every *non sequitur*, even where the form is a verbal one, produces a pronounced emotional effect. Where, however, such an effect is produced by the breach of logical propriety, we may react in either or both of two opposed ways. We may feel a sense of superiority, the amusement of the logician; we may also feel a sense of release, an anti-rational reaction which will be dealt with below in connexion with the distinction between directed thinking and dream or fantasy thinking. At present it is sufficient to note that when the perception of incongruity arouses an emotional response an impression of grotesqueness is created. This is the case even where the incongruity is of a relatively superficial kind which does not affect our human and

---

[1] cf. Robert Graves, *Poetic Unreason and Other Studies* (Cecil Palmer, London 1925), pp. 117 ff. Graves humorously justifies this classic *non sequitur* by treating it as a logical syncope, supplying the 'missing' idea that the innkeepers of Stratford are too miserly to provide clean bed linen.

animal nature as deeply as, say, physical deformity. Two examples may be given from the *N.E.D.*:

(1870) The grotesque doctrine that it is good for trade (R. W. Dale, *Week-day Sermons*, XII. 246).[1]

(1862) Where so much is beautiful, the occasional anomalies and grotesqueries of taste fail to offend you (B. Taylor, *Home and Abr.*, Ser. II. II. 339).[1]

In analysing the term grotesque, then, we must associate with the idea of incongruity the sense of strangeness. The word strange does, indeed, invariably imply conflict with existing standards (though this 'conflict' need not, of course, entail a rejection of the strange phenomenon), but it may do so to a slight degree only, as in the sentence: 'I can't play well with a strange racket.'[2] 'Strange' may mean merely 'unfamiliar, not previously experienced'.

The difference between the merely unfamiliar and the incongruously strange, that is, between the ephemeral strangeness which is simply due to novelty and the positive, discordant strangeness which is directly opposed to 'the natural conditions of organisation', is emphasized by Wolfgang Kayser. The grotesque in art, he maintains, is 'the alienated world'; not, that is to say, a world which is merely alien, but, as he puts it, our own world, so distorted that we no longer wish to live in it: 'Zugleich spüren wir, daß wir in dieser verwandelten Welt nicht zu leben vermöchten.'[3]

As it stands, however, the bald statement that we do not wish to live in the world of grotesque art requires qualification.

20. According to Kayser, the world depicted by the grotesque artist is our own world turned upside down; our standards, conventions, convictions are upset, and 'all melts under our feet'.

In the tragic universe, he tells us,[4] amid the prevailing absurdity, there is a gleam of sense; the moral growth of the protagonist gives us something to cling to. In grotesque art, on the other hand, all is absurd and we are unable to orientate ourselves: 'Die verfremdete Welt erlaubt uns keine Orientierung, sie erscheint als absurd.'[5]

Kayser is concerned to emphasize the revulsion of feeling induced in the reader or spectator by grotesque art. This revulsion, however, is not our only emotional response to such art. 'What the natural standards of our world reject belongs to the structure of the grotesque' (Zur Struktur des Grotesken gehört, daß die Kategorien unserer

---

[1] See Appendix.   [2] cf. *C.O.D.* (1954).   [3] cf. Kayser, op. cit., p. 199.
[4] ibid., p. 200.   [5] ibid., p. 199.

Weltorientierung versagen).[1] Clearly, it cannot be maintained that we are invariably satisfied with the natural standards of the world in which we live. We do not, perhaps, wish to live in an alienated world —the pejorative force of the word alienated makes the remark a tendentious one. It is another thing to ask whether we should like to live in 'a state of autonomous existence unsubjected to necessity, a state of perfect freedom, without time or age',[2] a description in which there is equal prejudice, but in the opposite direction.

In any case, it would clearly be going too far to say that we do not wish to *experience* a world which upsets natural standards. The curiosity value of grotesque art—to put its appeal in the most superficial way—is considerable. If, for example, our attitude to the work of Salvador Dali were simply one of rejection, then, notwithstanding his technical brilliance, it would scarcely be possible to account for his success.

To compare the appeal of such art with that of the freak show is to some extent valid; Graham Greene speaks of a freak show as being 'created to satisfy some horrifying human need for ugliness',[3] a phrase which well suggests the ambiguous reaction of the human mind to grotesqueness:

Odi et amo; quare id faciam, fortasse requiris.
nescio, sed fieri sentio et excrucior.[4]

Grotesqueness is not, of course, synonymous with ugliness; there may be grotesqueness of a kind without the introduction of deformity—possible or impossible—and without the introduction of 'monstrous' phenomena (the dinosaur, the rhinoceros, the dragon) or any of the 'uncanny' phenomena to which Kayser draws our attention—the bat, the puppet, the skeleton, &c.[5] It may lie in the juxtaposition of objects.

In the centaur image[6] the two elements involved are placed in an impossible relationship to each other, physically speaking. This is only partly true of Lear's poem 'The Owl and The Pussy-Cat', where the odd effect is not wholly due to the impossible events, but is already inherent in part in the simple juxtaposition of the two creatures.

[1] cf. Kayser, op. cit., p. 199.
[2] cf. David Gascoyne, *Hölderlin's Madness* (J. M. Dent and Sons Ltd., London), p. 11.
[3] cf. *The Lawless Roads* (Heinemann Uniform ed., 1955, p. 25).
[4] cf. Catullus, LXXXV.
[5] cf. Kayser, op. cit., pp. 195–8 (see above, p. 64).
[6] See pp. 16, 56.

The nature of contingency is a familiar question in scholastic philosophy, the question of whether any relationship could be discovered between such contingent facts as the colour of an orange and its shape and so on, a question ancillary to the problem of relationship in general. David Hume's best-known contribution to philosophy is, of course, the conclusion that necessary (*propter hoc*) relationship cannot be demonstrated and his attribution of the idea of cause and effect to constant psychological association.

The psychological tendency to seek a relationship between contiguous objects is exploited in grotesque art, notably in the *collage* creations of Dadaism. The juxtaposition of, say, an egg, a pistol, and a goldfish in a painting creates an effect of strangeness which is more remarkable than any impression created by the chance juxtaposition of these objects in real life, because we feel that our attention is being directed towards some kind of significant relationship between the objects in question. Such 'odd' juxtapositions are much employed by the detective-story writer; in the detective story, however, a logical connexion is eventually established between the objects involved.[1]

It is characteristic of the practical, 'progressive'[2] aspect of mind that it should either reject such deliberate juxtapositions as pointless or seek to establish a logical connexion between them. The 'regressive'[2] aspect of mind, on the other hand, luxuriates in their inexplicable 'significance'. To the first frame of mind the novels of Mrs. Ann Radcliffe, with their ultimate explanation of the mysterious occurrences, are satisfying; to the second frame of mind they are ultimately disappointing. Keats's famous remark about 'negative capability' admirably describes the second, regressive, attitude:

. . . *Negative Capability*, that is, when a man is capable of being in uncertainties, mysteries, doubts, without any irritable reaching after fact and reason—Coleridge, for instance, would let go by a fine isolated verisimilitude caught from the Penetralium of mystery, from being incapable of remaining content with half-knowledge.[3]

Both these attitudes of mind must be taken into consideration in examining our emotional response to grotesque art; we are not only repelled by it, we are also fascinated. The chief objection to Kayser's. assertion that we do not wish to live in the 'alienated world' of the

---

[1] cf. Chesterton's story 'The Honour of Israel Gow' for a particularly brilliant example.

[2] See below, pp. 75–76.

[3] Letter to George and Thomas Keats, 21 Dec. 1817. cf. *Letters of Keats*, ed. Maurice Buxton Forman, O.U.P. (3rd ed., 2nd imp., 1948), p. 72.

grotesque is not so much that there may be a difference of reaction in different persons as that every personality, however stable, contains opposed tendencies. In order to describe the effect of grotesque art on the reader or spectator, and to attempt a satisfactory explanation for the creation of grotesque art, something must be said about the nature of this opposition.

21. Opposing tendencies in the human personality were, of course, recognized long before the advent of the various modern systems of psychology. The list of opposed terms: soul and body, head and heart, reason and intuition, fancy and imagination, the Promethean and the Dionysian, the naïve and the sentimental, &c., is as familiar as it is endless. Perhaps the most significant thing about these pairs of terms is that, even where they are not regarded as mutually exclusive alternatives but as coexisting contraries, they give rise to alternative theories of conduct which arouse fierce controversy. Plato's rigorous criticism of the *furor poeticus*, especially in the tenth book of *The Republic*, where he objects to the exciting of passions which would upset the system of education he has outlined, is a classic example of the recognition of such an opposition.

Modern psychology takes a more balanced view of the opposed elements in the human personality, regarding neither the conscious nor the subconscious (or unconscious) mind as being malignant of itself, though in its medical, psychiatrical, aspect psychology naturally concerns itself with malignant and abnormal conditions of the subconscious. Jung, to a greater extent than Freud, is concerned with the exploration of the 'normal' condition of mind, and it is on his work that the following remarks are principally based.

J. A. Symonds, in making use of the phrase 'real conditions of man's subjective being' in his remarks on the origins of fantasy,[1] anticipates the more enlightened attitude of the twentieth century towards mental events. It is essential to our purpose to appreciate that the human mind, at birth, is not a mere *tabula rasa* or *intellectus ektypus* of which the ultimate character is entirely determined by individual experience. Like the acorn, both the human body and the human mind develop according to a certain pattern if they develop at all. Though ideas themselves are not, of course, inherited, propensities to develop certain characteristic ideas are. To take only the most obvious of these propensities, the sense of eternity or of 'the numinous':

[1] See p. 55.

. . . the same physiological and psychological processes that have been man's for hundreds of thousands of years still endure, instilling into our inmost hearts this profound intuition of the 'eternal' continuity of the living. But the self, as an inclusive term that embraces our whole living organism, not only contains the deposit and totality of all past life, but is also a point of departure, the fertile soil from which all future life will spring. This premonition of futurity is as clearly impressed upon our innermost feelings as is the historical aspect. The idea of immortality follows legitimately from these psychological premises.[1]

With such proclivities as this more or less unconscious conviction of its eternal nature—'real conditions of man's subjective being'— the mind must adjust itself to the problems and limitations of every-day life. The following convincing attempt to describe the polarization of the mind in the simplest terms incidentally suggests plausible reasons for both the creation and the appeal of some kinds of grotesque art:

The natural movement of the libido is forwards and backwards—one could almost think of it as the movement of the tides. Jung calls the forward movement which satisfies the demands of the conscious, *progression*, the backward movement, satisfying the demands of the unconscious, *regression*. Progression is concerned with the active adaptation to one's environment, and regression with the adaptation to one's inner needs. Regression therefore (contrary to some points of view) is just as normal a counterpole to progression as sleeping is to waking, so long as the libido is functioning in an unhindered manner, . . . when it must eventually turn over into a progressive movement. Regression may mean, among other things, a return to a dreamy state after a period of concentrated and directed mental activity, or it may mean a return to an earlier stage of development; but these are not necessarily 'wrong', rather can they be looked on as restorative phases—'*reculer pour mieux sauter*'. If there is an attempt to force the libido into a rigid channel, or repression has created a barrier, or for one reason or another the conscious adjustment has failed (perhaps because outer circumstances became too difficult), the natural forward movement becomes impossible. The libido then flows back into the un-conscious, which will eventually become over-charged with energy seeking to find some outlet. Perhaps the unconscious will then leak through into consciousness as fantasy, or as some neurotic symptom, perhaps it will manifest itself in infantile or even animal behaviour. It may even over-whelm consciousness so that there is a violent outburst, or a psychosis

[1] cf. Jolande Jacobi, *Complex/Archetype/Symbol in the Psychology of C. G. Jung*, trans. Ralph Manheim (Bollingen Series LVII, Pantheon Books Inc., New York, 1959), p. 65.

develops; when this happens it is as if a dam had burst and all the land was flooded. In extreme cases, where there is a complete failure of the libido to find an outlet, there is a withdrawal from life, as in some psychotic states; this is a pathological regression, and is unlike normal regression, which is a necessity of life. A man is not a machine who can continually and steadily adapt himself to his environment; he must also be in harmony with himself, i.e. adapt to his own inner world; 'Conversely, he can only adapt to his inner world and achieve unity within himself when he is adapted to the environmental conditions.'[1]

It is essential to notice these opposed tendencies in order to appreciate fully the differences between the various kinds of art to which the term grotesque is applied.

22. Before describing these in detail, however, a further distinction, intimately connected with the polarization of the mind remarked above, must be considered; the distinction between *directed thinking* and *dream or fantasy thinking*. Briefly, directed thinking is the activity of the mind in its progressive aspect, rigorously selective and systematic, expressing itself in 'common sense', logical organization, and reason. Dream or fantasy thinking is the activity which characterizes the regressive aspect of mind, expressing itself in wilful distortion, 'wishful thinking', and a rejection of the 'natural conditions of organisation' of the external world:

The first, working for communication with speech elements, is troublesome and exhausting; the latter, on the contrary, goes on without trouble, working spontaneously, so to speak, with reminiscences. The first creates innovations, adaptations, imitates reality and seeks to act upon it. The latter, on the contrary, turns away from reality, sets free subjective wishes, and is, in regard to adaptation, wholly unproductive.[2]

Directed thinking is not invariably conscious. Consciousness, certainly, implies order and control: '. . . exclusion, selection and discrimination are the root and essence of everything that lays claim to the name "consciousness".'[3] But the unconscious has also a progressive as well as a regressive aspect, and is capable of organized thinking:

There is no doubt in my mind that all the activities ordinarily taking place in consciousness can also run their course in the unconscious. There

---

[1] cf. Frieda Fordham, *An Introduction to Jung's Psychology* (Pelican Books No. A273, revised ed., 1959), pp. 18–19.

[2] cf. C. G. Jung, *The Psychology of the Unconscious*, trans. B. M. Hinkle (Kegan Paul, London, 1933), p. 11.

[3] cf. Jung, *The Archetypes and the Collective Unconscious* (Bollingen Series XX, Pantheon Books Inc., New York, 1959), trans. R. F. C. Hull, p. 288.

are many examples of an intellectual problem attaining no solution during the waking state, but being solved in a dream.[1]

Some subconscious faculty was at work while he slept and he would wake to find a complete set of facts, the proper arrangement of which had given him much thought on the previous night, neatly sorted and pigeon-holed in his mind on the following morning.[2]

The term 'dream or fantasy thinking' must therefore be understood in the sense 'of the kind characteristic of dreams', rather than as being invariably found in dreams.

The theory that personal repressions influence our dreams is, of course, a familiar one. Everyday anxieties and frustrations recur in dreams, winnowing and kneading their content.

To these influences, of which the effects can generally be interpreted in terms of individual experience, we must, however, add those influences which, like the sense of eternity or of 'the numinous' previously remarked, emanate from a deeper psychic level.

The raw material of dreams, our sensory experience, is in general simultaneously subjected to the influence of both our personal repressions and of these deeper, supra-personal impulses. Where the former influence predominates the content of a dream may be merely a re-creation, coloured and distorted by our personal desires and fears, of our waking experience. The dreamer runs after the eight-fifteen hampered by a ball and chain, argues with an office manager of gigantic proportions, loses all his hair, wins a fortune on the football pools and so on; the imagery may be much more obscure without ceasing to be ultimately explicable in terms of personal frustration, as is frequently the case with a neurosis of long standing, where the mental condition is more or less abnormal.

Where the chief influences are those which come from a deeper level of the unconscious mind, however, the imagery of a dream may be strange and obscure without any implication of neurosis. Such dreams often create a powerful feeling of significance.[3] The experience of discovering the key to the universe in a dream and hastily

---

[1] cf. Jung, *Contrib. Anal. Psych.*, trans. H. G. and C. F. Baynes (Kegan Paul, London, 1928), p. 101.

[2] *Rufus Isaacs by his Son* (1943), p. 108. cf. Sir Percy Nunn, *Education: Its Data and First Principles* (Edward Arnold, London, 1949), p. 53.

[3] 'Tatham tells how [Blake] was very much accustomed to get out of his bed in the night to write for hours, and return to bed for the rest of the night after having committed to paper pages and pages of his mysterious phantasies.' Mona Wilson, *Life of Wm. Blake* (Peter Davis Ltd., London, 1932), p. 69.

writing it down during the night, only to discover that the profound idea has turned into unintelligible gibberish on the following morning, is a common one.

Jung's account of the unconscious supplies a convincing reason for this feeling of significance in dreams of the deeper kind:

It is the mind of our unknown ancestors, their way of thinking and feeling, their way of experiencing life and the world, gods and men. The existence of these archaic strata is presumably the source of man's belief in reincarnation and in memories of 'previous existences'. Just as the human body is a museum, so to speak, of its phylogenetic history, so too is the psyche. We have no reason to suppose that the specific structure of the psyche is the only thing in the world which has no history outside its individual manifestations . . . The unconscious psyche is not only immensely old, it is also capable of growing into an equally remote future. It moulds the human species and is just as much a part of it as the human body, which, though ephemeral in the individual, is collectively of immense age.[1]

In dreams, the unconscious is capable of bringing 'into our ephemeral consciousness an unknown psychic life belonging to the remote past'.[2]

In the deepest kind of dreams the images and ideas are often of an elemental nature far removed from the experience of everyday life, images and ideas which frequently echo those to be found in mythology. Jung speaks of such images as 'archetypal', maintaining that they derive from a level of the mind where there is no individuality, identical in all human beings. We need not concern ourselves here with the more specific types of image described by Jung as archetypal.[3] It is sufficient for our purpose to mention the sense of eternity as one of the most powerful impulses of the supra- (or infra-) individual level of the mind, which manifests itself not only in dreams of the deepest kind but also in dreams of which the imagery is recognizably that of our everyday life, imbuing them with the air of significance remarked above, and even continuing to exert an influence on the fully conscious mind in its waking state.

It is, of course, primarily with the kind of dream or fantasy thinking

---

[1] cf. Jung, *The Archetypes and the Collective Unconscious*, pp. 286–7.
[2] ibid., p. 286.
[3] For detailed accounts of such 'archetypal' images, cf. especially *The Archetypes and the Coll. Uncon.* (See p. 76); Jung, *Symbols of Transformation* (Pantheon Books, 1956); C. G. Jung and C. Kerényi, *Essays on a Science of Mythology* (Pantheon Books, 1949).

pursued by the waking mind that we must deal in connexion with the creation of grotesque art.

Consciousness, as has already been remarked, is of its very nature exclusive, selective, and discriminating; in a word, progressive. However, 'consciousness succumbs all too easily to unconscious influences'.[1] Where there is a return to a strongly progressive attitude of mind on waking, the sense of 'significance' we have noticed as characteristic of some dreams is dissipated. Cinderella's coach turns back into a pumpkin. Dissatisfaction with one's material circumstances, however—whether because of social frustration or because of a natural tendency to introversion in the individual—may reduce the resistance of the conscious mind to unconscious influences, and result in the qualities of exclusion, selection, and discrimination being placed at the disposal of the unconscious. Thus, these qualities may be devoted to the creation of a poetic fantasy as well as to, say, a problem in engineering, though the former is 'in regard to adaptation, wholly unproductive'.[2] It is this domination of the conscious by the unconscious mind to which Kayser refers in his definition: 'The grotesque is the creation of an impersonal force (the "Es").'[3] The same idea of an automous power making use of the artist is apparent in Plato's remark:

It is the testimony of the ancients, that the madness which is of God is a nobler thing than the wisdom which is of men . . . He who sets himself to any work with which the Muses have to do without madness, thinking that by art alone can he do his work sufficiently, will be found vain and incapable, and the work of temperance and rationalism will be thrust aside and obscured by that of inspiration.[4]

The idea of the creative process as being in control of, rather than controlled by, the artist is a familiar one.

FOUR KINDS OF ART

23. Both the creation of and the reaction to grotesque art are illuminated by considering them in terms of the progressive-regressive polarization of the mind, and the corresponding opposition between directed thinking and dream or fantasy thinking.

It will be convenient to consider first the reactions of the audience.

---

[1] cf. Jung, *The Archetypes and the Coll. Uncon.*, p. 282.
[2] See note 2, p. 76.
[3] See p. 65.
[4] *Phaedrus.* cf. Ruskin, *The Stones of Venice*, III. III. §LX (footnote).

The more strongly marked the progressive aspect of mind in the individual experiencing such art, the more he will be inclined to dismiss it as meaningless, unless there is an obviously 'practical' reason for its existence, as in caricature (a genre which will be discussed later in connexion with the creation of grotesque art). The extrovert will tend to explain grotesque art away as the product of a deranged mind; or to regard the artist as disingenuously attempting to make capital out of sensationalism and mystification, like the weavers of 'The Emperor's New Clothes'. At best, he will be prepared to tolerate such art only in so far as it is clearly labelled 'Not to be taken seriously'.[1] Of such 'harmless' varieties of nonsense, the progressive-minded reader will perhaps be more attracted to the subtle *non sequiturs* and wayward logic of Lewis Carroll than to the cruder incongruities of Edward Lear.

The introvert, on the other hand, the reader or spectator in whom the regressive influence of the unconscious is marked, will be inclined to regard grotesque art as significant, either in a negative way, shattering to bits the sorry scheme of things with which he is dissatisfied, or as remoulding it nearer to the heart's desire, full of significant suggestions of a deeper, freer, more enduring world.[2]

The two chief kinds of usage of the term grotesque, with, and without, a pejorative force, largely correspond to these two opposed attitudes of mind. Where the progressive attitude occurs the term is employed to indicate antagonism, a violation of the accepted standards. Where the regressive aspect of mind is dominant, however, whilst the conscious mind, always selective, exclusive, and discriminating, recognizes the incongruity of the phenomenon described as grotesque with progressive standards, the effect of unconscious influences—the sense of the eternal or 'numinous' in particular—is to make this incompatibility appear a merit rather than an objectionable characteristic; hence the relish with which the term is employed by the obviously regressive-minded Poe.[3]

If we apply the ideas above to a consideration of the mental conditions in which grotesque art is created, it at once becomes clear that we must distinguish several kinds of such art.

[1] cf. pp. 60–61.

[2] cf. p. 61, footnote 3 (R. Petsch).

[3] The term may also be employed, of course, in directed thought—in literary criticism, for example—more or less colourlessly as a descriptive term, in which case it is to be compared with the use of 'absurd' in the geometrical sense without any emotion being involved.

Grotesque art, in the nature of things, cannot be as completely the work of an autonomous impulse as is the imagery of a dream. However great the extent to which the artist is possessed by 'the madness which is of God', he is able to some extent to stand back from his work and view it critically; but such critical examination, and the ability to organize and present the content of the work so as to produce the strongest possible effect on others, all characteristics of the conscious mind, may be subordinated to a creative impulse which originates in the unconscious. It will be convenient to distinguish four chief kinds of art according to the extent to which the conscious mind of the artist is influenced by, or makes use of, the impulses of the unconscious; in other words, the extent to which the mind of the artist is regressively or progressively orientated. In point of fact these four kinds, which will be referred to as regressive-positive, regressive-negative, progressive-negative, and progressive-positive, shade off into one another. Art which is deliberately grotesque in form belongs to the two middle categories.

Regressive-positive art is the kind of art which approximates most closely to the nature of the dream or vision. Its most characteristic type is the myth. Such art possesses a strongly synthetic quality. Its imagery is never merely anarchical, but highly evocative and symbolic, deriving its significance from something more positive than a mere reaction against the conditions of the material world. The primitive myth, the Revelation of St. John, the 'prophetic books' of Blake, are examples of such art, in which the artist is more concerned to construct a picture of the 'greater reality' which transcends the world of natural phenomena than merely to escape from the dictates of that world.

Such art is full of images of the type which Jung describes as 'archetypal'; images like the witch and the vampire, which, continually recurrent in art and religion, correspond to something permanent in the relationship of the human mind to its environment.

The greater the role played in grotesque art by consciousness, the factor which recognizes the material of such art *to be grotesque* and not merely dreadful or significant,[1] the less positive the work produced

[1] In dreams, which are experienced in a 'darkly conscious' state, we are not aware of the grotesqueness of the images and occurrences, however forcibly this may strike us on recalling the dream in a waking state: 'I think a nightmare can be more real than the real thing; for you do not know it is a nightmare when you are sleeping, but when you are awake you can pretend life is all a dream' (Richard Mason, *The Wind Cannot Read*, Hodder and Stoughton Ltd., 1947, p. 8).

tends to be in the sense above. It is from the unconscious that these powerful images emerge,[1] and they naturally occur only to the extent to which the unconscious is dominant. The second kind of art which we may usefully distinguish, regressive-negative art, is that in which, whilst the attitude of the artist is clearly regressive, unconscious influence is weaker, supplying emotion rather than actual imagery. The result is a concentration, so far as grotesque art is concerned, on the negative aspect of grotesqueness—incongruity with the normal. We may recall at this juncture Santayana's remark: 'We call these inventions comic and grotesque when we are considering their divergence from the natural, rather than their inward possibility.'

Regressive-positive art concerns itself with this 'inward possibility'; its suggestive, symbolic imagery, however strange when judged by common-sense standards, is not intentionally grotesque. The conception of the witch, for example, was felt to 'explain' a mystery, not to create one.

Regressive-negative art, on the other hand, shows a deep awareness of the everyday circumstances with which it is in conflict; so far as specifically grotesque art is concerned, emphasis is laid on the 'divergence from the natural' (or the conventional) of the imagery employed; where such images as the witch or the vampire appear in such art, it is largely for their 'shock value', their eeriness, and so on.

The difference between these two types of regressive art—which, admittedly, shade off into one another—may perhaps be related to Schiller's distinction between the naïve and the sentimental types of literature, the spontaneous and unforced naturalness of the one standing in contrast to the sophisticated and self-conscious attitude apparent in the other.

Briefly, then, whereas the former, regressive-positive, type of art is visionary, re-creating as nearly as possible in a waking state the 'significant' imagery and the 'numinous' atmosphere of the deep dream, the latter, regressive-negative, type of art is much less involuntary or 'inspired', and, so far as grotesque art in this category—to which all romantic art also belongs—is concerned, is generally dis-

---

[1] '. . . the unconscious displays contents that are utterly different from conscious ones . . . It is not a question of more or less normal contents that become unconscious just by accident. They are, on the contrary, products whose nature is at first completely baffling. They differ in every respect from neurotic material, which cannot be said to be at all bizarre' (Jung, *The Archetypes and the Coll. Uncon.*, p. 277).

ruptive, expressing dissatisfaction with the 'shallow
phenomenal world through deliberate anarchy, as in Da
example.

Something should also be said here about the remaining two k.
of art distinguished above in order to outline the general thesis of th.
present chapter before proceeding to a closer examination of each of
the four kinds in turn.

Just as the extreme manifestations of regressive-positive thinking—
the 'numinous' dream, the religious vision—lie outside the sphere of
art in the ordinary sense of the word, being wholly spontaneous and
autonomous, so, too, one is reluctant to describe as 'art' work which
is wholly the product of directed thought, of the progessive activity
of the mind: the mathematical treatise, for example. In so far as one
can speak of progressive-positive art, the term must be restricted to
work in which fantasy plays little or no part, and the artistic merit
inheres chiefly in the judicious arrangement of statements of fact or
logical conclusions, as in works of scholarship.

Progressive-negative art is best described as work in which fantasy
is employed for practical ends. The influence of the unconscious mind
is not strong enough to produce a regressive attitude; instead, its
power of suggestion is, so to speak, put to use by the conscious mind,
often to create an effect of absurdity, as in caricature and burlesque.
Grotesque imagery is, of course, a common feature of progressive-
negative art, and this category requires to be considered fully in consequence. First, however, it will be expedient to examine the regressive categories of art in greater detail.

REGRESSIVE-POSITIVE ART

24. It is important to understand the sense in which such imagery as
that of mythology and the folk-tale can be spoken of as 'regressive'.
The psychological value of these images, as of those of religion, resides
—or resided—in the fact that they provided a satisfactory 'objective
correlative' for both the regressive and the progressive aspects of
mind, helping to balance the personality. Thus the explanation of the
phenomenon of thunder as the sound of Thor's hammer afforded an
outlet both for the sense of the eternal and for curiosity about natural
phenomena. The superseding of this explanation, with all its implications, was thus both a triumph for man's practical sense and a
defeat for his feeling of contact with the divine.

Such images as Thor's hammer were the product of an associative, pre-logical type of thinking in which the various phenomena of human existence—dreams, fears of the dark, and the more intangible, subjective experiences, as well as thunder and lightning, day and night, and various external phenomena—were provided with a *raison d'être*. Some of these 'explanations' are logically obvious, as in the case of Thor's hammer. Others remain obscure and are open to various interpretations, like the *uroboros* (circular snake) image[1] which has been a feature of human art from time immemorial.[2]

The latter type of image, symbolizing subjective rather than objective conditions, naturally tends to persist in serious fashion longer than those images and ideas which, like Thor's hammer, were intimately connected with natural phenomena and could thus be ousted readily with the advance of knowledge about the phenomenal world.

To the twentieth-century European adult Thor and Neptune, and even the more commonly employed images of Mars and Cupid which retain considerable metaphorical value, can scarcely be more than poetic playthings. On the other hand, there remains a traditional body of imagery with a 'numinous' force which has not been reasoned away; the imagery of Christianity is, of course, the most obvious such group, stoutly resisting critical 'demythologizing'. The ghost and the poltergeist retain much of their power over the conscious mind even in twentieth-century Europe, where directed thinking has advanced farthest. Outside this area the number of images which are still dynamically 'numinous' may be multiplied indefinitely. In many parts of the world the witch and the wizard are accepted as part of the structure of reality, and the vampire and the werwolf have not had their fangs drawn by progressive thought.

If we confine our examination to the Western world, however, it is clear that, indestructible though the impulses of the unconscious may be, it has become increasingly difficult for them to find expression in forms recognized as significant, or at least as unexceptionable, by the conscious mind in its normal progressive state. So far as the traditional images of the supernatural are concerned, the present highly progressive Western type of education tends increasingly to be an education in iconoclasm.

In a period when there is a socially vigorous body of 'numinous' imagery, the artist is able to find an 'objective correlative' for his sense of the supernatural which is readily acceptable to his conscious

---

[1] cf. Jung, *The Arch. and the Coll. Uncon.* (Appendix).

[2] *Jormundgandr*. the serpent which, in Northern mythology, encircles Midgard, may be mentioned as an example.

mind. He need neither create his art in a state of frenzy, in which the critical eye of consciousness is closed, nor in a mood of defiance, in which conscious standards are deliberately rejected, as the only alternatives to accepting the physical world as ultimate reality. Thus the Greek and Northern myths, the books of the Bible, *Piers the Plowman*, were written with the collaboration of the conscious mind. They are confident affirmations of a supernatural reality, statements of facts accepted by their countless creators quite consciously. All are examples of regressive-positive creation.

We have already noticed Scott's acute remarks on the common content of folk tales:[1]

What are we to think when we find the Jutt and the Fin telling their children the same traditions which are to be found in the nurseries of the Spaniard and Italian; or when we recognise in our own instance the traditions of Ireland or Scotland corresponding with those of Russia?

Scott makes two guesses: that they are derived from a common oral tradition and that the similarity is due to 'the paucity of human invention'.

The latter idea comes close to the mark. Folk tales draw their content from the common well of human nature, and in their naïve form are characterized by a strong sense of the supernatural. The witch, the ogre, the lindworm, the princess in the tower, the simple hero, and so on, reflect 'real conditions of man's subjective being'.

As long as they are not subjected to progressive criticism, the preternatural figures and events of the folk-tale, like religious imagery, perform a useful task in providing an outlet for the 'numinous' impulse of the unconscious. Once persuaded of the absurdity of traditional supernatural images, the artist will tend to pursue one of the following courses:

(i) Where the unconscious impulse is very powerful, he may, like Blake for example, create an obscure system of 'numinous' images as a personal 'objective correlative' for the impulse, which constitutes a new mythology.[2]

---

[1] See p. 32 ff.

[2] '. . . there is a considerable difference between the archetype (i.e. unconscious tendency to form a certain type of image) and the historical formula that has evolved. Especially on the higher levels of esoteric (i.e. mystical or religious) teaching the archetypes appear in a form that reveals quite unmistakably the critical and evaluating influence of conscious elaboration. Their immediate manifestation, as we encounter it in dreams and visions, is much more individual, less understandable, and more naïve than

(ii) The artist may be obsessed with the desire to objectify his sense of the supernatural without being able to find an adequate form in which to do so.

He may accordingly pour his feelings into traditional forms, Greek mythology, the 'Gothic' ballad, &c., in a sophisticated fashion; utilize some such ephemeral symbol as the skylark, the cloud, the nightingale, as a makeshift; or fall back on anarchy, expressing his dissatisfaction with the phenomenal world by representing it in distorted and grotesque perspective.

(iii) In more progressive vein, the artist may continue to employ traditional imagery as useful artistic material in allegorical fashion— like Mars or Cupid—for a progressive purpose. Archetypal images used in this way, especially when the image arises spontaneously from the artist's unconscious, may retain much of their visionary, mythical quality in spite of the artist's attempt at rationalization, at drawing moral conclusions and so on. *Don Quixote*, *Moby Dick* are examples of such work. The case of Stevenson's *Dr Jekyll and Mr Hyde* is particularly significant:

> In his own well-known phrase, he has acknowledged his debt for it to his 'Brownies'; and the story of that night when he received this amazing gift from dreamland, and of the next three days when he wrote thirty thousand words almost without pausing, is one of the most startling among the curiosities of literature.[1]

His wife objected that the result was insufficiently allegorical, and Stevenson flung the entire manuscript into the fire and rewrote the story in its present form, obviously a more didactic one than the original.

In regressive-positive art a vision which the artist finds significant is expressed. Such art is primarily an unconditional assertion, made not defiantly nor in conscious conflict with accepted standards (though criticism of society may be incidentally included, as in *Piers the Plowman*); nor is it a picture of how the world ought to be—

---

in myths, for example. The archetype is essentially an unconscious content that is altered by becoming conscious and by being perceived, and it takes its colour from the individual consciousness in which it happens to appear' (Jung, *The Arch. and the Coll. Uncon.*, p. 5). The 'numinous' impulse can thus only objectify itself satisfactorily in a form which the conscious mind can tolerate. Blake was able to find such a form, the elusive goal sought in vain by the romantic artist.

[1] cf. Introduction to *Dr Jekyll and Mr Hyde* by John Kelman (Collins ed.), pp. 8–9.

Utopias belong to progressive art. The ideas and images of regressive-positive art are self-explanatory; they are significant, and there an end.

Such art, as has already been observed, is not deliberately grotesque; but as its images and ideas are frequently such as to arouse a strong feeling of incongruity with 'common-sense' standards, they are generally to be described as grotesque from the progressive point of view. However, it is important to note that the incongruity must be such as to arouse strong emotion before it produces an effect of grotesqueness.[1]

Wolfgang Kayser insists that the world of the fairy-tale is not grotesque. One can to some extent agree with this without necessarily accepting the reasons which Kayser gives for his assertion.[2] The witch, the ogre, the goblin, and so on may be regarded as familiar fancies, traditional absurdities which no longer have a strong emotional effect on the adult mind, no longer conflict *seriously* with common sense.

The idea, permissible in Pope's poor Indian, that 'his faithful dog shall bear him company' in heaven,[3] strikes us as grotesque in a twentieth-century spiritualist. Behaviour which might seem fitting enough in a primitive context appears grotesque when indulged in by such a person as Samuel Johnson: 'Sometimes he seemed to be obeying some hidden impulse, which commanded him to touch every post in a street or tread on the centre of every paving-stone, and would return if his task had not been accurately performed.'[4]

Johnson's rituals, some of which were very peculiar,[5] have obvious affinities with regressive-positive art of a personal and esoteric kind like that of Blake. Unconscious impulses dominate the conscious mind and express themselves in forms which, whilst they may appear completely illogical from a progressive point of view, have always their roots in a primitive, associative 'logic' like that of the witches' brew, or the reciting of the Our Father backwards to raise the devil. In this respect, regressive-positive art contrasts strongly with such deliberately anarchic confections as the *collages* of Dadaism. No doubt Blake's work has a 'defiant' negative side—he was vociferously opposed to much in the intellectual climate of his time and was fond of 'shock tactics' in social intercourse; but the fact remains that his work is genuinely a picture of truth as he saw it—a meaningful vision.

---

[1] See p. 70.   [2] See pp. 64–65.   [3] cf. *Essay on Man*, Epistle I, ll. 99–112.
[4] cf. Leslie Stephen, *Samuel Johnson* (Engl. Men of Letters Series, Macmillan, London, 1878), p. 3.
[5] ibid.; cf. also Boswell's *Life of Dr Johnson*, ch. IV.

REGRESSIVE-NEGATIVE ART

25. Something has already been said about the nature of regressive-negative art; but this category requires to be examined in greater detail, particularly as it is one of the two groups in which 'deliberately' grotesque art is to be found.

The chief characteristic of such art is its 'escapist' attitude. Whilst the influence of the unconscious is sufficiently strong to evoke dissatisfaction with the limitations and 'superficiality' of the material world and the standards which it imposes, it is not strong enough to dictate the manner in which this dissatisfaction is to express itself. At its weakest it may be no more than an addition to the restlessness and dissatisfaction caused by immediately personal frustrations and grievances which compel the artist to create, like Walter Mitty, a world of wish-fulfilment as a compensation. The stronger the 'numinous' impulse is, relative to the influence of such personal factors, the less 'worldly' the symbol of escape tends to become: the 'blue flower' of the German romantics is an example of this less materialistic type of image, or the bird—Wordsworth's cuckoo, Shelley's skylark, Keats's nightingale. The more vehement, too, becomes the rejection of the phenomenal world

> Where palsy shakes a few sad, last grey hairs
> Where youth grows pale and spectre-thin and dies.

and of the myopic frame of mind which applies itself wholly to that world:

> Is there so small a range
> In the present strength of manhood, that the high
> Imagination cannot freely fly
> As she was wont of old? prepare her steeds,
> Paw up against the light, and do strange deeds
> Upon the clouds?[1]

In contrast to the self-sufficiency of the genuine vision, such art is characterized by a sense of futility. The artist knows that his wings are the waxen ones of Icarus, not the iron ones of Volund the Smith. Hegel, as we have seen,[2] finds romantic art all the more poignant for this sense of the inadequacy of its images. The romantic artist can only express himself in the optative mood:

[1] cf. *Sleep and Poetry* (Keats), ll. 162–7.
[2] See p. 31.

I'd rather be
a pagan suckled in a creed outworn

.   .   .   .

I would build that dome in air
That sunny dome! Those caves of ice!

.   .   .   .

If I were a dead leaf thou mightest bear;
If I were a swift cloud to fly with thee

.   .   .   .

That I might drink, and leave the world unseen,
And with thee fade away into the forest dim:

The conscious mind cannot voluntarily relinquish its sophistication.

A particularly interesting type of regressive-negative art, in which
the search for 'the significant' is highly sophisticated but the influence
of the unconscious very obvious, is that exemplified by Virginia
Woolf. Mrs. Woolf's art is devoted to the attempt to capture 'the
significant moment'; she seeks it in 'the stream of consciousness':

> The mind receives a myriad impressions—trivial, fantastic, evanescent,
> or engraved with the sharpness of steel. From all sides they come, an in-
> cessant shower of innumerable atoms; and as they fall, as they shape them-
> selves into the life of Monday or Tuesday, the accent falls differently from
> of old; the moment of importance came not here but there . . . Life is not
> a series of gig lamps symmetrically arranged; life is a luminous halo, a
> semi-transparent envelope surrounding us from the beginning of con-
> sciousness to the end.[1]

Her characters are haunted by the feeling that

> We had the experience but missed the meaning.[2]

Significantly, she writes of herself: 'I insubstantise, wilfully to some
extent, distrusting reality—its cheapness.'[3]

In such work there is a subtle kind of ambivalence; the author is
strongly aware of the human tendency to look for an enduring
significance in experience, and, feeling this impulse herself, finds an
'objective correlative' for it in describing the psychological effect of
this impulse on her characters. In other words, the significant thing
to her is that people should seek significance in experience—'the
moment of illumination': 'Nelly Jenkinson, the typist, crumbled her

---

[1] cf. V. Woolf, *The Common Reader* (First Series, 1923), p. 189.
[2] cf. T. S. Eliot, *Four Quartets*, II (*The Dry Salvages*).
[3] cf. Woolf, *A Writer's Diary* (Hogarth Press, London, 1953), p. 57.

cake indifferently enough. Every time the door opened she looked up. What did she expect to see?'[1]

Mrs. Woolf's journal provides a striking account of the effects of the 'numinous' impulse upon her, personally:

> I enjoy almost everything. Yet I have some restless searcher in me. Why is there not a discovery in life? Something one can lay hands on and say 'This is it'? My depression is a harassed feeling. I'm looking: but that's not it—that's not it. What is it? And shall I die before I find it? Then (as I was walking through Russell Square last night) I see the mountains in the sky: the great clouds; and the moon which is risen over Persia; I have a great and astonishing sense of something there, which is 'it'. It is not exactly beauty that I mean. It is that the thing is in itself enough: satisfactory; achieved. A sense of my own strangeness, walking on the earth is there too: of the infinite oddity of the human position; trotting along Russell Square with the moon up there and those mountain clouds. Who am I, what am I, and so on: these questions are always floating about in me: and then I bump against some exact fact—a letter, a person, and come to them again with a great sense of freshness. And so it goes on. But on this showing, which is true, I think, I do fairly frequently come upon this 'it'; and then feel quite at rest.[2]

The last sentence confirms what has already been stated above; that Mrs. Woolf discovered the 'significant', for which the 'numinous' impulse impelled her to search, in the sense of the numinous itself; a subtlety which, however satisfactory to the conscious mind, could not, of course, put an end to the promptings of the unconscious:

> I wish to add some remarks to this, on the mystical side of this solicitude; how it is not oneself but something in the universe that one's left with. It is this that is frightened and exciting in the midst of my profound gloom, depression, boredom, whatever it is. One sees a fin passing far out. What image can I reach to convey what I mean? Really there is none, I think. The interesting thing is that in all my feeling and thinking I have never come up against this before. Life is, soberly and accurately, the oddest affair; has in it the essence of reality. I used to feel this as a child—couldn't step across a puddle, once, I remember, for thinking how strange—what am I? etc.[3]

The problem of regressive-negative art is that of the irresistible force meeting the immovable object; the sense of the infinite clashing with a critical intelligence which frustrates its attempts to achieve a

[1] cf. Woolf, *Jacob's Room* (Hogarth Press, London, 1922, repr. 1960), p. 119.
[2] cf. Woolf, *A Writer's Diary*, 27 Feb. 1926, p. 86.
[3] ibid., 30 Sept. 1926, p. 101.

satisfactory objectification. We have dealt so far in this section with the type of regressive-negative art in which the artist makes some attempt to ignore the objections of common sense, to pretend that such objections do not exist for the moment: 'One sees a fin passing far out.'

There is an occasional note of defiance, an explicit rejection of phenomenalistic standards:

> O Cuckoo! shall I call thee Bird,
> Or but a wandering Voice?
>
> .   .   .
>
> Hail to thee, blithe Spirit!
> Bird thou never wert

but on the whole, however, the romantic artist endeavours to give positive expression to his sense of the divine or 'numinous', to find an image which he can seriously regard as divine. The more he feels himself obliged to 'defy' common sense the more negative his art becomes; 'Bird thou never wert' detracts from the spontaneity of Shelley's vision.

The tale of wonder or 'tall story' evidences a weakened sense of the supernatural; the artist feels obliged to pile Pelion on Ossa, to amaze the critical objections of the audience into silence. The louder the shout, the more obvious the fear of contradiction. One must, of course, distinguish between the tale of wonder which is intended to impress the audience as true, and that which is merely meant to be humorously received. It is with the former that we are at present concerned; the fantastic narrative of Mandeville's *Travels* may be quoted in illustration:

In these isles there are many manners of folk of diverse conditions. In one of them is a manner of folk of great stature, as they were giants, horrible and foul to the sight; and they have but one eye and that is in the middle of the forehead; they eat raw flesh and raw fish. In another isle are foul men of figure without heads, and they have eyes, in either shoulder one, and their mouths are round, shapen like a horse-shoe, in midst their shoulders . . . In another isle are folk whose ears are so long that they hang down to their knees . . . In another isle are men that have their overlip so great that when they sleep in the sun they cover all the visage with that lip . . . There is an isle where the folk have but one foot and that foot is so broad that it will cover all the body and owmbre it from the sun. Upon this foot will they run, so fast that it is a wonder to see. Many other manner of folk there are in other isles thereabouts which were too long to tell all.[1]

[1] cf. M. D. Anderson, *Animal Carvings in British Churches* (C.U.P., 1938), pp. 20–21.

The point at issue is not whether the author is convinced of the actual existence of these monstrosities (though in a fourteenth-century work which is almost entirely a compilation from earlier works[1] the scepticism of the author must not be too readily assumed) but whether the narrative is intentionally jocose, like *The True History* of Lucian, *Gulliver's Travels*, or *The Adventures of Baron Münchausen*. Like Poe, Mandeville may be writing fiction; but both writers are giving expression to their sense of wonder, objectifying in significant form their deep-seated belief that the possibilities of the world are infinite.

Closely associated with the kinds of regressive-negative art above, but still more negative in character, are the various developments of irrationalism in art from the late nineteenth century onward, popularly —and significantly—referred to as 'lunatic fringe' art, of which sur-realism and Dadaism are the most widely known movements. The term surrealistic in particular has come to be applied to any markedly bizarre work of art. Santayana, as we have seen,[2] maintains that it is the 'inward possibility' of grotesque art which constitutes its real charm; at all events, incongruity for incongruity's sake, which at first sight appears to be the doctrine of such movements as surrealism and Dadaism, may strike one as being a barren and unrewarding pro-gramme for an artist.

One's attitude to such art varies, however, according to whether one regards it as the product of frustration or of cynicism, as the work of a man who, imprisoned by his own scepticism,

> scrawls
> With desp'rate charcoal round his darkened walls[3]

or as a catchpenny freak show. Needless to remark, most such work is the product of both frustration and cynicism, but it will be con-venient for the moment to disregard the disingenuous aspect.

Whereas the religious visionary, or the individual with a deep con-viction of the objective reality of a traditional body of supernatural imagery, has a positive outlet for his intuition of the divine and of his own immortality, the surrealistic artist, with no such conviction, has no such outlet. The advance of empirical thinking, of a purely phenomenalistic attitude of mind, has tended to make the twentieth-century European sceptical about the reality not merely of religious

---

[1] cf. K. Sisam, *14th Century Verse and Prose* (O.U.P., 1948), p. 94.
[2] See p. 16.
[3] cf. Pope, 'Epistle to Dr Arbuthnot', ll. 19–20.

images but of all metaphysical values and abstractions. In such an age the power of the conscious mind to resist the suggestions of the unconscious regarding the supernatural is greatly increased. The only alternative which the artist can conceive to 'the natural conditions of organisation' is not supernatural but 'unnatural' conditions. The pressure of the 'numinous' impulse obliges him to fall back on this alternative; the conscious mind can be made ancillary to the rejection of the phenomenal world, but cannot, under such conditions, be induced to depict an integrated image of a transcendental world which it can regard as objectively real.

It has been remarked that in surrealistic art there is a strong awareness of the incongruity of the imagery employed with common-sense standards; it is characterized by self-consciousness, by 'wilfulness'. Such art, as one would expect, unlike the naïve myth, is accompanied by elaborate theories and justifications, attempts to placate and persuade the sceptic. The following extract from the first *Manifesto of Surrealism* (1924) is representative:

We still live under the reign of logic; that, as you will well understand, is what I want to come to. But the methods of logic are applied nowadays only to the resolution of problems of secondary interest. The absolute rationalism which is still the fashion does not permit consideration of any facts but those strictly relevant to our experience. Logical ends, on the other hand, escape us. Needless to say that even experience has had limits assigned to it. It revolves in a cage from which it becomes more and more difficult to release it. Even experience is dependent on immediate utility, and common sense is its keeper. Under colour of civilisation, under pretext of progress, all that rightly or wrongly may be regarded as fantasy or superstition has been banished from the mind, all uncustomary searching after truth has been proscribed. It is only by what must seem sheer luck that there has recently been brought to light an aspect of mental life—to my belief by far the most important—with which it was supposed that we no longer had any concern. All credit for these discoveries must go to Freud. Based on these discoveries a current of opinion is forming that will enable the explorer of the human mind to extend his investigations, justified as he will be in taking into account more than mere summary realities. The imagination is perhaps on the point of reclaiming its rights. If the depths of our mind harbour strange forces capable of increasing those of the surface, or of successfully contending with them, then it is all in our interest to canalise them, to canalise them first in order to submit them later, if necessary, to the control of reason.[1]

[1] cf. D. Gascoyne, *A Short Survey of Surrealism* (Cobden-Sanderson, 1936), pp. 59–60.

The significant thing about the passage above is the emphasis placed upon the positive, constructive nature of surrealism. The contrast between theory and practice may be illustrated by quotation:

POETS

'The circle is a figure surrounded by a circular line'
Raymond Lulle.

The melancholy of illiterates in the mystery of bottles
The imperceptible disquiet of cartwrights
Pieces of money in the slender vase
In the cockle-shell of the anvil
Dwells the lonely poet
Great wheelbarrow of the swamps.
(René Char, from The Masterless Hammer, 1934.)[1]

We have seen that Mrs. Woolf, unable to objectify her sense of the 'numinous' in a wholly satisfactory image ('What image can I reach to convey what I mean? Really there is none, I think'),[2] derives some intellectual consolation from the simple fact that man has an appetite for the supernatural; it is something significant which she can consciously accept as real. In similar vein, Chesterton concludes his essay 'A Defence of Nonsense' as follows:

Nonsense and faith (strange as the conjunction may seem) are the two supreme symbolic assertions of the truth that to draw out the soul of things with a syllogism is as impossible as to draw out Leviathan with a hook. The well-meaning person who, by merely studying the logical side of things, has decided that 'faith is nonsense', does not know how truly he speaks; later it may come back to him in the form that nonsense is faith.'[3]

Faith in what? one asks. A fervent Christian, with 'his soul in a safe bank', as Shaw puts it, Chesterton has independent spiritual capital to draw on. He is able to recognize the appetite for the 'numinous' which causes the artist to show his dissatisfaction with the phenomenal world by depicting its forms in a chaotic manner; but he stands outside the vicious circle—faith is nonsense and nonsense is faith—in which the surrealistic artist is imprisoned. His detachment enables him to employ a term to describe these expressions of dissatisfaction which is taboo for the surrealist; the term nonsense.

[1] ibid., p. 143 (trans. by Ruthven Todd).
[2] See p. 90.
[3] cf. Chesterton, from 'The Defendant' (cf. *A Book of English Essays.* ed. W. E. Williams (Penguin Books, 1942, repr. 1962), p. 214).

It is, of course, the role played by the *conscious* mind in such art which is especially difficult to describe. In general it may be pointed out that the perception of incongruity, of grotesqueness, of the 'shocking' so strongly developed in surrealistic art shows how highly conscious such art is. Nevertheless, the surrealistic artists insist on regarding their work as the product of pure 'inspiration', of 'strange forces' welling up from the depths of the mind. André Breton, author of the *Manifesto of Surrealism* (1924), defines surrealism as follows:

SURREALISM, n. Pure psychic automatism, by which it is intended to express, verbally, in writing, or by other means, the real process of thought. Thought's dictation, in the absence of all control exercised by the reason and outside all aesthetic or moral preoccupations.

ENCYCL. *Philos.* Surrealism rests in the belief in the superior reality of certain forms of association neglected heretofore;[1] in the omnipotence of the dream and in the disinterested play of thought. It tends definitely to do away with all other psychic mechanisms and to substitute itself for them in the solution of the principal problems of life.[2]

The 'philosophy' of surrealism is, of course, an attempt at rationalization which has obvious affinities with the conclusions of Mrs. Woolf and G. K. Chesterton described above. In the absence of a satisfying image Mrs. Woolf points to the image-seeking impulse as a significant reality. Chesterton, too, sees the manufacture of unreal forms as evidence of a real faith in the supernatural. Breton believes in the reality not, we may note, of 'certain forms', but of 'certain forms of association'; it is not so much the images created as the process which creates them to which he draws our attention.

The reference to Freud in the first extract quoted from *The Manifesto of Surrealism* indicates another means of justification, namely that, however incongruous with objective reality the images of the surrealistic artist may be, they are real because they exist. Moreover, they symbolize 'real conditions of man's subjective being', taking on a positive aspect when regarded as reflections of 'strange forces' harboured in the infinite depths of the mind. Dali's sophisticated monstrosities are deeply indebted to Freud. They are the very reverse of surrealism as defined by Breton i.e. 'pure psychic automatism'.

The type of surrealistic art of which Dali is the most notable

[1] cf. p. 73.
[2] cf. Gascoyne, op. cit., pp. 61–62.

exemplar is that in which the characteristics of consciousness—exclusion, selection, discrimination—are most in evidence. The images employed in such art are frequently constructs based on psychological theory, in particular on the work of Freud. The degree to which Dali's own 'shock tactics' are calculated and 'disingenuous' is apparent from his 'paranoiac method of criticism';[1] briefly, his contribution to surrealist theory is the idea of simulating various kinds of mental disease. Such simulation is unquestionably to be found in his own work. It would be difficult to find a more deliberately anarchical species of art than that produced in conformity with such an idea.

The type of surrealistic art produced more in the fashion indicated by André Breton's definition of surrealism as 'pure psychic automatism' is perhaps fundamentally more sincere in intention. The artist attempts to thwart the 'common-sense' objections and restrictions of consciousness by expressing himself quite spontaneously, a method obviously suggested by the psychoanalytical technique of 'free association' in which the patient is encouraged to say the first thing that comes into his head; the process is exactly summarized in the old witticism, 'How do I know what I think until I hear what I say?'

Unfortunately, the method of 'free association' is one which the patient finds extraordinarily difficult, even when he is not hampered by such extraneous considerations as the need to write his reverie down and the desire to produce something *éclatant*:

This method consists in asking the patient to abandon all conscious control and direction of his thoughts and emotions and to say everything that comes into his head without hindrance or criticism. Absurdly simply as this may sound, and simple as it is indeed in theory, it is yet very far from easy in practice. It constitutes a radical departure from the speech habits of everyday life, in which we are (with good reason) constantly controlling and adapting our words and thoughts in accordance with the circumstances of our environment. The nearest approach to such a mental attitude as is required is that of reverie or day-dreaming (a condition which we regard as quite peculiarly private and unsuitable for communication to others). Day-dreaming apart, there is always some task to accomplish, some line of thought to pursue, some special pre-determined chain of association to follow up—all of them circumstances in which, checking our tendency to 'wander', we have constantly to keep attention upon the matter in hand . . . In free association . . . even this degree of control must be abandoned, the subject being instructed to say literally everything that occurs to him, even though . . . the saying of it may involve a complete flouting

[1] cf. Gascoyne, op. cit., pp. 96–103.

of all the intellectual, moral, aesthetic and social canons of our thought and speech. Let the reader try the process for but a few minutes, and (if he is honest) he will rapidly convince himself that . . . he has already begun to edit or censor his associations, for the sake of his own feelings or those of his collaborator. Indeed even in the special conditions of the analyst's consulting-room the procedure is at best only partially adhered to; the process of analysis constantly meets with 'resistances' which interrupt the flow of associations.[1]

In surrealistic literature the very anxiety of the artist to flout 'all the intellectual, moral, aesthetic and social canons of our thoughts and speech', to create strange and startling images, to give utterance to nothing remotely conventional, makes the method a thoroughly self-conscious one; the 'pure psychic automatism' of Breton's definition remains a pious hope; most surrealistic fantasy is no more spontaneous than *Alice in Wonderland*. Where there is spontaneity its manifestations are subsequently edited or interpreted in a sophisticated fashion. Thus the paintings of Paul Klee are often clearly akin to the absent-minded 'doodling' we indulge in whilst telephoning and so on; but they were subsequently 'improved', particularly as regards colour, and furnished with brilliantly wayward titles. The following newspaper report describes a similar kind of 'sophisticated spontaneity':

An artist who covers vast canvases with a personal pattern of dots and splashes, who charges at his work with a cavalry-like rush, with his brush fixed like a bayonet on the end of a 3yd.-long stick, flew into London last night.

French-born Georges Mathieu is, at 39, surely the most energetic of all action-painters.

He limbers up like an Olympic athlete before he publicly attacks his huge canvases *before audiences*[2] in the world's capitals.

The muscular Mathieu arrived for the opening this week of his first exhibition at the West End's New London Gallery in Bond-street.

Twenty-five of his 'pictures', *elaborately titled after great events in medieval French history*[2] will be offered for sale at up to £5,000 each.

He started to paint in 1942 when he enlarged picture postcards of London scenes by night. From these examples of black on black—with little spots of colour—he turned without any transitional phase to his own discovery of a 'lyrical configuration'.

[1] cf. J. C. Flügel, *Theories of Psycho-Analysis* (*An Outline of Modern Knowledge Series*, Victor Gollancz Ltd., London, 1931, pp. 353–4).
[2] The italics are mine.

Mathieu started squirting paint straight from the tube on to the canvas—
he calls it 'tubism'. He ran up and down step-ladders, blotted and dabbed
with his hands.

In 1956 at the theatre Sarah Bernhardt, in Paris, he painted a great
canvas called 'Homage to the Poets of the Whole World' in 20 minutes.
He almost brought the house down.

Says Britain's Sir Herbert Read of Mathieu's work: 'It is an unpremeditated paroxysm, as unselfconscious as a child's scribble or the auto-
graph of a caliph.'[1]

Here, of course, the exhibitionistic, 'enfant terrible' aspect of surrealistic art is very much in the ascendancy; but the account illustrates admirably the dilemma of the surrealistic artist, torn between
the desire to give free and spontaneous expression to the strange,
significant forces harboured in the depths of the mind,[2] and the
iconoclastic scepticism which at best scarcely allows these forces any
more positive form of expression than a sincere rejection of the
standards and processes of progressive thought, and gives free rein to
exhibitionism.

The work of Hoffmann, as we have seen, is by no means uniform
in type; 'The Entail' is a classic example of a Gothic romance, 'The
Sandman' a study of a persecution complex. The main body of his
work, however, may be classified as lying somewhere between the
romantic and the surrealistic kinds of regressive-negative art, more
consciously subjective than the former, less anarchic than the latter
in its imagery. Hoffmann's attitude is admirably suggested by the
concluding paragraph of 'The Golden Pot':

> Then Archivarius Lindhorst patted me gently on the shoulder, and
> said: 'Soft, soft, my honoured friend! Lament not so! Were you not even
> now in Atlantis; and have you not at least a pretty little copyhold Farm
> there, as the poetical possession of your inward sense? And is the blessed-
> ness of Anselmus aught else but a Living in Poesy? Can aught else but
> Poesy reveal itself as the sacred Harmony of all Beings, as the deepest
> secret of Nature?'[3]

The ambivalence of regressive-negative art is clearly shown in
the above passage; the poetic vision is simultaneously 'a pretty
little copyhold Farm' in Atlantis, and 'the sacred Harmony of all
Beings'.

[1] cf. *Daily Express*, 24 Oct. 1960.
[2] See p. 93.
[3] cf. *Tales from Hoffmann*, ed. J. M. Cohen (Bodley Head, 1951), p. 108.

J. M. Cohen, in his introduction to Hoffmann's stories, speaks of Hoffmann's 'caricaturist's style',[1] presumably in reference to the tongue-in-cheek attitude to his own fantasies which is often evident in Hoffmann's narrative tone and in his asides to the reader; certainly, there is often an element of mockery in Hoffmann's employment of such folk-tale images as the witch—in 'The Golden Pot', for example—which provides some justification for the term 'caricaturist's style'.

A contrast has already been made, by implication, between the tale of wonder, such as Mandeville's *Travels*, in which, however deliberate the inventions and exaggerations, the reader is meant to be astonished rather than amused, and the comic 'tall story'—*Gulliver's Travels*, *Münchausen*—which is intended to amuse rather than to astonish, or to astonish, so to speak, with its very outrageousness.[2]

The first type of narrative, to which the Gothic horror story belongs, is clearly regressive in character. The second, in which the bizarre and monstrous is meant to be regarded as ridiculous, is as clearly a vindication of common-sense standards, and is thus progressive in character.

Between these two kinds, however, there are ambivalent forms which sprawl across the watershed between regressive and progressive art, forms of which it is difficult to say whether they are primarily intended to astonish or to amuse; the one reaction does not inhibit the other.

John Addington Symonds considered an element of caricature or mockery to be an invariable ingredient of grotesque art. He found this element in 'Scandinavian poetry of the best period'.[3]

One of the narratives which best bear out Symonds's contention is Thor's journey to Utgard,[4] in which he and Loki spend the night in the thumb of Skrymir's glove, a giant who flabbergasts them by taking Thor's hammer-blow for a leaf dropping on his head; Thor fails to lift up the giants' cat or empty one of their drinking-horns, is worsted in a wrestling bout by an old woman, and so on. All is subsequently explained as being due to a magic spell cast over the gods by Utgard-Loki; the hammer-blow never struck Skrymir, the cat was the World-Snake, the end of the horn was in the sea, the old woman was Death, &c.

[1] ibid., p. 17.
[2] See pp. 91–92.
[3] See p. 52.
[4] cf. *Gylfaginning* (The Prose Edda).

The whole story is highly sophisticated in its attitude towards the gods; but it is not entirely sceptical in tone. Still more deliberately comic is the well-known account of Thor's masquerade as a bride in order to deceive the giant who demanded the hand of Freya in return for the stolen hammer Mjöllnir. Such stories were both recounted and heard in a state of mind in which a disbelief of the particular events did not destroy a more general belief in the existence of the gods involved in them—though in the long run this may indeed have been the case. There may be a touch of cynicism in these narratives, but they are not deliberately outrageous, like the 'traveller's tales' of Lucian or Swift.

A similar ambivalence can be seen in much surrealistic art; in the 'wildly fantastic humour' of Benjamin Péret,[1] for example:

HONEST FOLK

The quarrel between the boiled chicken and the ventriloquist
had for us the meaning of a cloud of dust
which passed above the city
like the blowing of a trumpet
It blew so loudly that its bowler hat was trembling
and its beard stood up on end
to bite off its nose
It blew so loudly
that its nose cracked open like a nut
and the nut spat out
into the far distance
a little cow-shed
wherein the youngest calf
was selling its mother's milk
in sausage-skin flasks
that its father had vulcanised.

(From *From Behind the Faggots*, 1934.)[2]

The difference between this 'poem' and, say, the verse of Edward Lear is that whereas Lear's verse is not only intended to be comic but also ridiculous, Péret's work is not meant to be regarded as *mere* nonsense. It is nonsense with pretensions, the work of a man who is simultaneously defying common-sense standards and tacitly accepting them to produce a comic effect, a kind of convulsion of futility caused

[1] cf. Gascoyne, op. cit., p. 54.
[2] Gascoyne, op. cit., p. 155.

by the conflict between the regressive and the progressive aspects of the mind: *Est aliquid fatale malum per verba levare.*[1]

PROGRESSIVE-NEGATIVE ART

26. It will be convenient to consider next those genres which are associated with grotesque art by Thomas Wright and John Addington Symonds,[2] namely burlesque and caricature. In doing so we graduate to the forms of art in which the impulses of the unconscious are made to serve the turn of progressive thought.

In regressive-negative art the objective physical world and the attitude of mind which devotes itself exclusively to that world are regarded as trivial and ephemeral. The passage previously quoted from Walter Bagehot[3] admirably describes this regressive mood of 'All the world's a stage': 'The soul ties its shoe; the mind washes its hands in a basin. All is incongruous.'

Where the progressive attitude is dominant, the boot is on the other foot; one may recall Johnson's 'refutation' of solipsism by 'striking his foot with mighty force against a large stone, till he re-bounded from it'.[4] Whatever is incongruous with accepted standards of behaviour or with directed thinking, all that is absurd by the canons of common sense, is utilized to further the ends of progressive thought—usually, though not invariably, as the object of ridicule— in what we may term progressive-negative art.

Several kinds of such art may be distinguished; for convenience these may be grouped under three main headings: the nonsensical story, burlesque and caricature, and fantastic (or fanciful) allegory.

Nonsense is the most negative in character of art forms which

[1] cf. Ovid., *Trist.*, vi. 59. A recent art form which seems to me to be potentially much more important than surrealism is science fiction, a term which has now, of course, become scarcely less inclusive than the term surrealism itself. Most of the great flood of stories in this category are more or less straightforward romanticism, and it is usual for critics to assess the quality of such work, still considered in a general way to be mere light reading, with regard to the 'shock value' (I do not use the phrase with a moral connotation) of the ideas it contains. The enormous popularity of science fiction with all classes of reader seems to me to be significant, considering the highly progressive attitude of mind induced by our present culture, of the fact that here is a form of art which induces a particularly ready suspension of disbelief, and which might conceivably offer imagery of a positive kind whether regarded from the regressive, 'magical', or the progressive, realistic, point of view.

[2] See ch. 3.
[3] See p. 43.
[4] cf. Boswell's *Life of Johnson*, ch. XIV.

G.E.L.—H

evidence a progressive frame of mind. It is a Janus-faced form in which the rejection of 'the natural conditions of organisation' is at once permitted and ridiculed; permitted on the understanding that the work is mere mental horseplay with no more signifiance than the antics of a clown. Lewis Carroll's ingenious puns and *non sequiturs*, Edward Lear's odd juxtapositions

> He reads but he does not speak Spanish
> He cannot abide ginger beer

are alike in having no pretensions to a mystical significance. All the same, however deliberate, gross, open, and palpable the nonsense, such art, whilst paying lip-service to progressive standards, is commonly a cloak for regression:

> Wer heiter im Absurden spielt
> Den wird auch wohl das Absurde ziemen.[1]

The anarchic tendencies of surrealistic art may be detected, for instance, in the following passage of deliberate nonsense by Keats:

> Give my sincerest respects to Mrs Dilk(e) saying that I have not for-given myself for not having got her the little Box of Medicine I promised for her after dinner flushings, and that had I remained at Hampstead I would have made precious havoc with her house and furniture—drawn a great harrow over her garden—poisoned Boxer—eaten her Cloathes pegs,—fried her Cabbages fricaceed (how is it spelt?) her radishes—ragouted her Onions—belaboured her beat root—outstripped her Scarlet Runners—parlezvou'd with her french Beans—devoured her Mignon or Mignonette—metamorphosed her Bell handles—splinterd her looking glasses—bullock'd at her cups and saucers—agonized her decanters—put old Philips to pickle in the Brine-tub—disorganized her piano—dislocated her candle-sticks—emptied her wine bins in a fit of despair—turned her Maid out to Grass and Astonished Brown—whose Letter to her on these events I would rather see than the original copy of the Book of Genesis.[2]

Mrs. Dilke, one gathers, was a house-proud woman whose orderli-ness stirs Keats to a gleeful vision of chaos in her conventional house-hold, stimulating a deep-rooted feeling of dissatisfaction.

In caricature and burlesque the progressive, purposeful nature of the work is more in evidence; though here, too, the avowed purpose of holding anti-social behaviour up to ridicule sometimes becomes an 'excuse' for fantasy thinking.

[1] See p. 66.
[2] Letter to Jane Reynolds, 14 Sept. 1817. cf. *Letters of Keats*, ed. M. Buxton Forman (O.U.P., 2nd impr. 1948).

In the more negative kind of satire—burlesque—and in caricature, directed thinking consists in the association of the victim with the ridiculous and unpleasant. In caricature, the simplest form of satire, the characteristic features of the victim are exaggerated and distorted to suggest that they are unpleasant and absurd, or tend towards the absurd. In burlesque the object to be ridiculed—or a distorted travesty of it—is surrounded with unpleasant, contemptible and absurd imagery:

> No Persian Carpets spread th' Imperial way,
> But scatter'd Limbs of mangled Poets lay:
> From dusty shops neglected Authors come,
> Martyrs of Pies, and reliques of the Bum.
> Much Heywood, Shirly, Ogleby there lay,
> But loads of Sh[adwell] almost choakt the way.[1]

In such work fantasy is applied, put to purposive use; the end, as it were, justifies the means—fantasy thinking. The 'flyting' matches, competitions in abuse popular in medieval Scottish literature, are a simple form of such art.

Satire, the term generally applied to a less farcical and more explicit kind of ridicule, is more positive in character in that it is more reasoned in its criticism; it is, of course, a term of extremely wide application, shading off into burlesque at the one extreme and at the other including much that can scarcely be described as progressive-negative at all, making no use of fantasy in its criticisms, apart from occasional metaphors such as occur in restrained and sparing fashion in *The Letters of Junius*, for example: 'Lord Bute . . . was forced to go through every division, resolution, composition, and refinement of political chemistry, before he happily arrived at the *caput mortuum* of vitriol in your Grace.'[2] Any considerable use of fantasy would naturally tend to destroy the tone of lucid common sense, of 'a calm appeal to the judgment of the people upon their own most essential interests'. We are here concerned with fantastic or consistently fanciful satire, usually, in the more burlesque forms, a comic 'vision', as in 'Mac Flecknoe', 'The Dunciad', 'The Vision of Judgment', &c., and in less farcical satire an allegory, as in 'Absalom and Achitophel' or 'The Hind and the Panther'. In these kinds of satire, fantasy is employed in order to associate the victim with absurdity, but also as

---

[1] cf. Dryden, 'Mac Flecknoe' (cf. *Dryden: Poetry, Prose and Plays*, selected by Douglas Grant, Rupert Hart-Davis, London, 1952, p. 137).
[2] *To His Grace the Duke of Grafton*, 8 July 1769.

'sugar coating' in order to make the progressive ideas emotionally more effective. The imagery of *Gulliver's Travels* is intended to amuse in the broad sense of the word; Swift deliberately appeals not merely to our sense of the ridiculous but to our appetite for the wonderful and outlandish, on the principle of 'Why should the devil have all the best tunes?':

> Now, he that will examine Human Nature with Circumspection enough, may discover several Handles, whereof the Six Senses afford one apiece, beside a great Number that are screw'd to the Passions, and some few riveted to the Intellect. Among these last, Curiosity is one, and, of all others, affords the firmest Grasp: Curiosity, that Spur in the side, that Bridle in the mouth, that Ring in the Nose, of a lazy, an impatient, and a grunting reader. By this Handle it is, that an Author should seize upon his Readers; which as soon as he has once compast, all Resistance and struggling are in vain; and they become his Prisoners as close as he pleases, till Weariness or dullness force him to let go his Gripe.[1]

Nevertheless, when one has given both these explanations for the fantastic imagery of Swift's satires—deliberate ridicule and deliberate fascination—it is apparent that they are not wholly adequate. Swift's delight in fantastic invention for its own sake is obvious, though he mockingly deprecates his own inclination to indulge in it:

> ... even I myself, the Author of these momentous Truths, am a Person whose Imaginations are hard-mouth'd, and exceedingly disposed to run away with his Reason, which I have observed from long Experience, to be a very light Rider, and easily shook off.[2]

In an odd passage Scott remarks:

> So far *Frankenstein*, therefore, resembles the *Travels of Gulliver*, which suppose the existence of the most extravagant fictions, in order to extract from them philosophical reasoning and moral truth. In such cases the admission of the marvellous expressly resembles a sort of entry-money paid at the door of a lecture-room—it is a concession which must be made to the author, and for which the reader is to receive value in moral instruction.[3]

It seems strange to regard the 'sugar coating' as something which must be tolerated for the sake of the pill: but at least Scott suggests that the fantasy is not merely a concession to the reader, but is some-

---

[1] cf. *A Tale of a Tub*, sect. XI (penultimate paragraph).
[2] ibid., sect. IX (last paragraph).
[3] cf. Scott, op. cit., pp. 211–12.

how congenial to the creative mood of the artist. Swift is the very antithesis of Coleridge. Both are endowed with astonishing imaginations—in the literal sense of the word—and with great ratiocinative power; but whereas in Coleridge's case the former faculty is dominant, so that the artist is preoccupied with his need to give the imagination a philosophical dignity and its creations an intellectual status, or concerned to exalt the 'vital' imaginative power above mere reason, Swift, on the other hand, in whom the progressive aspect of mind is dominant, makes all his images patently absurd and emphasizes the foolish and dangerous character of uncontrolled fantasy thinking. The imaginative power, for Swift, is a brute which must be ridden by reason and not allowed to get the bit between its teeth.

In some fantastic satire of an allegorical-burlesque nature—as in *The Battle of the Books*—the author may lead us by the rings of curiosity in our noses, but the violation of 'the natural conditions of organisation' is clearly not intended to be overlooked. Such work may therefore be regarded as more progressive in character than fantastic allegory in which the fantasy is not intended to seem absurd; the obvious example of the latter is *The Faerie Queene*, but the allegorical figures of Sin and Death in *Paradise Lost*, or the more fantastic passages of *The Pilgrim's Progress*, may also be mentioned. In serious allegory, which may be regarded as the myth of the progressive aspect of mind—just as ethics may be regarded as the progressive aspect of religion—the artist, appreciating the need for his allegorical narritive to move the reader emotionally, naturally tends to encourage belief in his symbols as living entities; it is significant that the most directly allegorical of Gulliver's four voyages, the voyage to Laputa, is at once the most farcical and the least effective emotionally. Swift does indeed accomplish the miracle of simultaneously inducing a 'willing suspension of disbelief' and conveying the impression that his tongue is firmly in his cheek; in this respect the voyage to Lilliput is a triumph of ambivalence. Spenser does not, of course, similarly hold the phenomenal absurdity of his dragons and monsters before our attention, and it is possible for the reader, like Hazlitt, to derive a primarily regressive and 'escapist' pleasure from his work without being entirely out of sympathy with the poet's own attitude towards his creations, though it is clearly going too far to say that 'his poetry was the essence of romance, a very halo round the bright orb of fancy'.[1]

[1] cf. W. Hazlitt, 'Of Persons One Would Wish to Have Seen'.

We are here concerned rather with the conditions in which art is created than with its subsequent interpretation; but Hazlitt's or Keats's romantic view of Spenser suggests the manner in which progressive, practically intended art may come to be regarded as romantic and escapist. Similarly, the myth or vision, when it is not simply dismissed by the progressive mind, is commonly adapted to its purposes by allegorical explanation. Medieval theologians thus interpreted the Bible on four levels: the literal (as historical fact), the allegorical, the tropological, and the anagogical. The search for the moral content of a work of art is a familiar feature of criticism.

The medieval Bestiaries are a particularly interesting type of allegorical art, standing in much the same relation to Spenser as Spenser does to Swift. The characteristics of the various animals described are given a Christian symbolic value; but the relationship between the symbol and the reality is clearly regarded as much more than a merely metaphorical one. It is a mystical one. One is reminded of Berkeley's remark that the world is a language spoken by God to be interpreted by men, or Blake's observation: 'There Exist in that Eternal World the Permanent Realities of Every Thing which we see reflected in this Vegetable Glass of Nature.'[1] It is true that Spenser regarded his creations as symbols of a transcendental reality; but his allegorical figments are entirely fictitious, whereas many of the descriptions of animal behaviour in the Bestiaries were believed to be factual by the artists. The lion, hiding in his den, is the type of Christ in the womb of the Blessed Virgin; the sweet breath of the panther symbolizes the holy discourses of Christ; the eagle rejuvenating itself in a spring suggests the efficacy of baptism, and so on. Naturally there is much sophisticated ingenuity. The dual nature of the siren, human and piscine, is pressed into service as an illustration of hypocrisy; the whale, sounding with mariners on its back which they have mistaken for an island, symbolizes the devil, and so on.[2] In such cases there is some approximation to deliberate fantasy, though —as in the case of Mandeville's Travels—it is doubtful whether many of the animal characteristics described were, in fact, invented by the artist, however far-fetched they may appear. Bestiary figures were much used in church decoration, and it may be remarked here that whilst allegorical interpretation, as we have seen, has made much

[1] cf. William Blake, *A Vision of the Last Judgment* (*Blake's Poetry and Prose*, Nonesuch ed., 1946, p. 639).
[2] cf. Joseph Hall, *Selections from Early Middle English, 1130–1250* (O.U.P., 1920), part I, pp. 176 ff.

regressive art acceptable to progressive standards, lack of understanding has led to many such examples of conscious ingenuity as
these animal symbols of Christianity being regarded as wilfully
grotesque. The following passage refers to both developments in
regard to church art, emphasizing that both *progressive*—allegorical—
and *regressive*—purely fantastic—figures occur in church art:

All the recognizable animals I have observed in English churches can
be fitted into one or other of the above categories; there remains only the
strange fauna of mediaeval fantasy, grotesques which defy classification,
hybrids no legend can justify, nightmare hordes with neither name nor
kind. When it was supposed that all medieval sculpture was necessarily
symbolical, the gargoyles on the outsides of churches were explained as
demons fleeing from the power of the Church, or baffled by it in their
attempts to enter and attack the congregations; the famous 'Lincoln Imp'
is supposed to have entered the cathedral with evil intent and there been
miraculously petrified. This theory has now been abandoned and the conception of these grotesque beings more reasonably attributed to the exuberance of creative fantasy among the carvers. But even though we give up the
attempt to explain gargoyles I think it would surprise the casual visitor to
know how many of the apparently meaningless grotesques could have been
used as illustrations of the text in Job xii.7.: 'Ask now the beasts, and they
shall teach thee; and the fowls of the air, and they shall tell thee.'[1]

PROGRESSIVE-POSITIVE ART

27. It has been remarked that the kind of satirical writing exemplified
by *The Letters of Junius* makes so little use of fantasy that it can
scarcely be said to belong to progressive-negative art. Briefly, we
may place in the category of progressive-positive art those works
which are entirely the product of directed thinking, presenting the
reader or spectator with conclusions derived from actual facts or with
realistic representations of actual objects. In such art there is no rejection of 'the natural conditions of organisation', of the physical laws
of the phenomenal world.

Strictly speaking, therefore, all fiction should be excluded from
this category. Even work of so realistic a quality as the Prologue to
The Canterbury Tales could be accepted as progressive-positive art
in the strict sense only if the people and events described in it could
be shown to be historically real. Such work is best regarded as being
on the borderline between the two progressive categories.

[1] cf. Anderson, *Animal Carvings in British Churches*, pp. 22–23 (see also
p. 61 above, footnote 1).

The first group of characteristically positive works in this last category which we may note is on the whole of a type in which aesthetic value is generally regarded as being of secondary importance, as in historical and biographical studies, scientific, philosophical, and critical works, and so on. Consciousness, of its nature, is selective, discriminating, and exclusive. The progressive aspect of mind endeavours above all to systematize man's relations with his environment through a national understanding of that environment. Work produced in this frame of mind is never deliberately grotesque, though it may be so described, pejoratively, by someone who is out of sympathy with ratiocinative thought; Blake, for example.

The presentation of imagery in such art is subordinated to the general purpose of the work, much as imagery of a fantastic nature is employed in progressive-negative art. It is never an end in itself. The following passage may be regarded as typical:

A salmon leaping in a limpid waterfall; a school of tunny-fishes swimming rapidly in the open sea; the silvery glitter of a sardine shoal on the move; the rainbow pink of surface cruising mackerel; the spectral brilliance of gentle coral fishes; the slaty coat of a shark or swordfish on the prowl—all these conjure up an idea of unbounded freedom in the protean world of nature. But this colourful splendour and this power and harmony of motion are merely appearances masking an implacable determinism which rules all living beings. All are swayed by definite laws appropriate to the surroundings in which they move, feed and multiply.[1]

The description or representation of actual objects may, of course, ultimately be due to an 'escapist' impulse; the construction of, say, a faithful model of a pirate ship, or a scholarly dissertation on the cultures of Polynesia, may well be the outcome of a 'romantic' desire to associate oneself with a mode of existence which is more exciting, happier, richer, &c., than that of the immediate present and one's actual surroundings. Just as fantasy may be made to serve a progressive purpose, so an 'escapist' impulse may find an 'objective correlative' in actual phenomena. Nevertheless, work which is the reasoned product of directed thought is clearly to be described as progressive-positive, whatever the emotional incentives of the creator.

It remains to speak of the accurate representation of actual objects which belong to the artist's immediate surroundings and which can

---

[1] cf. Edouard Le Danois, *Fishes of the World* (Harrap and Co., London, 1957), p. 13.

scarcely be said to have either romantic associations or an obvious practical intention. Roger Fry observes with regard to painting and sculpture: '. . . it would be no easy matter to persuade anyone who looked at life from a purely practical or ethical angle that there was any justification for the economic waste implied by these particular useless activities.'[1]

In such art, where familiar objects are portrayed accurately, it may be assumed that the artist is largely concerned with technique. The object appears as a problem to be resolved, a challenge to the artist's skill. Vincent Van Gogh's work often seems to be of this kind: his painting of his pipe on a rush-bottomed chair, for example, can hardly be said to have any symbolic significance—though, of course, one can never altogether rule out the possibility of some 'sentimental' association of a personal nature. Such work may reasonably be explained as being primarily of technical interest to the artist; the literary equivalent, perhaps, is the search for *le mot juste*.

However 'useless' from a 'purely practical . . . angle', as a manifestation of the human need for self-expression such purely descriptive or representational art does at least have progressive qualities; it is empirical, it embodies the results of close observation of natural phenomena in its productions, and it in no way rejects 'the natural conditions of organisation'. It is, in fact, the equivalent on the level of the emotions of the more obviously progressive creations of the intellect—scientific works, mathematical treatises, and so on—in its appeal to the reader or spectator.

SUMMARY OF CHAPTER 5

28. The chief ideas regarding grotesque art outlined above may be summarized for convenience as follows:

(i) Grotesqueness may appear in anything which is found to be in sufficiently grave conflict with accepted standards to arouse emotion. In theory, therefore, there is nothing which might not be regarded as grotesque from some standpoint: 'But taken as a whole the universe is absurd . . . All is incongruous.'[2] In point of fact it is human nature to regard some things—physical deformity for instance, or creatures which in some way suggest deformity like the ape or the snake—as being more deeply or abidingly grotesque than others.

[1] cf. R. Fry, *The Arts of Painting and Sculpture* (*An Outline of Modern Knowledge Series*, Gollancz, 1931, p. 910).
[2] See p. 43.

(ii) The peculiar fascination exercised by grotesque imagery which common sense rejects as ridiculous and/or repulsive may be accounted for by the polarity of the mind, of which the conscious and unconscious parts exert opposed influences. The influence of the conscious mind (progressive aspect) prompts us to be curious about the phenomenal world, to regard it as ultimate reality and to seek fulfilment through our relations with it. The influence of the unconscious (regressive aspect) leads us to regard the phenomenal world as superficial and transitory and to seek a reality of a transcendental or mystical kind. What we reject under the influence of one of these aspects may thus appeal to us, simultaneously or subsequently, under the influence of the other aspect. This polarity is an ineradicable characteristic of the human mind.

(iii) Where both these impulses, the regressive and the progressive, find satisfactory expression in the same objectification (e.g. in the image of Thor's hammer, evoking the gods and explaining a natural phenomenon), the objectification may be spoken of as 'positive' and without any inner conflict. From the twentieth-century point of view the regressive side of such positive imagery appears to be the salient one. In general, where no inner conflict is to be observed between the promptings of the two impulses the work may be described as positive: regressive-positive where the imagery is of a supernatural or mystical kind, as in the religious vision of myth, progressive-positive where the progressive attitude dominates and the content is of an empirical kind, as in the scientific treatise. Positive work is thus work which successfully expresses the artist's conception of reality.

(iv) Negative art is art in which the content is not wholly positive in the above sense, i.e. the artist does not regard his work as being completely 'factual'. In regressive-negative art, the artist is too strongly aware of the 'common-sense' objections to his vision to regard it as a completely genuine picture of reality. He therefore tends to 'justify' his work by appeasing common sense,[1] by denigrating it,[2] or by defying it.[3] Deliberately 'grotesque' imagery, in regressive-

---

[1] It has already been remarked that the 'tall story', 'nonsense', &c., which pays lip-service to progressive standards by openly admitting its own absurdity easily becomes a cloak for regressive feeling. The phrase 'the willing suspension of disbelief for the moment' suggests this sense of the need to appease or disarm scepticism.

[2] cf. Keats: Do not all charms fly
         At the mere touch of cold philosophy? ('Lamia', 229–30.)

[3] cf. Shelley: Hail to thee, blithe Spirit!
         Bird thou never wert.

negative art—in surrealist art, for example—is generally indicative of a highly negative attitude. The artist is not so much concerned to present a coherent picture of a supernatural reality as to express his 'claustrophobia', his rejection of the physical surroundings by which he feels himself to be imprisoned.

In progressive-negative art fantastic imagery is employed by the artist in either or both of the following ways:

(*a*) In order to capture the reader's emotions, as a 'ring in the nose of a lazy and impatient and a grunting reader',[1] the progressive end justifying the regressive imagery, which, of course, is not regarded by the artist as being significant in itself.

(*b*) In burlesque, caricature, and satire, in order to associate the object of ridicule with ridiculous ideas or images; in such art fantastic imagery is significant only in the sense of being barren, futile, and opposed to common sense; it signifies disorder and absurdity.

29. The hypothesis on which the above examination is based, that of innate propensities in the human mind (I have confined myself, in speaking of the unconscious, to consideration of a single propensity, the 'sense of infinity'), whilst it remains a hypothesis, has a considerable weight of professional opinion behind it. It is a central feature of the work of Jung, and is to some extent countenanced by Freud as well.[2]

[1] See p. 104 (Swift, *A Tale of a Tub*).
[2] 'Freud himself has been so struck with the frequency and similarity of certain "primal fantasies" . . . that he too is inclined to consider that they cannot be entirely accounted for in terms of the individual's own experience.' (cf. Flügel, *Theories of Psycho-Analysis; An Outline of Modern Knowledge Series*, p. 367.) cf. also Jung's remarks on Freud in *Symbols of Transformation* (ch. II).

6

SWIFT: THE FANTASY OF
EXTREME LOGIC

30. In the previous chapter we saw that there are good grounds for connecting the use of the grotesque with the religious sense in what has been termed regressive-negative art. This is equally true of progressive-negative art (fantastic satire) in cases where the creation of fantastic imagery is clearly a means of satisfying a strong inner compulsion. There is ample evidence that this was the case with Swift. He dwells repeatedly upon the absurd nature of his imagery; but his attitude towards it was, in fact, an ambiguous one. The general purpose of this study is to bring out this ambiguity and to indicate the general effects of such an attitude upon Swift's work. For this purpose some account requires to be given of Swift's view of the ideal state of mind—incurious, emotionally quiescent, rational—and of his religious opinions. My reason for dwelling on these at some length is to demonstrate how resolutely Swift rejects the more intellectual kinds of emotional outlet: scientific curiosity, philosophical speculation, religious zeal. In dealing with his attitude towards reason, my examination will be based chiefly upon the famous 'Fool among Knaves' passage in *A Tale of a Tub*, and in considering his religious views I wish to comment in some detail upon Professor Irvin Ehrenpreis's association of the Houyhnhnms with deism in *The Personality of Jonathan Swift*.

We have previously noted Jung's description of directed or progressive thinking as 'troublesome and exhausting', in contrast to fantasy thinking, which 'goes on without trouble'.[1] For Swift, whose attitude to reason is substantially that of Locke, the proper use of reason involves no such effort as Jung maintains. In Swift's view, what we need to know about reality is perfectly obvious. Locke's remark: 'God has not been so sparing to men to make them barely

---

[1] See note 2, p. 76.

two-legged creatures, and left it to Aristotle to make them rational',[1] is echoed in *Gulliver's Travels*:

The Lilliputians believe . . . that Providence never intended to make the Management of publick Affairs a Mystery, to be comprehended only by a few Persons of sublime Genius, of which there seldom are three born in an Age; But, they suppose Truth, Justice, Temperance, and the like, to be in every Man's Power.[2]

Reason, for Swift as for Locke, does not consist of syllogistic reasoning. The involved, futile ratiocination of the Laputians stands in contrast to the effortless common sense of the Houyhnhnms:

Neither is Reason among them a Point problematical as with us, where Men can argue with Plausibility on both Sides of a Question; but strikes you with immediate Conviction; as it must needs do where it is not mingled, obscured, or discoloured by Passion and Interest. I remember it was with extreme Difficulty that I could bring my Master to understand the Meaning of the word Opinion, or how a Point could be disputable; because Reason taught us to affirm or deny only where we are certain; and beyond our Knowledge we cannot do either . . . In the like Manner when I used to explain to him our several Systems of Natural Philosophy, he would laugh that a Creature pretending to Reason, should value itself upon the Knowledge of other People's Conjectures, and in Things where that Knowledge, if it were certain, could be of no Use.[3]

Novel facts, like ingenious speculations, are given short shrift. Whilst truth, even in trivial matters, is preferable to falsehood, and Gulliver has acquired 'a great Disgust against this Part of Reading (i.e. travel books), and some Indignation to see the Credulity of Mankind so impudently abused',[4] fact for fact's sake makes no appeal to Swift:

The Captain was very well satisfied with this plain Relation I had given him; and said, he hoped when we returned to England, I would oblige the World by putting it in Paper, and making it publick. My Answer was, that I thought we were already over-stocked with Books of Travels: That nothing could now pass which was not extraordinary; wherein I doubted, some

[1] cf. *An Essay Concerning Human Understanding* (1690), bk. IV, ch. XVII ('Of Reason'), ed. Raymond Wilburn (Everyman's Library, J. M. Dent & Sons Ltd., London, 1947), p. 327.
[2] cf. *Gulliver's Travels*, bk. I, ch. VI cf. *Swift/Gulliver's Travels and Selected Writings in Prose and Verse*, ed. John Hayward (Nonesuch Press, London, 1946), p. 55.
[3] ibid. bk. IV, ch. VIII (Nonesuch ed., p. 262).
[4] ibid. bk. IV, ch. XII (Nonesuch ed., p. 287).

Authors less consulted Truth than their own Vanity or Interest, or the Diversion of ignorant Readers. That my Story could contain little besides common Events, without those ornamental Descriptions of strange Plants, Trees, Birds, and other Animals; or the barbarous Customs and Idolatry of savage People, with which most Writers abound.[1]

In general, then, Swift's attitude of mind is well described, in Professor A. O. Lovejoy's well-known phrase, as 'rationalistic anti-intellectualism'. The following summary of the implications of the phrase admirably brings out the opposition of this attitude of mind to 'troublesome and exhausting' directed thinking:

The presumption of the universal accessibility and verifiability of all that is really needful for men to know implied that all subtle, elaborate, intricate reasonings about abstruse questions beyond the grasp of the majority are certainly unimportant, and probably untrue.[2]

Swift's profoundest expression of this attitude is perhaps to be found in a paradoxical and much-discussed passage in section IX of *A Tale of a Tub*:

In the Proportion that Credulity is a more peaceful Possession of the Mind, than Curiosity, so far preferable is that Wisdom, which converses about the Surface, to that pretended Philosophy which enters into the Depths of Things, and then comes gravely back with Informations and Discoveries, that in the inside they are good for nothing. The two Senses, to which all Objects first address themselves, are the Sight and the Touch; These never examine farther than the Colour, the Shape, the Size, and whatever other Qualities dwell, or are drawn by Art upon the Outward of Bodies; and then comes Reason officiously, with tools for cutting, and opening, and mangling, and piercing, offering to demonstrate, that they are not of the same consistence quite thro'. Now I take all this to be the last Degree of perverting Nature: one of whose Eternal Laws it is, to put her best Furniture forward. And therefore, in order to save the Charges of all such expensive Anatomy for the Time to come; I do here think fit to inform the Reader, that in such Conclusions as these, Reason is certainly in the Right; and that in most Corporeal Beings, which have fallen under my 'Cognizance, the Outside hath been infinitely preferable to the In: Whereof I have been farther convinced from some late Experiments. Last Week I saw a Woman flay'd, and you will hardly believe, how much it altered her Person for the worse. Yesterday I ordered the Carcass of a

---

[1] ibid. (Nonesuch ed., p. 145).
[2] cf. Gladys Bryson, *Man and Society: The Scottish Inquiry of the 18th century*, pp. 12–15.

Beau to be stript in my Presence; when we were all amazed to find so many unsuspected Faults under one Suit of Cloaths: Then I laid open his Brain, his Heart, and his Spleen; But, I plainly perceived at every Operation, that the farther we proceeded, we found the Defects encrease upon us in Number and Bulk: from all which, I justly formed this Conclusion to myself; That whatever Philosopher or Projector can find out an Art to sodder and patch up the Flaws and Imperfections of Nature, will deserve much better of Mankind, and teach us a more useful Science, than that so much in present Esteem, of widening and exposing them (like him who held Anatomy to be the ultimate End of Physick.) And he, whose Fortunes and Dispositions have placed him in a convenient Station to enjoy the Fruits of this noble Art: He that can with Epicurus content his Ideas with the Films and Images that fly off upon his Senses from the Superficies of Things; Such a Man truly wise, creams off Nature, leaving the Sower and the Dregs, for Philosophy and Reason to lap up. This is the sublime and refined Point of Felicity, called the Possession of being well deceived; The Serene Peaceful State of being a Fool among Knaves.[1]

Dr. F. R. Leavis regards this brilliant paragraph as a skilful trap which is sprung in the last sentence.[2] In agreeing that the reader is certainly meant to be taken unawares, however, we must not suppose that the whole passage is ironically intended. Swift's criticism of the misuse of reason is earnest enough; but he then leads us gradually to perceive that one can misuse reason in more than one way, by Amorphy and Oscitation as well as by Fastidiosity:[3] we are led through the passage from one extreme to the other.

The most significant thing about the passage as regards content is the insight which it affords us into Swift's attitude towards reason, here placed in opposition to common sense: '. . . then comes Reason officiously, with tools for cutting, and opening, and mangling, and piercing . . .' How is one to reconcile this with his remark: 'I am in all opinions to believe according to my own impartial reason, which I am bound to inform and improve, as far as my capacity and opportunities will permit'? The answer lies in the word *capacity*. Reason is a magnificent instrument, but it requires to be used properly, and this involves two other factors, the agent who uses it and the material upon which it is used. Human nature being the weak and fallible thing it is, any attempt to use our reason to penetrate

[1] cf. *A Tale of a Tub* (O.U.P., 1958, 2nd ed), pp. 173–4.
[2] cf. F. R. Leavis, 'The Irony of Swift' (*The Common Pursuit*, Chatto & Windus, London, 1953, pp. 80–84).
[3] cf. *A Tale of a Tub*, sect. V (O.U.P. ed., p. 124).

deeper than that which we are intended to know—the obvious—must result in one or more of the following evils:

(i) Error:

They (the Laputians) are very bad Reasoners, and vehemently given to Opposition, unless they happen to be of the right Opinion, which is seldom their Case.[1]

(ii) Triviality:

In the like Manner, when I used to explain to him our several Systems of Natural Philosophy, he would laugh that a Creature pretending to Reason, should value itself upon the Knowledge of other People's Conjectures, and in Things where that Knowledge, if it were certain, could be of no use.[2]

(iii) Moral culpability (especially pride):

Violent zeal for truth hath an hundred to one odds to be either petulancy, ambition, or pride.[3]

(iv) Destruction of the will to live:

Although reason were intended by providence to govern our passions, yet it seems that, in two points of the greatest moment to the being and continuance of the world, God hath intended our passions to prevail over reason. The first is, the propagation of our species, since no wise man ever married from the dictates of reason. The other is, the love of life, which, from the dictates of reason, every man would despise, and wish it at an end, or that it never had a beginning.[4]

It is perhaps true that, in the remark above regarding the improvement of reason 'as far as my capacity and opportunities will permit', Swift is thinking primarily of the variation in individual capacity; but it is legitimate to consider the remark in the wider sense of human capacity for reason, with which he is in general far more concerned.

Too intensive a use of reason, then, is an error of judgement and therefore unreasonable. This is clearly the general tenor of the passage quoted above from *A Tale of a Tub*. What, then, is to be made of the final sentence: 'This is the sublime and refined Point of Felicity, called, the Possession of being well deceived; The Serene

---

[1] cf. *Gulliver's Travels*, bk. III, ch. II (Nonesuch ed., p. 160).
[2] See p. 113.
[3] cf. *Thoughts on Religion* (7) (Nonesuch ed., p. 465). cf. Pope, *Essay on Man*, Epistle I. l. 123:
       In Pride, in reas'ning Pride, our error lies.
[4] cf. *Thoughts on Religion* (15) (Nonesuch ed., pp. 466–7).

Peaceful State of being a Fool among Knaves'? If Swift had written, say, 'of being a blind man in an ugly world', it would certainly have been more in keeping with the argument. It would also, however, have made the whole passage an inexact expression of Swift's attitude. What Swift is doing is to contrast two equally reprehensible frames of mind, 'the two principal Branches of Madness'.[1] The 'expensive anatomy' which cuts, opens, pierces, and mangles in order to confirm what we already know, that the world is a sorry place, is useless and absurd: 'Last Week I saw a Woman flay'd, and you will hardly believe, how much it altered her Person for the worse.' On the other hand, those who, like Epicurus, are content with 'Films and Images that fly off . . . from the Superficies of Things', though they may be happier than the 'anatomists', are equally lacking in common sense. Swift tells us that 'the great Introducers of new Schemes in Philosophy', such as Epicurus, Diogenes, Apollonius, Lucretius, Paracelsus, Descartes, 'generally proceeded in the Common Course of their Words and Actions, by a Method very different from the vulgar Dictates of unrefined Reason'.[2] and continues:

Now, I would gladly be informed, how it is possible to account for such Imaginations as these in particular Men, without Recourse to my Phae-nomenon of Vapours, ascending from the lower Faculties to over-shadow the Brain, and thence distilling into Conceptions, for which the narrowness of our Mother-Tongue has not yet assigned any other Name, besides that of Madness or Phrenzy.[3]

Swift is thus insisting on the need to take a common-sense view of life, lacking both in the fact-collectors and in the fools who wrap themselves up in their own delusions, the system-makers.

The latter, in Swift's view, are closely akin to the religious fanatics, men who claim special knowledge denied to the many, and attempt to win others over to their individual theories and creeds:

. . . when a Man's Fancy gets astride on his Reason, when Imagination is at Cuffs with the Senses, and common Understanding, as well as common Sense, is Kickt out of Doors; the first Proselyte he makes, is Himself, and when that is once compass'd, the Difficulty is not so great in bringing over others.[4]

[1] cf. *A Tale of a Tub*, sect. IX (O.U.P. ed. (1958), p. 174).
[2] ibid. (O.U.P. ed., p. 166).
[3] ibid. (O.U.P. ed., p. 167).
[4] ibid. (O.U.P. ed., p. 171).

G.E.L.–I

The kinship of the two types, the philosophical and the religious innovator, is apparent in Swift's pillorying of Wotton:

Surely, no Man ever advanced into the Publick, with fitter Qualifications of Body and Mind, for the Propagation of a new Religion. Oh, had those happy Talents misapplied to vain Philosophy, been turned into their proper Channels of Dreams and Visions, where Distortion of Mind and Countenance, are of such Sovereign Use; the base detracting World would not then have dared to report, that something is amiss, that his Brain hath undergone an unlucky Shake.[1]

In *A Discourse Concerning The Mechanical Operation Of The Spirit*, Swift explicitly identifies fanaticism in learning with that in religion:

. . . it is hard to assign one Art or Science, which has not annexed to it some Fanatick Branch: Such are the Philosopher's Stone; The Grand Elixir; The Planetary Worlds; The Squaring of the Circle; The Summum Bonum; Utopian Commonwealths . . . But, if this Plant has found a Root in the Fields of Empire, and of Knowledge, it has fixt deeper, and spread yet farther upon Holy Ground.[2]

The religious visionary, the enthusiast, is, of course, one of Swift's favourite targets. His view of enthusiasm is precisely that of Locke:

Enthusiasm laying by reason, would set up revelation without it; whereby in effect it takes away both reason and revelation, and substitutes in the room of it the ungrounded fancies of a man's own brain.[3]

Too intense a Contemplation [Swift remarks] is not the Business of Flesh and Blood; it must by the necessary Course of Things, in a little Time, let go its Hold, and fall into Matter.[4]

Swift nowhere, perhaps, summarizes his intellectual attitude more exactly than in the following passage:

. . . the Brain, in its natural Position and State of Serenity, disposeth its Owner to pass his Life in the common Forms, without any Thought of subduing Multitudes to his own Power, his Reasons or his Visions; and the more he shapes his Understanding by the Pattern of Human Learning, the less he is inclined to form Parties after his particular Notions; because that instructs him in his private Infirmities, as well as in the stubborn Ignorance of the People.[5]

[1] ibid. (O.U.P. ed., p. 169).
[2] cf. above (O.U.P.) ed., p. 266
[3] cf. Locke, *Essay Concerning Human Understanding; Of Enthusiasm.* (cf. Russell: *History of Western Philosophy*, p. 631.)
[4] cf. *Disc. Mech. Op. of the Spirit* (O.U.P. ed., p. 288).
[5] cf. *A Tale of a Tub*, sect. IX (O.U.P. ed., p. 171).

Man must be aware of his limitations; he must be content with the obvious and avoid abstract speculation, or at least avoid plaguing others with his speculations. This, however, is not to give him *carte blanche* to do nothing; in addition to the besetting sins of carping and enthusiasm, there is a third: 'Man's Epidemical Diseases being Fastidiosity, Amorphy, and Oscitation.'[1]

31. The above examination of Swift's attitude of mind requires to be completed with a consideration of his religious views before we can apply ourselves to his use of the grotesque.

The existence of God for Swift, as for Locke, is a matter of common sense:

> The idea of a supreme Being, infinite in power, goodness, and wisdom, whose workmanship we are, and on whom we depend; and the idea of ourselves, as understanding, rational creatures, being such as are clear in us, would, I suppose, if duly considered and pursued, afford such foundations of our duty and rules of action as might place *morality* among the *sciences capable of demonstration.*[2]

Locke's view is that we are certain of two things; our own existence and the existence of God as the author of our being. Like the necessity of morality, the existence of God is capable of being demonstrated—it is a logical conclusion that a creature requires a Creator—but 'the vulgar Dictates of unrefined Reason'[3] are thoroughly adequate to the task; it is a matter of common sense. This is essentially Swift's view. Belief in God is one of the cases in which '. . . Reason . . . strikes you with immediate Conviction; as it must needs do where it is not mingled, obscured, or discoloured by Passion and Interest.'[4]

The above passage, from the fourth book of *Gulliver's Travels*, naturally raises, however, the question of the role played by revelation in Swift's religious attitude. The Houyhnhnms, of course, have religion without revelation: '. . . . she made two Excuses, first for her Husband, who, as she said, happened that very Morning to *Lhnuwnh*. The Word is strongly expressive in their Language, but not easily rendered into English; it signifies, to retire to his first Mother.'[5]

---

[1] ibid., sect. V (O.U.P. ed., p. 124).
[2] cf. Locke, *Essay*, bk. IV, ch. III (*Of the Extent of Human Knowledge*), Everyman ed., p. 266. cf. Russell, *Hist. Western Philosophy* (1946), p. 639.
[3] See p. 117.
[4] See p. 113.
[5] cf. *Gulliver's Travels*, bk. IV, ch. VIII (Nonesuch ed., p. 269).

In his recent work *The Personality of Jonathan Swift* (1958),
Professor Irvin Ehrenpreis insists that, far from being a really
admirable model for men to follow, we are meant to regard the
Houyhnhnms as 'a false ideal for humanity' and intended as a satire
on the deistic belief in the all-sufficient nature of reason:

> . . . the rule of nothing-but-reason leads him to repudiate all human
> obligations and to detest his wife. Swift wished men to be as rational as
> possible; he believed that religion helps them to become so, and that
> reason leads them toward revelation. But the deistic effort to build a
> rational system of morals outside revelation, he regarded as evil and
> absurd.[1]

Ehrenpreis goes on to extend this hypothesis of religious satire to the
Yahoos:

> The representation of men as apes suggests Calvinistic doctrines. In
> depicting our case as hopeless, and denying our power in any way to move
> toward salvation except through the arbitrary action of unmerited, unpre-
> dictable grace, the Puritans sink us to the category of mindless beasts.[2]

Hence he concludes:

> As the truly Christian alternative to both deistic and Dissenting errors,
> Swift provides Captain Pedro de Mendez, 'the finest of all the European
> characters' in Gulliver. It is in this image of humility, compassion, and
> charity (disdained by the infatuated Gulliver) that he would like us to
> rest.[3]

Doubtless Ehrenpreis does not mean to suggest that the Houyhnhnms and Yahoos are *merely* satirical representations of deists and
Dissenters. Even so, he is surely wrong in regarding them as types of
religious error. The difference between the Houyhnhnms and the
deists lies in the fact that, whereas the deists chose to ignore the
special claims of Christian revelation,[4] the Houyhnhnms were merely
ignorant of them. Ehrenpreis remarks above that in Swift's opinion,
'reason leads [men] toward revelation' (i.e. toward accepting revelation). Are we to assume that this would not have held good also for
the Houyhnhnms? If Gulliver had attempted in vain to convert the

---

[1] cf. Ehrenpreis, op. cit. (Methuen and Co., London, 1958), p. 103.
[2] ibid., p. 109.
[3] ibid.
[4] cf. Bryson, op. cit. (see p. 114): 'Deism, being, when full blown, not
merely cosmopolitan but cosmical in its outlook and temper, could admit the
claim of no people and no planet to an exceptional or even distinctive role in
religious history.'

Houyhnhnms, the case would have been very different. As it is, their case is similar to that of the so-called heathen philosophers (Swift rejects the term heathen as applied to Plato, &c.), whose ignorance of revelation can scarcely be held against them: 'And therefore in this point, nothing can justly be laid to the Charge of the Philosophers further than that they were ignorant of certain Facts which happened long after their Death.'[1]

We should note, moreover, that it is not really a reflection on the Houyhnhnms and 'the rule of nothing-but-reason' that Gulliver is led 'to repudiate all human obligations and to detest his wife'; it is the very natural reaction of one who has been in contact with perfection and must now return to the imperfect. After all, social responsibility and family harmony are two of the chief virtues of the Houyhnhnms. The moral is very clearly not that Gulliver should become less like the Houyhnhnms, but that his wife and the world at large should become more like them. One need scarcely enlarge on the fact that Swift does not intend the Houyhnhnms to be a *religious* model for mankind; but this is far from implying that he regards them as heretics or free thinkers.

Ehrenpreis finds 'a rather light hint' of Swift's supposed satire on deism in 'the houyhnhnms' ignorance of bodily shame':[2] 'He said . . . he could not understand why Nature should teach us to conceal what Nature had given. That neither himself nor Family were ashamed of any Parts of their Bodies.'[3] But surely Swift is neither giving Gulliver *carte blanche* to run naked nor suggesting that horses should wear trousers. Deists must go clothed because they partake of the fallen nature of Adam; but the problems of sin and salvation do not concern the Houyhnhnms at all.

I have examined Ehrenpreis's assertions about the fourth book of *Gulliver's Travels* at some length, because he raises the important question of the nature of the relationship between Gulliver and the Houyhnhnms, emphasizing the fact that in Swift's opinion—opposed to that of the deists—reason is not enough without revelation. In so doing, he *contrasts* the dictum of Gulliver's Houyhnhnm master: 'Reason alone is sufficient to govern a rational Creature',[4] with Swift's statement in his sermon *Upon the Excellency of Christianity*: 'There

---

[1] cf. *A Letter To A Young Gentleman Lately Entered Into Holy Orders* (Nonesuch cd., p. 409).
[2] cf. Ehrenpreis, op. cit., p. 100.
[3] cf. *Gulliver's Travels*, bk. IV, ch. III (Nonesuch ed., p. 231).
[4] ibid., ch. VII (Nonesuch ed., p. 253).

is no solid, firm foundation of virtue, but in a conscience directed by the principles of religion.'[1] Now, so far as conscience is concerned, no discrepancy exists between the two passages; for Swift, as for Locke, conscience is entirely consonant with common sense: 'The preference of vice to virtue is a manifest wrong judgement.'[2]

We are left with the question, to what extent are the principles of religion, and adherence to those principles, a matter of common sense? (The term reason, as employed by the Houyhnhnms, is, of course, synonymous with common sense.) Clearly, acceptance of the Scriptures and their system of morality is rational behaviour; 'reason leads toward revelation.'[3] As regards the extent to which the principles of religion are discoverable by reason alone, we must notice Swift's highly significant comments on the distinction between the divine and the human or social aspects of religion in *A Letter To A Young Gentleman Lately Entered Into Holy Orders*, which require to be quoted at some length:

Before you enter into the common unsufferable Cant of taking all Occasions to disparage the Heathen Philosophers, I hope you will differ from some of your Brethren, by first enquiring what those Philosophers can say for themselves. The System of Morality to be gathered out of the Writings or Sayings of those ancient Sages, falls undoubtedly very short of that delivered in the Gospel, and wants besides, the divine Sanction which our Saviour gave to His. Whatever is further related by the Evangelists, contains chiefly, Matters of Fact, and consequently of Faith, such as the Birth of Christ, His being the Messiah, His Miracles, His Death, Resurrection, and Ascension. None of which can properly come under the Appellation of human Wisdom, being intended only to make us Wise unto Salvation. And therefore in this Point, nothing can justly be laid to the Charge of the Philosophers further than that they were ignorant of certain Facts which happened long after their Death. But I am deceived, if a better Comment could be any where collected, upon the Moral Part of the Gospel, than from the Writings of those excellent Men; even that Divine Precept of loving our Enemies, is at large insisted on by Plato, who puts it, as I remember, into the Mouth of Socrates. And as to the Reproach of Heathenism, I doubt they had less of it than the corrupted Jews in whose Time they lived. For it is a gross piece of Ignorance among us to conceive, that in those polite and learned Ages, even Persons of any tolerable Education, much less the wisest Philosophers did acknowledge or worship any more than one Almighty Power under several Denominations, to whom

[1] cf. Ehrenpreis, op. cit., p. 100.
[2] cf. Locke, *Essay*, bk. II, ch. XX (cf. Russell, op. cit., p. 637).
[3] See p. 120.

they allowed all those Attributes we ascribe to the Divinity: And as I take it, human Comprehension reacheth no further: Neither did our Saviour think it necessary to explain to us the Nature of God, because I suppose it would be impossible without bestowing on us other Faculties than we possess at present. But the true Misery of the Heathen World appears to be what I before mentioned, the want of a Divine Sanction, without which the Dictates of the Philosophers failed in the Point of Authority, and consequently the Bulk of Mankind lay indeed under a great Load of Ignorance even in the Article of Morality, but the Philosophers themselves did not. Take the Matter in this Light, and it will afford Field enough for a Divine to enlarge on, by shewing the Advantages which the Christian World has over the Heathen, and the absolute Necessity of Divine Revelations, to make the Knowledge of the true God, and the Practice of Virtue more universal in the World.[1]

The philosophers, then, who, like the Houyhnhnms but unlike the deists, could plead invincible ignorance of Christian revelation, were lacking neither in virtue nor the principles of religion, though they were guided by reason alone. If they were not wise unto salvation, they were certainly wise unto virtue; even in the point of salvation, is it not significant that in the third book of *Gulliver's Travels*, Brutus, Junius, Socrates, Epaminondas, Cato the Younger, are spoken of as being 'perpetually together' with one of Swift's great Christian heroes, Sir Thomas More, in 'A Sextumvirate to which all the Ages of the World cannot add a Seventh,?[2]

Swift does indeed observe that the ethics of the ancient philosophers fall very short of those of the Scriptures. It is nevertheless clear that he does not regard virtuous conduct as being the monopoly of Christians. Revelation was necessary 'to make . . . the Practice of Virtue *more* universal in the World', but did not introduce it.

The point is an important one. Ultimately, of course, as a devout Christian clergyman, Swift must put salvation before all else; but as a writer he is far more concerned with virtuous conduct in the Greek—or Houyhnhnm—sense than with personal holiness, with the social and political rather than the religious implications of morality. Significantly, the creatures whose exemplary conduct is held up to our admiration in the fourth book of *Gulliver's Travels* know nothing of Christianity. Swift's religious attitude is a far cry from that of Luther:

As the soul needs the word alone for life and justification, so it is

[1] cf. Nonesuch ed., pp. 409–10.
[2] cf. *Gulliver's Travels*, bk. III, ch. VII (Nonesuch ed., p. 192).

justified by faith alone, and not by any works . . . Therefore the first care of every Christian ought to be to lay aside all reliance on works, and to strengthen his faith alone more and more.[1]

Far from believing that 'the soul . . . is justified by faith alone, and not by any works', Swift gives the clearest indication, in his three prayers for Stella, that he regards her good works as being by no means the least of her claims upon God's mercy:

> We beseech thee also, O Lord, of thy infinite goodness to remember the good actions of this thy servant; that the naked she hath clothed, the hungry she hath fed, the sick and fatherless whom she hath relieved, may be reckoned according to thy gracious promise, as if they had been done unto thee.[2]

Accept, and impute all her good Deeds.[3]

It is the primary task of the preacher to describe the *duty* of the Christian: 'As I take it, the two principal Branches of Preaching, are first to tell the People what is their Duty, and then to convince them that it is so.'[4] His own sermon *Doing Good*—a significant title—perfectly illustrates these precepts, with its characteristic emphasis on public spiritedness and submission to authority:

> This love of the public, or of the commonwealth, or love of our country, was in antient times properly known by the name of *Virtue*, because it was the greatest of all virtues . . . In those times it was common for men to sacrifice their lives for the good of their country, although they had neither hope or belief of future rewards.[5]

To injure a neighbour, on the other hand, was to merit damnation: '. . . without our utmost endeavours to make restitution to the person injured, and to obtain his pardon, added to a sincere repentance, there is no hope of salvation given in the gospel.'[6]

It is unnecessary here to amass instances of Swift's concern, in his writings, with the external and social aspects of virtue rather than with salvation, with the moral, progressive aspect of religion rather than

---

[1] cf. Martin Luther, *Concerning Christian Liberty* (Wace and Buchheim, *Luther's Primary Works*, 1896, pp. 258–9). cf. R. H. Tawney, *Religion and the Rise of Capitalism*, ch. II, ii (Mentor Books ed. (1947), p. 90).

[2] cf. *Three Prayers for Stella* (I) (Nonesuch ed., p. 735).

[3] ibid. (III) (Nonesuch ed., p. 736).

[4] cf. *A Letter To A Young Gentleman*, &c. (Nonesuch ed. pp. 406–7).

[5] cf. *Doing Good: A Sermon, On the Occasion of Wood's Project* (*Irish Tracts 1720–1723* ed. Herbert Davis, *And Sermons* ed. Louis Landa, Basil Blackwell, Oxford, 1963, p. 233).

[6] ibid., p. 239.

the regressive, mystical one. It is so marked that Leslie Stephen, observing that 'Swift's religion . . . partook of the directly practical nature of his whole character', goes so far as to conclude that salvation was a matter of some indifference to Swift:

> . . . this state of mind carried with it the necessity of clinging to some religious creed: not because the creed held out promises of a better hereafter, for Swift was too much absorbed in the present to dwell much upon such beliefs; but rather because it provided him with some sort of fixed convictions in this strange and disastrous muddle.[1]

Stephen's own scepticism about religion led him to minimize the importance of the idea of salvation to Swift. The truth is rather that Swift does not regard belief, whether in God or in revelation, as something which must be inculcated. There is therefore little need for him to dwell on it in his writings, for it is natural for men to believe. They may, of course, merely be ignorant of Scripture, a matter which can be put right simply by informing them of the facts of Christian doctrine; but where this is not the case infidelity is the direct result of vice, and faith is thus the consequence of a return to virtuous behaviour:

> For in the Course of Things, Men always grow vicious before they become Unbelievers; but if you could once convince the Town or Country profligate, by Topicks drawn from the View of their own Quiet, Reputation, Health, and Advantage, their Infidelity would soon drop off.[2]

Here Swift lays bare the principle behind his much-criticized *Project for the Advancement of Religion*, the most 'external' of all his writings on religion, in which he argues that the observance of the forms of Christianity should be enforced 'by the power of the administration'. It is true that Swift regards such coercion as being to the public advantage, but he also regards it as being very much to the advantage of those coerced: 'You may force men, by interest or punishment, to say or swear they believe, and to act as if they believed: You can go no further.'[3] In Swift's opinion it is justifiable to go so far; to act like a Christian is a real step in the direction of becoming one.

He sees nothing cynical in appeals to self-interest: 'Nature directs every one of us, and God permits us, to consult our own private Good, before the private Good of any other person whatsoever. We

---

[1] cf. Stephen, *Swift* (Macmillan and Co., London, 1882), p. 50.
[2] cf. *A Letter To A Young Gentleman*, &c. (Nonesuch ed., p. 415).
[3] cf. *Thoughts On Religion* (5) (Nonesuch ed., p. 465).

are, indeed, commanded to love our Neighbour as ourselves, but not as well as ourselves.'[1] On the other hand, involved arguments and appeals to emotion are of little avail with the unbeliever, and a danger to the integrity of the preacher himself:

> Nor, lastly, are Preachers justly blamed for neglecting human Oratory to move the passions, which is not the Business of a Christian Orator, whose Office it is only to work upon Faith and Reason. All other Eloquence hath been a perfect Cheat to stir up Men's Passions against Truth and Justice for the Service of a Faction . . .[2]

With a Christian congregation, argument may be employed with caution, but appeals to emotion are another matter: 'A Lady askt a great Person coming out of Church, whether it were not a very moving Discourse? Yes, said he, I was extremely sorry, for the Man is my Friend.'[3] For Swift, religion and emotion go ill together: 'Religion . . . by laying Restraints upon human Nature is supposed the great Enemy of the Freedom of Thought and Action.'[4] He regards *religious emotion*, particularly of an intense kind, with abhorrence:

> Persons of a visionary Devotion, either Men or Women, are in their Complexion, of all others, the most amorous: For Zeal is frequently kindled from the same Spark with other Fires, and from inflaming Brotherly Love, will proceed to raise that of a Gallant . . . Too intense a Contemplation is not the Business of Flesh and Blood.[5]

32. It remains to consider the effects of Swift's attitude of mind, imposing itself upon an intensely emotional nature, on his work. The aspect of mind which is dominant in Swift's personality is the progressive one. He is convinced that men should restrict their interests to 'the common Forms': not merely to facts, but to facts which have an obvious, practical value for a simple, thoroughly ordinary existence. Moderation is essential in all things, in the activities of the mind as well as of the body. Berkeley, Swift's friend, idealistically observes: 'Whatever the world thinks, he who hath not much meditated upon God, the human mind, and the *summum bonum*, may possibly make a thriving earthworm, but will most

---

[1] cf. *Doing Good (Irish Tracts*, &c., p. 232).
[2] cf. *Upon Sleeping in Church*, ibid., p. 214.
[3] cf. *A Letter To A Young Gentleman*, &c. (Nonesuch ed., p. 406).
[4] cf. *An Argument to prove that the Abolishing of Christianity may . . . be attended with some Inconveniences*, &c. (Nonesuch ed., p. 396)
[5] cf. *Mech. Operation of the Spirit* (O.U.P. ed., pp. 287–8).

indubitably make a sorry patriot and a sorry statesman.'[1] In *A Discourse Concerning The Mechanical Operation Of The Spirit*, Swift dismisses the *summum bonum*, together with the squaring of the circle, as a subject for fanatics.[2] Not only ought we to restrict our interests to practical everyday matters, but we ought to pursue those interests without emotional excitement, in a mood of friendship and benevolence—the two principal virtues of the Houyhnhnms. God and religion are to be approached in the above spirit; they are matters of fact with which we must concern ourselves diligently but not too ardently.

Inevitably, as one continues to outline Swift's view of proper conduct with his own work in mind, the words acquire an ironic ring:

> Every man, as a member of the common wealth, ought to be content with the possession of his own opinion in private, without perplexing his neighbour or disturbing the public.[3]

> . . . this Talent of Ridicule, they value so much, is a Perfection very easily acquired and applied to all Things whatsoever; neither is it any Thing at all the worse, because it is capable of being perverted to Burlesque: Perhaps it may be the more perfect upon that Score; since we know, the most celebrated Pieces have been thus treated with greatest Success. It is in any Man's Power to suppose a Fool's Cap on the wisest Head, and then laugh at his own Supposition. I think there are not many Things cheaper than supposing and laughing; and if the uniting these two Talents can bring a thing into Contempt, it is hard to know where it may end.[4]

How is one to reconcile such remarks with, say, *The Battle of the Books* or *A Tale of a Tub*? Is not his own practice inconsistent with his principles?

First we may note that such 'inconsistencies' are only so to be described from a purely logical point of view; thus considered, what applies to one man applies to another, and all without exception ought to preserve silence and despise ridicule. It is at once the weakness and the strength of 'common sense' that it imposes no such restrictions on the individual. What Russell says of Locke:

> He is always sensible, and always willing to sacrifice logic rather than become paradoxical. He enunciates general principles which . . . are capable

---

[1] cf. *Siris*, 350. cf. Tawney, op. cit., p. 233. Tawney also makes use of the sentence as a motto.
[2] See p. 118.
[3] cf. *Thoughts on Religion* (6) (Nonesuch ed., p. 465).
[4] cf. *Upon Sleeping in Church* (*Irish Tracts*, &c., p. 217).

of leading to strange consequences; but whenever the strange consequences seem about to appear, Locke blandly refrains from drawing them.[1]

largely applies to Swift. It is *perplexing and disturbing opinions* which must be repressed, not his own correct ones; it is ridicule of *admirable* things which is undesirable, not of those things which are 'clearly' despicable. Common sense is necessarily autocratic.

Second, we should note that no man can be held to be inconsistent because he is unable to live up to his convictions or principles. The fact that Swift is unable to adopt the sober, dispassionate attitude to life which he regards as an ideal does not mean that he abandons that ideal. It is one which exerts a powerful influence upon his work. He acknowledges his weakness, albeit ironically: '. . . even I myself, the author of these momentous truths, am a person, whose imaginations are hard-mouth'd, and exceedingly disposed to run away with his reason, which I have observed from long experience, to be a very light rider, and easily shook off.'[2]

Leslie Stephen observes of Swift's character:

He shrank invariably . . . from any display of his emotion, and would have felt the heartiest contempt for the sentimentalism of his day. At once the proudest and most sensitive of men, it was his imperative instinct to hide his emotions as much as possible . . . He always masks his strongest passions under some ironical veil, and thus practised what his friends regarded as an inverted hypocrisy . . . this intense dislike to wearing his heart upon his sleeve, to laying bare the secrets of his affections before unsympathetic eyes, is one of his most indelible characteristics.[3]

There is, of course, evidence for this emotional inhibition to which Stephen refers as an 'imperative instinct'. Stephen cites Delany's account of how Swift concealed the fact that he prayed with his servants every day. He is said to have taken leave of his guests on one occasion with the words: 'Good night, God bless you, and I hope I never see you again.'

Stephen's use of the present tense 'masks', however, clearly shows that he is not merely referring to Swift's private conduct, but to his writings, when he observes that Swift concealed his passions under 'some ironical veil'; and this raises an important point. To what extent is one to regard Swift's affectation of a casual, dispassionate, humorous attitude in such a work as *A Modest Proposal* as the result

[1] cf. Russell, op. cit., p. 630.
[2] See p. 104 (cf. *A Tale of a Tub*, O.U.P. ed., p. 180).
[3] cf. Stephen, op. cit., pp. 48–49.

of a psychological inhibition which prevents him from writing in a violent and passionate vein; and to what extent is it to be regarded as a deliberate, enormously effective stroke of art?

In his book *The Masks of Jonathan Swift*, William Bragg Ewald asks much the same question: 'Writers frequently, of course, use *personae* for primarily artistic reasons . . . Did Swift . . . use masks for mainly literary reasons? Or were there more specific psychological causes?'[1] Ewald briefly considers the possibility that Swift's 'disguises' may be the result of a feeling of insecurity, but concludes that though the information we possess, particularly about Swift's childhood, is insufficient for us to make any definite pronouncement about his supposed feeling of insecurity, at all events such an inner compulsion towards concealment cannot have been very urgent:

> Much more illuminating than these biographical details is the fact that, unlike those writers for whom the device is an indispensable instrument for self-expression and who tend to identify themselves with their masks, Swift seems to have been able to use it or not as the occasion demanded.[2]

Similarly, we may point to the fact that Swift's irony is not 'an indispensable instrument for self-expression', even where his emotions are deeply involved. Indeed, on one occasion at least he assures us that his emotions are too deeply involved for irony:

> With what Envy and Admiration would these Gentlemen return from so delightful a Progress? What glorious Reports would they make when they went back to England?
> But my Heart is too heavy to continue this Irony longer, for it is manifest that whatever Stranger took such a Journey, would be apt to think himself travelling in Lapland or Ysland, rather than in a Country so favoured by Nature as Ours, both in Fruitfulness of Soyl, and Temperature of Climate. The miserable Dress, and Dyet, and Dwelling of the People. The general Desolation in most parts of the Kingdom. The old Seats of the Nobility and Gentry all in Ruins, and no new Ones in their stead. The Families of Farmers who pay great Rents, living in Filth and Nastiness upon Butter-milk and Potatoes, without a Shoe or Stocking to their Feet, or a House so convenient as an English Hog-sty to receive them . . . *Nostrâ miseriâ magnus est.*[3]

It is all too easy in considering the expressive aspect of a literary

---

[1] cf. Ewald, op. cit. (Basil Blackwell, Oxford, 1954), p. 1.
[2] ibid., p. 3.
[3] cf. *A Short View of the State of Ireland* (Nonesuch ed., p. 509).

work to convey the impression that the representative aspect, the deliberate calculation of the effect upon the reader, is comparatively unimportant. On the other hand, in examining the conditions of the creation of a work of literature the expressive aspect cannot merely be dismissed. In the case of Swift's use of irony, though Stephen's remark that he 'always masks his strongest passions under some ironical veil' needs qualifying, there is clearly a great deal of truth in it. The fact is that Swift, like everyone else, requires an outlet for two different movements of emotion: his practical, progressive interest in his material environment and his interest in the supernatural and eternal. His cast of mind, predominantly a progressive one, as we have seen, makes him much less concerned to discipline or conceal the first kind of emotion than the second. Religion must be divorced from emotion:

> Religion seems to have grown an Infant with Age, and requires miracles to nourish it, as it had in its Infancy.[1]

> Vision is the Art of seeing Things invisible[2].

Here there is a more serious conflict between conviction and instinct. Determined to practise and preach Christianity 'without the least tincture of enthusiasm', to quote the old joke, Swift is largely denying an outlet to the irrational, imaginative side of his nature, which, refusing to be denied, escapes in the form of fantastic imagery, justified or rationalized by Swift on the ground that it has a practical *raison d'être*. Such justification on rational, practical grounds is not to be regarded as in some way mistaken or superficial. The representative side of Swift's grotesque imagery—its satirical point—is no less significant than the expressive side. But as Swift himself was clearly aware, it is not the whole story: '. . . even I myself . . . am a person, whose imaginations are hard-mouth'd, and exceedingly disposed to run away with his reason.'

In actual fact, Swift manages the reins well enough. There is no question of the fantastic imagery in his work being the product of a kind of explosion of emotion which escapes his control. In connecting his compulsive need for self-expression through fantasy with his endeavours to keep emotion out of his religious life, one must take into consideration the fact that these endeavours are only partially successful. Just as his conviction that one ought to take a sober and

---

[1] cf. *Thoughts On Various Subjects* (7) (Nonesuch ed., p. 459).
[2] ibid. (46) (Nonesuch ed., p. 464).

dispassionate view of worldly affairs does not inhibit the display of emotion in his social and political writings, so his quietist attitude to religious matters, though very influential, does not serve to keep the emotion out of Swift's Christianity altogether. The three prayers for Stella are sufficient evidence to the contrary, full of genuine feeling. They represent, admittedly, Swift's religious feelings at their most intense; but they are a complete rebuttal of Stephen's view that salvation is a matter of some indifference to Swift. It is because he has a serious outlet for his powerful imagination in his religion that he is able to make his imaginative energy work in harness; but, equally, because he does his utmost to keep that outlet blocked, he is com-pelled to put the irrepressible energy of his imagination—his 'visionary emotion'—to use in some other form. That form, dictated by a strongly progressive consciousness so selective, discriminating, and exclusive as to reject even logical and systematic thinking when it is carried to extremes, is the absurd.

On the above hypothesis there is a clear connexion between the 'three Swifts' distinguished by Bonamy Dobrée:

And now we become aware of three Swifts; the plain straightforward thinker of the Enlightenment who is yet Christian, the hater of all pedan-tries of thought and useless ornaments of expression, the rationalist anti-intellectual; second, the imaginative artist, who can express with full force what the first Swift means only by putting plain thought into a shape which is as fantastic as he can conceive—even if it is the fantasy of extreme logic; and finally the exuberant comic writer, the wit, the mirth provoker, the man whose motto was *vive la bagatelle*.[1]

FANTASY AND LOGIC

33. The relationship between fantasy and logic in Swift's work is one which requires to be examined in detail. It will be most convenient to consider first those examples of his fantasy which have no satirical purpose.

The term fantasy, with its implication of unreality, is an apposite one to use in connexion with Swift's imaginative creations. Unlike the term imagination, it clearly conveys that the standpoint of the user is a practical, common-sense one. Swift invariably makes it clear that the products of his imagination are absurd; they may be used as sugar coating for a serious opinion, but in themselves they are merely meant

[1] cf. B. Dobrée, *English Literature in the Early Eighteenth Century 1700–1740* (O.U.P., 1959), p. 62.

to amuse, in the broad sense of that word. This is the most important means of discipline which Swift exercises over his 'hard-mouth'd' imagination; it is enforced where there is no question of his fantasy being informed by logic: 'Nite delest sollahs: farewell deelest Rives; rove poopoopdfr. farewell deelest richar Md, Md, Md FW FW FW FW FW Me Me Lele, Me lele lele richar Md.'[1] Swift's emotions escape for a moment from the political arena, and manifest themselves, significantly, in affectionate silliness. He can enjoy fantasy without a logical frame of reference; but not without some degree of absurdity.

His fondness for grotesque names may be given as a further example of fantasy for its own sake—or more accurately, absurdity for its own sake—Skyris Bolgolam (Galbet, or High Admiral), Glumdalclitch, Lorbrulgrud, the Struldbruggs; his preposterous 'languages' are a further instance: *'Fluft drin Yalerick Dwuldum prastrad mirplush*, which properly signifies, *My tongue is in the Mouth of my Friend*.'[2] Even here, however, it is clear that Swift derives additional pleasure from his inventions when they have a logical quality; Lilliput, for example, is obviously intended to suggest the diminutive, Brobdingnag the gigantic, Houyhnhnm the equine. In Gulliver's remark, '. . . I pronounced the following Words, as they had been taught me the Night before, *Ickpling Gloffthrobb Squut-serumm blhiop Mlashnalt Zwin tnodbalkquffh Slhiophad Gurdlubh Asht*',[3] the queer conglomerations of syllables are chosen not merely for their absurdity, but jocularly for their difficulty as well, for their 'shock value' after 'I pronounced the following words'. Swift's 'bagatelles' are predominantly of this kind—fantasy with logic but without satire. Leslie Stephen's disapproving account may be given:

He could no longer read by candle-light, and his only resource was to write rubbish, most of which he burnt. The merest trifles that he ever wrote, he says in 1731, 'are serious philosophical lucubrations in comparison to what I now busy myself about'. This, however, was but the development of a lifelong practice. His favourite maxim, *Vive la bagatelle*, is often quoted by Pope and Bolingbroke. As he had punned in his youth with Lord Berkeley, so he amused himself in later years by a constant interchange of trifles with his friends, and above all with Sheridan. Many of these trifles have been preserved; they range from really good specimens of Swift's rather sardonic humour down to bad riddles and a peculiar kind

---

[1] cf. *Journal to Stella*, Letter XLVII (31 May 1712) (Nonesuch ed., p. 710).
[2] cf. *Gulliver's Travels*, bk. III, ch. IX (Nonesuch ed., p. 201).
[3] ibid.

of playing upon words. A brief specimen of one variety will be amply sufficient. Sheridan writes to Swift. *Times a re veri de ad nota do it oras hi lingat almi e state.* The words are separately in Latin, and are to be read into the English: 'Times are very dead; not a doit or a shilling at all my estate.' Swift writes to Sheridan in English, which reads into Latin, 'Am I say vain a rabble is,' means *Amice venerabilis*—and so forth. Whole manuscript books are still in existence filled with jargon of this kind. Charles Fox declared that Swift must be a goodnatured man to have had such a love of nonsense.[1]

It would be a grave mistake to dismiss Swift's 'rubbish' as an unimportant by-product; to understand its character is to obtain a real insight into the nature of much of his art. Above all, we should inquire whether the phrase 'a love of nonsense' adequately describes the frame of mind in which Swift's bagatelles were created. The term nonsense, like the term absurdity, implies a rejection. In so far as Swift regards his bagatelles as nonsensical or absurd, he regards them with contempt; a contempt clearly in evidence in his remark about their triviality quoted by Stephen. What he enjoys is invention, the use of his imagination in a logical fashion, ingenuity. Strictly speaking, therefore, it is incorrect to say that Swift enjoys inventing absurdities or that he loves nonsense. It is truer to say that he derives pleasure from the use of his imagination, but endeavours to use it in such a way that he is protected against any accusation—whether made by others or by his own conscience—of 'escapism', of departing from common-sense standards. His attitude towards his 'bagatelles' is thus an ambivalent one, that of *odi et amo*. This, surely, is the lesson of Swift's 'manuscript books . . . filled with jargon', his 'rubbish, most of which he burnt'. Swift has a ready answer to the question: 'Are not the products of your imagination absurd, judged by common-sense standards?'—namely, 'Of course; I clearly intend them to be absurd.' Stephen's exasperation at the spectacle of Swift 'wasting the most vigorous intellect in the country upon ingenuities beneath that of the composer of double acrostics'[2] suggests, however, a more searching common-sense criticism: 'If we are to regard your fantasies as absurd, why waste time and energy on absurdity?'

There are two kinds of answer, both valid, neither adequate without the other. The first is that hinted at in the significant admission: '. . . even I myself . . . am a person, whose imaginations are hard-mouth'd, and exceedingly disposed to run away with his

---

[1] cf. Stephen, op. cit., p. 197.
[2] cf. Stephen, op. cit., p. 198.

reason, which I have observed from long experience, to be a very light rider, and easily shook off.'

One answer, then, is that Swift has a compulsion to employ a faculty on which his common sense impresses the stamp of absurdity.

The second kind of answer, of which there are several varieties, is concerned with the deliberate use of the absurd and the fantastic for practical purposes: '. . . curiosity, that spur in the side, that bridle in the mouth, that ring in the nose, of a lazy, an impatient, and a grunting reader.'[1]

In this second passage we see Swift justifying the fantastic element in his work as a calculated device for holding a reader's interest. The note of contempt is particularly worthy of attention; the implication is that a really intelligent reader, a reader after the writer's own heart, would not need to be coaxed into a receptive frame of mind; he would look for the bread and never miss the circuses. Against this we must set the imaginative artist described by Bonamy Dobrée, who 'can express with full force what the first [rationalistic] Swift means only by putting plain thought into a shape which is as fantastic as he can conceive.'

Dobrée adds, 'even if it is the fantasy of extreme logic'. It is important, however, to emphasize Swift's concern to mingle with the issue of his imagination not only logic but a more powerful extraction of his common sense—absurdity. Donne's sermons contain a wealth of examples of logical fantasy:

. . . thou passest through this world as a flash, as a lightning of which no man knows the beginning or the ending, as an *ignis fatuus*, in the air, which does not only not give light for any use, but does not so much as portend or signify anything; and thou passest out of the world as a hand passes out of a bason, or a body out of a bath, where the water may be the fouler for thy having washed in it, else the water retains no impression of thy hand or body, so the world may be the worse for thy having lived in it, else the world retains no marks of thy having been there.[2]

God's way is positive, and thine is privative: God made every thing something, and thou makest the best of things, man, nothing; and because thou canst not annihilate the world altogether, as though thou hadst God at an advantage, in having made an abridgment of the world in man, there in that abridgment thou wilt undermine him, and make man, man, as far as thou canst, man in thyself nothing. He that qualifies himself for nothing,

---

[1] See p. 104.

[2] cf. *Poetry and Prose of John Donne*, ed. W. S. Scott (John Westhouse, London, 1946), p. 361.

does so; he whom we can call nothing, is nothing: this whole world is one entire creature, one body; and he that is nothing may be excremental nails, to scratch and gripe others, he may be excremental hairs for ornament, or pleasurableness of meeting; but he is no limb of this entire body, no part of God's universal creature, the world.'[1]

In nature the body frames and forms the place; for the place of the natural body is that *proxima aeris superficies*, that inward superficies of the air, that invests and clothes, and apparels that body ... In nature the body makes the place, but in grace the place makes the body.[2]

Swift is the equal even of Donne in ingenuity; the difference between his conceits and Donne's lies in the jocular tone:

When I beheld this, I sigh'd, and said within my self, *Surely Man is a Broom-Stick*; Nature sent him into the World Strong and Lusty, in a Thriving Condition, wearing his own Hair on his Head, the proper Branches of this Reasoning Vegetable, till the Axe of Intemperance has lopt off his Green Boughs, and left him a wither'd Trunk: He then flies unto Art, and puts on a Peruque, valuing himself upon an Unnatural Bundle of Hairs, all cover'd with Powder that never grew on his Head; but now should this our Broom-Stick pretend to enter the Scene, proud of those Birchen Spoils it never bore, and all cover'd with Dust, tho' the Sweepings of the Finest Lady's Chamber, we should be apt to Ridicule and Despise its Vanity, Partial Judges that we are![3]

Look on this Globe of Earth, you will find it to be a very compleat and fashionable Dress. What is that which some call Land, but a fine Coat faced with Green? or the Sea, but a Wastcoat of Water-Tabby? Proceed to the particular Works of the Creation, you will find how curious Journeyman Nature hath been, to trim up the vegetable Beaux: Observe how sparkish a Perewig adorns the Head of a Beech, and what a fine Doublet of white Satin is worn by the Birch. To conclude from all, what is Man himself but a Micro-Coat, or rather a compleat Suit of Cloaths with all its Trimmings? As to his Body, there can be no dispute; but examine even the Acquirements of his Mind, you will find them all contribute in their Order, towards furnishing out an exact Dress: To instance no more; Is not Religion a Cloak, Honesty a Pair of Shoes, worn out in the Dirt, Self-love a Surtout, Vanity a Shirt, and Conscience a Pair of Breeches, which, tho' a Cover for Lewdness as well as Nastiness, is easily slipt down for the Service of both.[4]

In his classic work on Swift, Ricardo Quintana remarks that the

[1] ibid., pp. 361–2.
[2] ibid., p. 363.
[3] cf. *A Meditation upon a Broom-Stick* (Nonesuch ed., p. 457).
[4] cf. *A Tale of a Tub*, sect. II (O.U.P. ed., p. 78).

analysis of Swift's ideas, in itself, may give no indication of the intensity of his writing:

It is possible . . . to analyse his controlling ideas with some accuracy, and yet to miss entirely that quality of the man which sets him apart from all of his contemporaries. There is in Swift a Dantesque intensity of appre-hension which has little to do with his formal thought . . . Not until we have felt what we shall call Swift's moral realism should we venture to explore Swift's formal ideas, which enforced the emotional intensity and canalized it but did not generate it.[1]

Something similar may be said about Swift's imaginative intensity in relation to his ideas and his artistic technique. However important it is to examine such a work as *A Tale of a Tub* in terms of the ideas it contains and the methods by which they are communicated, we must also recognize the fact that Swift's satisfaction in his work is not only that of the preacher, of putting his views in an effective way, but equally that of the poet, of having created something excellent in itself.

It has often been argued that the two kinds of satisfaction are not altogether compatible. A. M. Clark, in an examination of satirical poetry, remarks:

It is quite true that poets have sometimes written with a didactic inten-tion. But more often they have sought no end beyond the work itself and no justification beyond the art and delight thereof. Or, if they did indeed have a didactic intention at the outset, that intention was quickly relegated to the background when once they had actually begun; it had served their turn and it might come forward again when the work was completed. But in the process of creation a purely artistic intention supervened and dis-placed the didactic, for the creative process generates an artistic potential far more powerful than any which is not artistic.[2]

Clark quotes De Quincey's essay 'The Poetry of Pope', where this view of the conflict between preaching and poetry is uncompromisingly expressed:

What is didactic poetry? What does 'didactic' mean when applied as a distinguishing epithet to such an idea as a poem? The predicate destroys the subject; it is a case of what logicians call *contradictio in adjecto* . . . No poetry can have the function of teaching.[3]

---

[1] cf. R. Quintana, *The Mind and Art of Jonathan Swift* (O.U.P. Inc., New York, 1936), p. 51.
[2] cf. A. M. Clark, *Studies in Literary Modes* (Oliver and Boyd, Edinburgh, 1946), p. 34.
[3] ibid.

The point, of course, is not that the poet may not produce work which has moral or educational value, but that he cannot do so *qua* poet; that the creative process is not entirely under the control of the artist.

The view of art as the production of an autonomous force, 'the madness which is of God', is one which naturally has a special appeal for the romantic critic. It may be objected to such a view that technique and purpose are not negligible elements in a work of art, but it would be equally objectionable to ignore the compulsive or expressive aspect of art altogether.

A Tale of a Tub, apart from being a powerful onslaught upon what Swift considered to be perversions of Christianity, of reason, and so on, is also a great feat of imagination. It is entirely to our purpose to examine the uses to which Swift puts his imagination in the course of his satire. Basically, it is directed into two connected forms, the conceit or ingenious simile and the allegory or extended metaphor. In both forms Swift endeavours to keep the absurd nature of his inventions, and their triviality, firmly impressed upon the reader, by grotesque exaggeration, by jocularity of tone, and by 'admitting' a regrettable inclination towards wit:

> I myself, the Author of these momentous Truths, am a Person, whose Imaginations are hard-mouth'd, and exceedingly disposed to run away with his Reason. . .[1]
>
> In my Disposure of Employments of the Brain, I have thought fit to make Invention the Master, and to give Method and Reason, the Office of its Lacquays. The Cause of this Distribution was, from observing it my peculiar Case, to be often under a Temptation of being Witty, upon Occasions, where I could be neither Wise nor Sound, nor any thing to the Matter in hand. And, I am too much a Servant of the Modern Way, to neglect any such Opportunities, whatever pains or Improprieties I may be at, to introduce them.[2]

Such passages convey something of the ambiguity of Swift's attitude towards the products of his imagination.

Whilst Swift's fantastic satires reflect a general tendency, the settling of the metaphysical style at the level of comic and satirical writing, it is equally clear that the inclination towards ingenious and fantastic forms of expression is much more urgent in Swift than in Dryden or Pope. From his most 'traditional' burlesque, *The Battle*

---

[1] cf. *A Tale of a Tub* (O.U.P. ed., p. 180), sect. IX.
[2] ibid. (the Conclusion) (O.U.P. ed., p. 209).

of the Books, onwards Swift's satire is at once more intellectual—closer to the style of Donne—and more inventively bizarre than that of either Dryden or Pope. If his fantastic style can be related loosely to a genre, it is none the less a deeply personal form of expression.

To a much greater extent than in the use of the simile by Romantic poets, the metaphysical conceit depends for its effect upon its aptness, the point-for-point relevance of the comparison. The more dissimilar the objects compared, the greater the feat of ingenuity. Since the perception of relationships between objects is normally thought of as an attribute of reason, we may inquire what role the imagination plays in the metaphysical conceit as employed by Donne and Swift. It will be best, in attempting an answer, to replace the terms 'reason' and 'imagination' by the terms 'directed thinking' and 'fantasy thinking.' In both, association or the perception (or supposition) of relationships occurs. The chief difference lies in the selective nature of directed thinking, which sifts its way through the mass of relationships with the the establishment of 'necessary' relationships only as its purpose. Directed thought is thus concerned with reducing rather than increasing the number of associations. In 'metaphysical' writing the perception of congruities which subserves everything else is not in itself directed thinking:

> Much of our thinking consists of trains of images suggested one by another, of a sort of spontaneous revery of which it seems likely enough that the higher brutes should be capable . . . As a rule, in this sort of irresponsible thinking, the terms which fall to be coupled together are empirical concretes, not abstractions. A sunset may call up the vessel's deck from which I saw one last summer, the companions of my voyage, my arrival into port, etc.; or it may make me think of solar myths, of Hercules' and Hector's funeral pyres, of Homer and whether he could write, of the Greek alphabet, etc. If habitual contiguities predominate, we have a prosaic mind; if rare contiguities, or similarities, have free play, we call the person fanciful, poetic, or witty.[1]

Many metaphysical conceits are simply the perception of an unexpected relationship between objects normally thought of as incongruous with one another. More characteristically, however, this relationship is then used as a basis for selective thinking; the further associations which it suggests are winnowed, and logical or mock-logical inferences drawn from the relationships selected. The subtle

[1] cf. William James, *Psychology* (*Briefer Course*) (Macmillan, London), p. 353.

non sequitur to which Swift, like Donne, was especially addicted is precisely the kind of 'irresponsible thinking' to which James refers, on the plane of abstractions.

In Swift the ability to perceive relationships was abnormally developed. In describing *A Tale of a Tub* as a great feat of imagination, it is primarily this faculty to which one refers. As Browning could devise a rhyme for anything, so Swift could devise a relationship; it is, perhaps, his most impressive gift. His puns and bagatelles are examples of this faculty at its weakest, and evidence of its irrepressible nature. Unlike the metaphysical poets, and to a much greater extent than either Dryden or Pope, Swift both revels in his talent and feels obliged to emphasize its irrational and trivial character:

I made a good pun on Saturday to my lord keeper. After dinner we had coarse Doiley napkins, fringed at each end, upon the table to drink with: my lord keeper spread one of them between him and Mr. Prior; I told him I was glad to see there was such a Fringeship between Mr Prior and his lordship. Prior swore it was the worst he ever heard: I thought so too; but at the same time I thought it was most like one of Stella's that ever I heard.[1]

In his satires this perception of relationships manifests itself in miracles of aptness:

The most accomplisht Way of using Books at present, is two-fold: Either first, to serve them as some Men do Lords, learn their Titles exactly, and then brag of their Acquaintance. Or, secondly, which is indeed the choicer, the profounder, and politer Method, to get a thorough Insight into the Index, by which the whole Book is governed and turned, like Fishes by the Tail. . . . For the Arts are all in a flying March, and therefore more easily subdued by attacking them in the Rear. Thus Physicians discover the State of the whole Body, by consulting only what comes from Behind. Thus Men catch Knowledge by throwing their Wit on the Posteriors of a book, as Boys do Sparrows with flinging Salt upon their Tails. Thus Human Life is best understood by the wise man's Rule of Regarding the End. Thus are the Sciences found like Hercules's Oxen, by tracing them Backwards. Thus are old Sciences unravelled like old Stockings, by beginning at the Foot.[2]

This typical flight of fancy can be 'justified' on practical or rational grounds in three ways. First, the comparisons are humorous; second,

---

[1] cf. *Journal to Stella*, Letter XXI, London, 23 April 1711 (Nonesuch ed., p. 669).
[2] cf. *A Tale of a Tub*, sect. VII (O.U.P. ed., p. 145).

they are congruous or 'logical'; third, they are satirical, are intended
to disparage. These are the three hoops through which Swift's imagination must jump in order to satisfy both the writer and his readers
that it is under control.

GULLIVER'S TRAVELS, A TALE OF A TUB

34. The result is a fascinating paradox which lies at the heart of Swift's
use of the fantastic and the grotesque. Bonamy Dobrée speaks of
Swift's compulsion, as an imaginative artist, to put 'plain thought
into a shape which is as fantastic as he can conceive—even if it is the
fantasy of extreme logic'.[1] The question arises, to what extent such
an artist can draw our attention to the absurdity of that fantastic
shape without detriment to the 'plain thought' which it is intended to
convey. Clearly, much depends upon the nature of the thought. If the
form is that of an allegory, whether it is humorous, like *Animal Farm*,
or non-humorous, like *The Pilgrim's Progress*, the figures are meant to
have a serious significance, and the aim of the artist is to induce a
'willing suspension of disbelief', not to draw our attention to the fact
that he is describing the impossible. On the other hand, if he is writing
a satirical burlesque, like Lucian, the more obviously absurd the
imagery the better.

The affinities between Lucian's *True History* and *Gulliver's Travels*
have often been pointed out:

> *Gulliver's Travels* belongs to a literary genus full of grotesque and
> anomalous forms. Its form is derived from some of the imaginary travels
> of which Lucian's *True History*—itself a burlesque of some early traveller's
> tales—is the first example.[2]

Stephen continues: 'It may be compared, again, to the *Pilgrim's
Progress*, and the whole family of allegories.'[3]

There is no question of Lucian's grotesque having symbolic
significance:

> Whoever would pass for a beauty among [the Selenites] must be bald
> and without hair; curly and bushy heads are an abomination to them. But
> in the comets it is just the reverse: for there only curly hair is esteemed
> beautiful, as some travellers, who were well received in those stars, in-
> formed us. Nevertheless they have somewhat of a beard a little above the
> knee. On their feet they have neither nails nor toes; for the whole foot is

---

[1] See p. 131.
[2] cf. Stephen, op. cit., p. 174.
[3] ibid., p. 175.

entirely one piece. Every one of them at the point of the rump has a large cabbage growing, in lieu of a tail, always green and flourishing, and which never breaks off though a man falls on his back.

They sneeze a very sour kind of honey; and when they are at work or gymnastic exercises, or use any exertion, milk oozes from all the pores of the body in such quantities that they make cheese of it, only mixing with it a very little of the said honey.[1]

In his introduction Lucian roundly declares that his whole narrative is impossible:

I resolved, however, to adopt an honester mode of lying than the generality of my compeers: for I tell at least one truth, by saying that I lie . . . Accordingly I hereby declare, that I sit down to relate what never befell me; what I neither saw myself, not heard by report from others; aye, what is more, about matters that not only are not, but never will be, because in one word they are absolutely impossible.[2]

Moreover, he attacks the symbolic use of fantasy:

Their great leader and master in this fantastical way of imposing upon people was the famous Homeric Ulysses, who tells a long tale . . . about King Aeolus and the winds, who are his slaves, and about one-eyed men-eaters and other the like savages; . . . For my part I was the less displeased at all the falsehoods, great and numerous as they were, of these honest folks, when I saw that even men who pretend that they only philosophize, act not a hair better; but this has always excited my wonder, how they could imagine their readers would fail of perceiving that there was not a word of truth in all their narratives.[3]

Such a work as *Animal Farm* would obviously incur Lucian's criticism as the work of one of those who indulge in fantasy thinking and 'pretend that they only philosophize'.

On one level of significance, *Gulliver's Travels*, like Lucian's *True History*, is a burlesque of the traveller's tale; as such, it is essential to the writer's purpose that it should be regarded as wholly incredible. This aspect of the work is explicitly communicated in the concluding chapter of the Voyage to the Houyhnhnms: 'I could perhaps like others have astonished thee with strange improbable Tales; but I rather chose to relate plain Matter of Fact in the simplest Manner and

[1] From Lucian's *True History*, cf. *The International Library of Famous Literature*, ed. R. Garnett, vol. II (London, issued by the *Standard*, 1900), p. 588.
[2] ibid., p. 579.
[3] ibid., p. 579.

Style; because my principal Design was to inform, and not to amuse thee.'[1]

Swift's irony would lose its effect if the phenomena described in the narrative were probable, or even possible; they must be grotesque, exaggerated, absurd—monkeys as big as elephants, flying islands, talking horses. We must read and disbelieve, however much we are entertained.

On another more important level of significance, however, the allegorical or symbolic level, it is equally essential to Swift's purpose that the phenomena he describes should have some relationship, however tenuous, with reality. They must have a serious meaning; in other words, they must, at bottom, depict either the actual or some idealized form of the actual. Whereas Lucian's burlesque flaunts its implausibility, the allegorist or symbolic writer must aim at plausibility—he is presenting truth in a new light. Milton's Sin and Death, for example, are both 'lies' and striking representations of truth; it is, of course, the second view we are meant to take.

There is, in addition, a third level of significance in *Gulliver's Travels*; the ideal. Both Ehrenpreis and Stephen refer to the affinities of the work with More's *Utopia*, and it is certainly an important aspect of Swift's satire, particularly in the fourth book of *Gulliver's Travels*, to contrast the social, moral, and political corruptions of England with a perfect state, as More does. It is ironic, and of great significance, that for all Swift's admiration of St. Thomas More, who is included in his 'Sextumvirate to which all the Ages of the World cannot add a Seventh',[2] 'Utopian Commonwealths' are derided in *A Discourse Concerning the Mechanical Operation of the Spirit*, together with the squaring of the circle, &c., as serving 'for nothing else, but to employ or amuse this Grain of Enthusiasm, dealt into every Composition'.[3] The consequence is that the perfect state of the Houyhnhnms must fulfil two quite different functions. First, it must be absurd and impossible, a burlesque of the serious 'Utopian Commonwealth'; second, it must be a vision of perfection which will have a serious import for the reader.

To what extent does Swift succeed in integrating these three different aspects of *Gulliver's Travels*, the absurd, the humorously allegorical, and the ideal? The simplest answer is that it is the mingling of the absurd and the ideal, in the fourth book, which gives

[1] cf. *Gulliver's Travels*, bk. IV, ch. XII (Nonesuch ed., p. 286).
[2] cf. *Gulliver's Travels*, bk. III, ch. VII (Nonesuch ed., p. 192).
[3] cf. *A Tale of a Tub*, &c., O.U.P. ed., p. 266.

Swift most difficulty. The reconciling of the absurd and the allegorical is rather a matter of tone than of imagery. It would be impossible to set a 'reasonable' limit to the amount of distortion and
grotesqueness which we are prepared to accept as justified by a symbolic or allegorical intention. Such serious allegorical images as
Milton's Sin and Death, Spenser's Blatant Beast, and the beasts of
the Apocalypse are far more grotesque than any of the figures of
Gulliver's Travels, as regards mere physical distortion. What matters
most is the attitude of mind suggested by the artist. Lucian's Selenites strike us as preposterous because we adopt the author's point of
view. The equally grotesque Selenites of H. G. Wells's *The First Men
in the Moon* do not, for the same reason. Swift does not keep the
impossibility of his figures—what might be called their negative
significance—before the reader's attention; on the contrary, he goes
to great lengths to make them as plausible as they are fascinating.
Instead of openly parading his mendacity, like Lucian, he contents
himself with a tongue-in-cheek tone and occasional digs at our
credulity:

> And, as Truth always forceth its Way into rational Minds; so, this honest
> worthy Gentleman, who had some Tincture of Learning, and very good
> Sense, was immediately convinced of my Candor and Veracity.[1]
> My Answer was, that I thought we were already over-stocked with
> Books of Travels: That nothing could now pass which was not extra-
> ordinary; wherein I doubted, some Authors less consulted Truth than
> their own Vanity or Interest, or the Diversion of ignorant Readers. That
> my Story could contain little besides common Events . . .[2]
> I thought this Account of the Struldbruggs might be some Entertain-
> ment to the Reader, because it seems to be a little out of the common way;
> at least, I do not remember to have met the like in any Book of Travels
> that hath come to my Hands:[3]

In the first and second books of *Gulliver's Travels* the use of the
fantastic is precisely similar to that of Orwell's *Animal Farm* or
Aesop's *Fables*. It provides an entertaining vehicle for satire. The
change of scale is readily assimilated in each case and gives a 'reasonable' air to all the wonders which flow from it. All is consistent.
Moreover, at a period when 'the terrestrial globe needed the light of
reason as much as the nature of the physical universe or the mysteries

[1] cf. *Gulliver's Travels*, bk. II, ch. VIII (Nonesuch ed., p. 144).
[2] ibid. (Nonesuch ed., p. 145).
[3] ibid., bk. III, ch. XI (Nonesuch ed., p. 210).

of God',[1] perhaps even the stature of the Lilliputians and the Brobdingnagians conflicted less powerfully with the reader's conception
of the possible than is the case today. In these books the chief source
of conflict is Swift's introduction of the ideal level into what is predominantly a presentation of the actual in novel perspective. Thus the
satirical purpose of the first book is fundamentally that of the
triviality and insignificance of human affairs:

GOLBASTO MOMAREN EVLAME GURDILO SHEFIN
MULLY ULLY GUE, most Mighty Emperor of Lilliput, Delight and
Terror of the Universe, whose Dominions extend five thousand Blustrugs,
(about twelve Miles in Circumference) to the Extremities of the Globe:
Monarch of all Monarchs: Taller than the Sons of Men; whose Feet press
down to the Center, and whose Head strikes against the Sun: . . .[2]

The introduction, into this world of rope-dancing politicians and
Big- and Little-Endians, of a Utopian element in chapter VI is
artistically weak. It illustrates the difficulty which even Swift experiences in manipulating three levels of significance. In Professor
Dobrée's words, 'the philosopher overcame the artist'.[3] In the second
book Dobrée finds no such inconsistency and insists that 'nothing
ruffles us as we read'.[4] Whilst this may be acceptable as an overall
impression, however, there are inconsistencies between the allegorical satire and the Utopian element which appears later in the
narrative.

In general, Swift avoids conflict between these two levels by concentrating his allegorical satire principally upon the physical aspect of
the Brobdingnagians:

The Nipple was about half the Bigness of my Head, and the Hue both
of that and the Dug so varified with Spots, Pimples and Freckles, that
nothing could appear more nauseous . . . This made me reflect upon the
fair Skins of our English Ladies . . .[5]
For, they would strip themselves to the Skin, and put on their Smocks
in my Presence . . . which, I am sure, to me was very far from being a
tempting Sight, or from giving me any other Motions than those of Horror
and Disgust.[6]

[1] cf. J. H. Plumb, *England in the 18th Century* (Pelican Books, 1950),
p. 30.
[2] cf. *Gulliver's Travels*, bk. I, ch. III (Nonesuch ed., p. 38).
[3] cf. Dobrée, op. cit., p. 451.
[4] ibid.
[5] cf. *Gulliver's Travels*, bk. II, ch. I (Nonesuch ed., p. 88).
[6] ibid., ch. V (Nonesuch ed., p. 115).

There was a Woman with a Cancer in her Breast, swelled to a monstrous Size, full of Holes, in two or three of which I could have easily crept, and covered my whole Body. There was a Fellow with a Wen in his Neck, larger than five Woolpacks; and another with a couple of wooden Legs, each about twenty Foot high. But the most hateful Sight of all was the Lice crawling on their Cloaths: I could see distinctly the Limbs of these Vermin with my naked Eye, much better than those of an European Louse through a Microscope.[1]

It is consistent for Swift to combine such satire—he assures us that the giants were in point of fact 'a comely Race of People'[2]—with the satire of contrast, representing their culture, politics, &c., as admirable. Nevertheless, there are inconsistencies, conflicts between the allegorical and the Utopian levels. The most obvious example is the pedantic speculation of the 'three great Scholars' who attempt to classify Gulliver 'with many learned Arguments':

After much Debate, they concluded unanimously that I was only *Relplum Scalcath*, which is interpreted literally *Lusus Naturae*; a Determination exactly agreeable to the Modern Philosophy of Europe: whose Professors . . . have invented this wonderful Solution of all Difficulties, to the unspeakable Advancement of human Knowledge.[3]

Clearly these pedants belong to the Academy at Lagado, rather than in a culture described approvingly as follows:

The Learning of this People is very defective; consisting only in Morality, History, Poetry and Mathematicks; wherein they must be allowed to excel. But the last of these is wholly applied to what may be useful in Life; to the Improvement of Agriculture and all mechanical Arts; so that among us it would be little esteemed. And as to Ideas, Entities, Abstractions and Transcendentals, I could never drive the Least Conception into their Heads.[4]

Apart from the cupidity of Gulliver's first master, the chief impression gained from the first chapters of the second book is that of a good-natured, rough-mannered people who are thus an apposite vehicle for satire of affectation and ceremony by contrast. It is somewhat surprising to find Swift attributing floridity of style to them:

But as I was out of all fear of being ill treated under the Protection of so good an Empress, the Ornament of Nature, the Darling of the World,

[1] ibid., ch. IV (Nonesuch ed., p. 109).
[2] ibid., ch. I (Nonesuch ed., p. 89).
[3] ibid., ch. III (Nonesuch ed., p. 100).
[4] ibid., ch. VII (Nonesuch ed., p. 133).

the Delight of her Subjects, the Phoenix of the Creation; so, I hoped my late Master's Apprehensions would appear to be groundless; for I already found my Spirits to revive by the Influence of her most August Presence.

This was the Sum of my Speech, delivered with great Improprieties and Hesitation; the latter Part was altogether framed in the Style peculiar to that People, whereof I learned some Phrases from Glumdalclitch, while she was carrying me to Court.[1]

The satirical tone is obvious; and the passage is clearly inconsistent with the Utopian view of the Brobdingnagians which emerges in the later chapters, where we read: 'Their Stile is clear, masculine, and smooth, but not Florid; for they avoid nothing more than multiplying unnecessary Words, or using various Expressions.'[2]

The fact that there is an army of 'twenty five thousand Foot, and six thousand Horse' in this Utopia is explained by Swift, in similar vein to his 'lame excuse'[3] for the admirable laws and customs of the Lilliputians, as a kind of relic of former times:

For in the Course of many Ages they have been troubled with the same Disease, to which the whole Race of Mankind is Subject; the Nobility often contending for Power, the People for Liberty, and the King for absolute Dominion. All which, however happily tempered by the Laws of that Kingdom, have been sometimes violated by each of the three Parties; and have more than once occasioned Civil Wars, the last whereof was happily put an End to by this Prince's Grandfather in a general Composition.[4]

In its context, the passage above is something of an anti-climax; we have been told that the King 'was perfectly astonished with the historical Account I gave him of our Affairs during the last Century; protesting it was only an Heap of Conspiracies, Rebellions, Murders, Massacres, Revolutions, Banishments'.[5] Now we discover that two generations previously Brobdingnag was in much the same state. On the whole, however, Swift switches levels with great dexterity in the Voyage to Brobdingnag. For our purposes the most significant thing about the first two books is the absence of effects calculated to strike the reader as utterly absurd; we are coaxed into a state of acquiescence by a wealth of plausible detail. It is the congruities between his

---

[1] ibid., ch. III (Nonesuch ed., pp. 98–99).
[2] ibid., ch. VII (Nonesuch ed., p. 134).
[3] cf. Dobrée, op. cit., p. 451.
[4] cf. *Gulliver's Travels*, bk. II, ch. VII (Nonesuch ed., p. 136).
[5] ibid., ch. VI (Nonesuch ed., p. 129).

imaginary countries and our own circumstances that Swift is concerned to emphasize, not the incongruities.

Perhaps the most interesting example of a difficulty produced by conflict of techniques in the third book of *Gulliver's Travels* is the case of the flying island. We are expressly told that the Laputians, 'though they are dextrous enough upon a Piece of Paper', are a 'clumsy, awkward, and unhandy People':[1] 'Their Houses are very ill built, the Walls bevil, without one right Angle in any Apartment; and this Defect ariseth from the Contempt they bear for practical Geometry; . . .'[2] In short, they are 'very bad Reasoners'.[3] As a description of the inventors of a flying island, this criticism is as unexpected as though Jules Verne had suddenly assured us that Captain Nemo knew nothing about engineering: it is clear from chapter III that the flying island is in fact an invention.

The point is that we are meant to regard the flying island as an absurdity in the sense of an impossibility. Like the preposterous experiments carried out at the Academy of Lagado, it is a burlesque of the crazy notions of 'virtuosos'. Whereas the former, however, are represented in the narrative itself as hopelessly ineffectual, the flying island actually flies. The result is that in order to enjoy the satire the reader is obliged to shift his perspective in an awkward fashion. The 'intellectuals' of Laputa and Lagado and their activities are an exaggeration of the truth; the flying island—in so far as it flies—is an ironic misrepresentation of the truth. There is, of course, the important difference between, say, Lucian's absurd Selenites and Swift's absurd flying island that as a mere 'projection' the island has an allegorical function; as things stand, however, the picture of the clumsy and impractical Laputians manipulating their flying island contains a real inconsistency which is perhaps most simply indicated by saying that whereas the important thing about the Laputians—for all that 'one of their Eyes turned inward, and the other directly up to the Zenith'—is that they are a representation of the truth, the important thing about the flying island is that it is a contradiction of the truth.

The most powerful satire in the third book is generally considered to be Swift's account of the Struldbruggs, undying but perpetually ageing. Here we see Swift employing his imagination in a thoroughly congenial manner, exorcizing the fear of death which he felt as

[1] ibid., bk. III, ch. II (Nonesuch ed., p. 160).
[2] ibid. (Nonesuch ed., pp. 159–60).
[3] ibid. (Nonesuch ed., p. 160).

strongly as any man by conjuring up a vision of the still more fearful alternative. There is nothing in his work to which Dobrée's phrase 'the fantasy of extreme logic' can be applied more aptly. The fantasy —the immortality of the Struldbruggs, like the change of scale in the first two books, is a hypothesis which the artist develops in a logical and consistent fashion. It is imperative that we should accept the initial supposition; if we reject it as absurd, the whole effect is spoiled.

The attitude of mind required for the proper appreciation of the Struldbruggs is thus very different from that required for the proper appreciation of the Selenites. Dobrée's remark, '. . . in Book III Swift might have said as frankly as Lucian did, "I humbly solicit my readers' incredulity" ',[1] though perhaps applicable to the third book in the sense that it is less convincing than the earlier books, scarcely holds good as a description of its prevailing tone.

In view of Swift's contemptuous comments on the 'dark conceit', and those 'Grubaean Sages' who 'have always chosen to convey their Precepts and their Arts, shut up within the Vehicles of Types and Fables', in the Introduction to *A Tale of a Tub*,[2] it is ironic that the fourth book of *Gulliver's Travels* should have given rise to so many differing interpretations.

Perhaps the chief point of contention has been the attitude we are meant to take towards the *modus vivendi* of the Houyhnhnms. We have already noticed one extreme view, that of Ehrenpreis, who maintains that we are meant to regard the completely rational behaviour of the Houyhnhnms as 'a false ideal for humanity'.[3] Ewald, on the other hand, observes:

Swift does not condemn the Houyhnhnms for being completely rational, without either numerous or non-rational (i.e. non-social) emotions. . . . Before singling out the Houyhnhnms for their cold and inhuman rationality, one should compare Houyhnhnm-land with Plato's Republic and Lycurgus's Sparta.[4]

For J. M. Bullitt, the Houyhnhnms present Gulliver with a 'vision of an ideal perfection', 'an unattainable and desirable ideal'.[5] Dobrée says of Swift:

. . . he is not really arguing that man could be, or even should be, with-

---

[1] Dobrée, op. cit., p. 456.
[2] cf. O.U.P. ed., p. 66.
[3] See p. 120.
[4] cf. Ewald, op. cit., p. 161.
[5] cf. J. M. Bullitt, *Jonathan Swift and The Anatomy of Satire* (Harvard U.P., 1953), p. 15.

out the element of irrationality which makes him able to recognize the divine. For though it might be pleasanter to dwell among his horses than among his anthropoid apes (he is careful to make the distinction between civilized man and the Yahoos), to be a Houyhnhnm might be a good deal duller than to be a Yahoo.[1]

Are we, then, intended to reject the Houyhnhnm Utopia as undesirable, to accept it with reservations, or to accept it unreservedly as a vision of perfection? Are the conflicting interpretations a mere matter of personal idiosyncrasy, or do they correspond to a conflict in the work itself?

In the fourth book of *Gulliver's Travels*, Swift attempts to kill three birds with one stone; first, to write a moral tract of the 'Go to the ant, thou sluggard' variety; second, to contrast the imperfections of human society with a Utopian perfection; and third—a minor aim —to write a 'wonderful' plausibly absurd narrative to satirize the mendacious traveller's history.

Swift explicitly refers to the Biblical text mentioned above: '. . . it was no Shame to learn Wisdom from Brutes, as Industry is taught by the Ant, and building by the Swallow'.[2] The horse is cleanly and decorous, man is dirty and depraved. Horses are therefore superior to men, and ought to be their masters. As it stands, however, the objection to this idea as the basis for a moral lesson is that men are not horses. The Biblical proverb continues:

> Go to the ant, thou sluggard;
> Consider her ways, and be wise:[3]

Swift must establish that the virtues of the horse are to some extent at least within the province of man; he must persuade us that these virtues are both desirable and to some extent obtainable.

This difficulty is vastly increased when the horse becomes the Houyhnhnm, which 'signifies a Horse; and in its Etymology, the Perfection of Nature'.[4] If the perfect horse is merely *contrasted* with man, whilst there may be an emotional effect, there can be little more than 'insult value' in it; it is like contrasting, say, the beauty of the deer with the ugliness of the human form. It is thus essential to Swift's moral intention to provide some link between man—in particular, Gulliver—and the Houyhnhnms. That link is 'reason'.

[1] cf. Dobrée, op. cit., p. 459.
[2] cf. *Gulliver's Travels*, bk. IV, ch. IX (Nonesuch ed., p. 267).
[3] cf. *Proverbs* vi. 6.
[4] cf. *Gulliver's Travels*, bk. IV, ch. III (Nonesuch ed., p. 229).

In the Third Epistle of his *Essay on Man*, Pope contrasts instinct with reason:

> One must go right, the other may go wrong.[1]

It is vital to Swift's purpose to avoid any suggestion that the intelligence of the Houyhnhnms is different in *kind* from that of man. If they are represented as creatures of instinct, their perfection is simply irrelevant to the human condition. But it is equally important that he should avoid conveying the idea that their intelligence is different in *quantity*. In so far as they are more admirable because they are more intelligent, man is exonerated of blame for being less perfect. We are as God made us, as far as our intelligence is concerned. Swift does not altogether succeed in avoiding the latter danger; we are nowhere given to understand that Gulliver is at least potentially as intelligent as the Houyhnhnms, unless there is a hint in Gulliver's initial reaction to the Houyhnhnms, when they seem to him still little more than 'ordinary cattle': '. . . however this confirmed my first Opinion, that a People who could so far civilize brute Animals, must needs excel in Wisdom all the Nations of the World.'[2] Subsequently, however, the general impression created by Gulliver's awe of the Houyhnhnms and the contemptuous remarks made by Gulliver's master about his pretensions to reason is that he is less intelligent than the Houyhnhnms:

. . . he looked upon us as a Sort of Animals to whose Share . . . some small Pittance of Reason had fallen.[3]

. . . he observed in me all the Qualities of a Yahoo, only a little more civilized by some Tincture of Reason; which however was in a Degree as far inferior to the Houyhnhnm Race, as the Yahoos of their Country were to me.[4]

For, they alledged, That . . . I had some Rudiments of Reason.[5]

This impression is deepened by the suggestions that many human characteristics are a kind of instinct in the Yahoos, such as 'their strange Disposition to Nastiness and Dirt', their fondness for 'shining stones', their habit of intoxicating themselves, and so on.[6]

The difficulty, for Swift, arises from the fact that in Lockian fashion, he regards vice as a kind of stupidity: 'The preference of vice

[1] cf. op. cit., Epistle III, l. 94.
[2] cf. *Gulliver's Travels*, bk. IV, ch. II (Nonesuch ed., p. 222).
[3] ibid., ch. VII (Nonesuch ed., p. 253).
[4] ibid., ch. IX (Nonesuch ed., p. 267).
[5] ibid., ch. X (Nonesuch ed., pp. 274–5).
[6] cf. ch. VII, *passim*.

to virtue is a manifest wrong judgment.'[1] Thus Gulliver remarks, regarding his banishment: '. . . in my weak and corrupt Judgment, I thought it might consist with Reason to have been less rigorous'.[2] The problem, left unresolved by Swift, is whether the weakness of human judgement is the consequence of human corruption, or the corruption due to weakness of judgement.

Wherever human reason is mentioned it is seen not as a counteraction to human vice but as an aggravating factor: '. . . he looked upon us as a Sort of Animals to whose Share . . . some small Pittance of Reason had fallen, whereof we made no other Use than by its Assistance to aggravate our natural Corruptions, and to acquire new ones which Nature had not given us.'[3]

Swift's general thesis that creatures which have the intelligence of Houyhnhnms are morally culpable if they behave like Yahoos is obscured by the general impression he conveys that we are less intelligent than the Houyhnhnms and that we have much more in common with the Yahoos by nature than with their masters.

The source of human evil is our unwillingness to control our passions; mere *inability* to control them is scarcely a just ground for censure. The chief cause of dissatisfaction felt by the reader with the ideal held up to us by Swift is the fact that the Houyhnhnms, unlike the saint or martyr, are represented as being devoid of any Yahoo element, and are therefore devoid of moral grandeur. The suggestion that the uncomplicated, mechanically rational behaviour of the Houyhnhnms, from whom Gulliver learns 'excellent Lessons of Virtue',[4] is *morally* superior to our own, leaves us with a sense of irritation. Ehrenpreis understandably concludes that Swift is therefore contrasting the robot-like Houyhnhnms to their detriment with the really admirable behaviour of Pedro de Mendez, who succours the wretched outcast at the end of the voyage. The significance of the introduction of de Mendez, however, is not so much that Swift is implying that the Houyhnhnm Utopia is a 'false ideal' as distinct from a true one—a satire on deism—as that, having confronted Gulliver with a vision of perfection, Swift is now portraying Gulliver as something of a fanatic, depicting the harmful effect which idealism has upon common sense:

After Dinner Don Pedro came to me, and . . . assured me he only meant

[1] See p. 122.
[2] cf. *Gulliver's Travels*, bk. IV, ch. X (Nonesuch ed., p. 275).
[3] ibid., ch. VII (Nonesuch ed., p. 253).
[4] ibid., ch. XII (Nonesuch ed., p. 291).

to do me all the Service he was able; and spoke so very movingly, that at last I descended to treat him like an Animal which had some little Portion of Reason.[1]

My Wife and Family received me with great Surprize and Joy, because they concluded me certainly dead; but I must freely confess, the Sight of them filled me only with Hatred, Disgust and Contempt . . . my Memory and Imaginations were perpetually filled with the Virtues and Ideas of those exalted Houyhnhnms.[2]

Gulliver's subsequent conduct is clearly 'fanatical': 'My Horses understand me tolerably well; I converse with them at least four Hours every Day.'[3]

There are indeed hints of Gulliver's increasing fanaticism earlier in the book. At the beginning of chapter XII, for example, in excusing himself for giving his master 'so free a Representation' of the evils of life in Europe, Gulliver observes:

. . . I must freely confess, that the many Virtues of those excellent Quadrupeds placed in opposite View to human Corruptions, had so far opened my Eyes, and enlarged my Understanding, that I began to view the Actions and Passions of Man in a very different Light; and to think the Honour of my own Kind not worth managing; which, besides, it was impossible for me to do before a Person of so acute a Judgment as my Master, who daily convinced me of a thousand Faults in my self, whereof I had not the least Perception before, and which with us would never be numbered even among human Infirmities. I had likewise learned from his Example an utter Detestation of all Falsehood or Disguise; and Truth appeared so amiable to me, that I determined upon sacrificing every thing to it.[4]

The last sentence in particular acquires an extra significance when it is juxtaposed with Swift's aphorism: 'Violent zeal for truth hath an hundred to one odds to be either petulancy, ambition, or pride.'[5]

How is one to interpret Gulliver's behaviour on his return from the country of the Houyhnhnms—his stopping of his nose with rue, his daily converse with his horses, &c.? To regard it simply as a final instance of Swift's misanthropy, as has so often been the case, and to take the opposite extreme and argue that because the attitude of the returned Gulliver is wrongheaded and absurd, the criticism of

---

[1] ibid., ch. XI (Nonesuch ed., p. 282).
[2] ibid. (Nonesuch ed., p. 285).
[3] ibid. (Nonesuch ed., p. 286).
[4] ibid., ch. VII (Nonesuch ed., p. 252).
[5] cf. *Thoughts on Religion* (7) (Nonesuch ed., p. 465).

human society by contrast with the Houyhnhnm Utopia is not seriously intended, are equally incorrect views. The significant thing about Swift's description of the Houyhnhnm Utopia and its effect upon Gulliver is its ambiguity. In the fourth book of *Gulliver's Travels* human life is first criticized from the Gigadibs point of view with burning seriousness and contrasted with a Utopian society which we are meant to find seriously significant. Swift gives free rein to his dissatisfaction with the dirtiness and imperfections of his surroundings and creates a vision of perfect sanity and serenity. Having done so, he scrutinizes the results and brings Gigadibs firmly to earth again:

> The common problem, yours, mine, every one's
> Is not to fancy what were fair in life
> Provided it could be,—but, finding first
> What may be, then find how to make it fair
> Up to our means—a very different thing!
> No abstract intellectual plan of life
> Quite irrespective of life's plainest laws,
> But one, a man, who is man and nothing more,
> May lead within a world which (by your leave)
> Is Rome or London—not Fool's-paradise.[1]

The conflicting interpretations of the fourth book of *Gulliver's Travels* are a reflection of a conflict in the narrative itself, of the Gigadibs-Blougram, regressive-progressive opposition in Swift's own personality. Swift's lesson, that Gulliver cannot reasonably live with his head in Utopia and his feet in the world of men, implies only one serious criticism of the world of the Houyhnhnms, that it is impossible. Attempts to find deliberately conceived flaws in the Houyhnhnm way of life seem to me to be mistaken. The Houyhnhnms are at once grotesque and ideal; Gulliver is both crazed and ennobled by contact with them. The real source of the book's lasting fascination is that it gives expression to the enduring paradox of human nature.[2]

[1] cf. Robert Browning: 'Bishop Blougram's Apology', ll. 87 ff.

[2] It must not be lost sight of that contact with the world of the Houyhnhnms, whilst it unbalances Gulliver, is also a moral revelation to him. The way of life of the Houyhnhnms was conceived by Swift as a species of perfection, and the contrast between the beauty and harmony of this life and the discords of human society is forced upon us as a serious moral lesson in precisely the same way as in More's *Utopia*. We can neither ignore the exemplary perfection of the Houyhnhnms nor transplant this perfection into human society. It is this ambiguity which has largely been neglected in those examinations of the fourth book of *Gulliver's Travels* which rightly, in my opinion, point to Gulliver's derangement as a lesson in the necessity to compromise with an imperfect world. M. Price (*Swift's Rhetorical Art; A Study*

The simultaneous perfection and grotesqueness of the Houyhnhnms is one expression of the prevailing ambiguity in Swift's use
of fantastic symbolism. By describing the absurd behaviour of
Gulliver on his return, Swift ultimately leads our attention away from
the positive, ideal side of the role played by the Houyhnhnms, that
of stalking-horses for an attack upon English society, and directs it
towards the negative, fantastic side. It is rather as though Raphael
Hythloday, at the end of his discourse on Utopia, had been represented as mentally unhinged, the difference being that Swift keeps us
—and himself—in touch with the absurd, with talking horses and
ape-men, throughout the fourth book, leaving himself a loophole of
escape even in the most earnest passages.

35. The uncertainty of attitude continually induced in the reader
by Swift's work, evident in the case of the Houyhnhnms, is much
more pronounced in *A Tale of a Tub*. It is certainly true that the sheer
complexity of the work has a bewildering effect: 'The Tale is so many
different things all at once, it is moving round so many different axes,
that description from a single point of reference is impossible.'[1] The
chief cause of uncertainty, however, is that we are kept in doubt as to
what is seriously intended and what is merely frivolous, and whilst
there is no doubt that Swift deliberately keeps us guessing, this uncertainty is ultimately due to the ambiguity of his own attitude.
Bonamy Dobrée, as we have seen, describes the method of 'Swift the
imaginative artist' as that of putting plain thought in a fantastic form.

---

in *Structure and Meaning*, O.U.P., 1953) stresses the black and white opposition of Houyhnhnm and Yahoo, a deliberate oversimplification: '. . . the
impossible choice of Gulliver between Houyhnhnm and Yahoo' is one of
'Swift's devices for dissolving the reductive simplicity he has opposed to an
uncritical complacency. A middle view is left for the reader to define' (p. 76).
   A. E. Case (*Four Essays on Gulliver's Travels*, Princeton University Press,
1945) remarks both the perfection of the Houyhnhnms and its unsettling
effect upon Gulliver: 'Mendez is a paragon . . . Yet Gulliver, controlled by
the exalted conception of virtue he had acquired from living with Houyhnhnms, and by his now fixed belief in the utter worthlessness of all yahoos,
with whom he has come to group the human race, is unable to perceive even
the most extraordinary goodness when it manifests itself in one of the hated
species . . . after five years, Gulliver is able in retrospect to appreciate the
virtues of Mendez . . . and he gradually becomes more accustomed to his
family' (p. 121). Mr. Case insists, however, that 'the opinions concerning
mankind which Gulliver gives vent to are his own, not those of his creator'.
In my opinion both the conversations between Gulliver and his master regarding life in Europe, and Gulliver's fulminations against pride at the end
of Book IV, are a serious expression of Swift's own views.

[1] cf. Quintana, *Swift; An Introduction* (O.U.P., 1955), pp. 59–60.

The central allegory of *A Tale of a Tub* is an obvious example. Swift is also concerned in this work, however, to ridicule such barren forms of thought as nebulous theory and the dark conceit by parodying them, the point about the parodies being that they are meaningless and ridiculous.

Frequently these two uses of fantasy, that in which the fantasy is meant to be a humorous way of putting the truth and that in which it is meant to be an exposure of fallacious thinking, interpenetrate each other, and we find Swift ridiculing something by means of a 'theory' which bewilderingly compounds sense and nonsense, as in the 'Aeolist' theory of section VIII and the 'vapours' theory of section IX.

Swift continually insists upon the triviality and absurdity of the allegorical manner of writing which he is himself pursuing. The whole Tale is to be regarded as a burlesque of the allegory or dark conceit, an empty tub designed to distract 'unquiet spirits' from interfering in matters of real moment. At the same time, it is intended to 'expose the Abuses and Corruptions in Learning and Religion',[1] a thoroughly serious programme.

In point of fact, the central allegory of *A Tale of a Tub* demonstrates not the absurdity of the allegorical method but its effectiveness. The story of the three brothers is a humorous allegory, not an absurd one. It is significant that whilst Swift puts plain thought into a fantastic form in obedience to the promptings of his imagination, he inundates the reader with warnings against

> such, whose converting Imaginations dispose them to reduce all Things into Types; who can make Shadows, no thanks to the Sun; and then mold them into Substances, no thanks to Philosophy; whose peculiar Talent lies in fixing Tropes and Allegories to the Letter, and refining what is Literal into Figure and Mystery.[2]

We are rebuked for our inability to digest plain fact plainly stated. We must be led by a ring in the nose: 'as Mankind is now disposed, he receives much greater Advantage by being Diverted than Instructed; His Epidemical Diseases being Fastidiosity, Amorphy, and Oscitation.'[3]

It is this conflict in Swift's nature, between the need to express himself imaginatively and the equally imperious need to convince

---

[1] cf. *A Tale of a Tub* (O.U.P. ed., p. 12).
[2] cf. *A Tale of a Tub*, sect. XI (O.U.P. ed., pp. 189–90).
[3] ibid., sect. V (O.U.P. ed., p. 124).

himself and his readers that symbolic writing is an absurdity to which
he resorts against his better judgement, mere 'varnish and tinsel',[1]
which makes his imagery grotesque.

NOTES TO CHAPTER 6

I have given in some detail my reasons for disagreeing with Professor
Ehrenpreis's view that the Houyhnhnms are intended as a satire on
deism. In doing so I have assumed that Ehrenpreis considers the
world of the Houyhnhnms to be not merely 'a false ideal for humanity
to pursue', but in itself imperfect. I have argued that the only respect
in which the world of the Houyhnhnms is imperfect is in its lack of
revelation, which no more invalidates the behaviour of the Houyhnhnms as an ideal for mankind than it does that of Socrates. Thus
the Houyhnhnm contempt for 'our several Systems of Natural
Philosophy', which Swift tells us was in entire agreement with the
views of Socrates, is merely one instance, which could be multiplied
almost indefinitely, of an attitude which mankind would do well to
imitate. It would, on the other hand, be difficult to find any feature
of the lives of the Houyhnhnms which Swift clearly intends us to
find objectionable—apart from the primitive religious ideas of the
Houyhnhnms, which cannot reasonably be said to have the purpose
of exciting our disapproval; no parade is made of them whatever.

Whereas the Houyhnhnms stand in the same position as the
ancient philosophers with regard to revelation, Gulliver does not, and
his subsequent behaviour—it is perhaps significant that the question
of Gulliver's religion does not arise whilst he is with the Houyhnhnms—may be fairly regarded as satirizing the ideal of 'nothing
but reason'. This may be considered as an attack on deism, though I
prefer to interpret his attitude in a more general fashion as an object
lesson in the dangers of 'Fastidiosity', of the misuse of reason by a
creature too weak to stand long exposure to the direct sunlight of
Houyhnhnm-land. Ehprenpreis's views are largely shared by Miss
Kathleen Williams,[2] who emphasizes the 'remote, unsympathetic,
and in the end profoundly unsatisfying' nature of Houyhnhnm life
and suggests that Swift intended the Houyhnhnms to seem unsympathetic and 'sometimes faintly absurd'.[3] Absurd they certainly
are in so far as they are impossible figures, particularly when

[1] ibid., sect. IX (O.U.P., ed., p. 172).
[2] cf. Kathleen Williams, *Jonathan Swift and the Age of Compromise*
(University of Kansas Press, Lawrence, 1958).
[3] op. cit., p. 190.

one considers them from the physical point of view: but they are scarcely absurd in the sense of behaving foolishly. The fact that they are unsympathetic is not without significance in view of the contrast with de Mendez, whose warmth drives home the point that this is the world in which Gulliver properly belongs. But one cannot argue from this fact that the Houyhnhnms are not intended to seem admirable:

> Friendship and Benevolence are the two principal Virtues among the Houyhnhnms: and these not confined to particular Objects, but universal to the whole Race. For, a Stranger from the remotest Part, is equally treated with the nearest Neighbour, and where-ever he goes, looks upon himself as at home.[1]

Chapter VIII seems to me to be of particular importance; the Houyhnhnm attitude towards controversy, natural philosophy, &c., their friendship and benevolence—cool, but not cold terms—are clearly features which Swift regarded as admirable. The Spartan upbringing of their children—a 'cold' trait—echoes the Lilliputian method of educating children, which is described in a chapter intended to emphasize the wisdom of the Lilliputians. The obvious question is whether the manner of life of the Houyhnhnms is seriously intended to excite our disapproval. I cannot accept that it is meant to do so.

In general, my interpretation of the effects of Gulliver's intercourse with the Houyhnhnms is close to that of Ehrenpreis and Miss Williams; Gulliver is smitten with pride, becomes anti-social, and so on; but I see his predicament as part of an enduring paradox. Browning's Gigadibs is similarly frustrated, and proud of his refusal to accept the imperfect nature of things: yet ideals of a kind there must be. Miss Williams has in one admirable passage, with reference to *A Tale of a Tub*, laid bare the central idea of the main allegory in words which fairly adequately summarize my own attitude towards the Fourth Book of *Gulliver's Travels*:

> There are, as so often, two satiric standards: the will, by which all the churches, as all humanity, stand condemned, and the compromise standard, the best that can practically be achieved by half-blind humanity, the conduct of the reformed Martin.[2]

This seems to me to suggest excellently the contrast between the role of Houyhnhnm-land, with its social perfection, and the role which must be played by Gulliver in a fallen world.

[1] *Gulliver's Travels*, bk. IV (Nonesuch ed., pp. 262–3).
[2] cf. op. cit., p. 134.

7

COLERIDGE: THE ORGANIZATION
OF A DREAM

COLERIDGE'S 'NATIVE BIAS'

36. In his recent book on Coleridge, Professor J. V. Baker observes:
'. . . if Coleridge's ghost ever looked over Lowes's shoulder, how
fascinated he would have been at the play of the hooked atoms there
laid bare.'[1] Perhaps the most congenial aspect of Lowes's great book,
to Coleridge, would have been its scholarly simplicity. It is true that
The Road to Xanadu[2] is subtitled 'A Study in the Ways of the
Imagination', and that there is sufficient speculation in the work to
justify Baker's reference to 'Lowes's theory of poetic creation'—
'Gerard's theory of the preternaturally rapid and subtle associations
of genius with the conception of the unconscious added'.[3] First and
foremost, however, *The Road to Xanadu* is a compilation of materials,
an investigation of what Coleridge used rather than why he used it,
of 'the pieces that compose the pattern'.[4] A great deal naturally
emerges in the course of Lowes's examination regarding the characteristic activities of Coleridge's imagination; but Lowes makes no
attempt to 'see all round' Coleridge, to 'explain' his work in terms of
his duty-feelings towards Sara, his feelings of guilt about his use of
laudanum, and so on.[5] Such considerations may provide useful ideas
of an incidental kind, but—as Coleridge himself insisted—the creative activity of the imagination cannot be accounted for merely in
terms of personal experience;

We shall do well, I think, to make fully explicit all the implications of
that way of accounting for artistic creation which consists in reducing it
to personal factors. We should see clearly where it leads. The truth is that
it takes us away from the psychological study of the work of art, and con-

---

[1] cf. J. V. Baker, *The Sacred River; Coleridge's Theory of the Imagination*
(Louisiana State University Press, 1957), p. 278.
[2] cf. J. L. Lowes, *The Road to Xanadu; A Study in the Ways of the
Imagination* (Constable, London, 1930).
[3] cf. Baker, op. cit., p. 239.
[4] cf. Lowes, op. cit., p. 434.
[5] cf. Baker, op. cit., p. 244; cf. also Lowes, op. cit., pp. 593 ff (note 128).

fronts us with the psychic disposition of the poet himself. That the latter presents an important problem is not to be denied, but the work of art is something in its own right, and may not be conjured away.[1]

Miss Maud Bodkin, who attempts to identify suprapersonal, 'archetypal' images in Coleridge's work, along Jungian lines, comments critically upon Lowes's hypercautious attitude towards psychology: '. . . in his general theory Lowes seems to take no account of emotional forces as determining either the selection or the fashioning of the material of the poem. Such forces he appears to regard as necessarily personal.'[2] In contrast to Lowes, Miss Bodkin's examination of 'The Ancient Mariner' is subjective, relying chiefly upon her own responses as a sensitive reader:

> The reader, looking back from this stanza to the suggestion in Cook's page of a windless sea glowing red in the night, may guess from his own response to Coleridge's line what was the emotional symbolism of Cook's description for the imagination of the poet. Here, as always, it is through our sense of the emotional forces stirring in the experience communicated to ourselves that we can discern something of what the forces were that first gripped the significant aspects in the material to the poet's hand, and then held and fashioned this into perfect expressiveness.[3]

The question arises to what extent one can apply to a deliberate work of art—in the case of 'The Ancient Mariner', a highly sophisticated work with a considerable philosophical content—methods of examination which are appropriate to the myth and the genuine religious vision. It is, for example, difficult to agree with Miss Bodkin's assertion:

> In *The Ancient Mariner* the magic breeze, and the miraculous motion of the ship, or its becalming, are not, of course, like the metaphor, symbolic in conscious intention. They are symbolic only in the sense that, by the poet as by some at least of his readers, the images are valued because they give—even though this function remain unrecognized—expression to feelings that were seeking a language to relieve their inner urgency.[4]

Miss Bodkin here underestimates Coleridge as a conscious artist. To deny the deliberately symbolic nature of the breeze, the calm, &c.,

---

[1] cf. Jung, *Modern Man In Search Of A Soul* (Kegan Paul and Co., London, 1936), p. 185.

[2] cf. M. Bodkin, *Archetypal Patterns In Poetry; Psychological Studies Of Imagination* (O.U.P., 1934, 3rd Impr. 1951), p. 40.

[3] ibid., p. 43.

[4] cf. Bodkin, op. cit., p. 35.

in 'The Ancient Mariner' is like denying the deliberately symbolic nature of the storm on the heath in *King Lear*.

It is essential to an understanding of the role of the grotesque in Coleridge's work—we are primarily concerned with 'The Ancient Mariner', 'Christabel', and 'Kubla Khan'—to give proper weight to an aspect of that work which is sometimes lost sight of, or paid only lip-service to, in the by no means unrewarding search for 'the hooks-and-eyes of memory', for archetypal imagery, for unconscious wish-fulfilments, and the like. However profound the resources of Coleridge's reading, and however rich the levels of his mind which can be discerned in his poems, Coleridge was above all an *artist*, intensely aware of the representative aspect of his work, not merely expressing his feelings, but *communicating* both emotions and ideas. In vindicating Shakespeare from the popular misconception of him as 'a sort of beautiful *lusus naturae*, a delightful monster', Coleridge emphasizes the deliberate nature of Shakespeare's art. He is 'a nature humanized, a genial understanding directing self-consciously a power and an implicit wisdom deeper even than our consciousness'.[1]

It is the *directed* nature of Coleridge's own work which must be kept to the fore in the present examination, even if that work furthers the ends of an impulse of which he is thoroughly aware but which is beyond his control. Even in the case of 'Kubla Khan', it must be borne in mind that we have to do with a *composition*, not an example of 'free association'.

A work of art may, as we have seen, be considered grotesque through lack of sympathy or familiarity with its attributes even when no grotesque effect was intended; conversely, what was intended as grotesque may lose much of its impact, as in the case of the centaur, through increasing familiarity with its characteristics. The latter development has certainly occurred in the case of the 'Gothic' elements in romantic literature, many of which have become hackneyed and conventional.

The imagery of the true myth or vision, though it may strike us as grotesque, is not deliberately so. It is a statement of truth as the writer sees it which is not made in conscious conflict with an alternative conception of reality; it is not made with a sense of inadequacy or in a mood of defiance.

In romantic literature, on the other hand, the rejection of an

[1] cf. S. T. Coleridge, *Lectures on Shakespeare* (1818). cf. *Coleridge; Poetry and Prose*, ed. H. W. Garrod (O.U.P., 1954), p. 169.

alternative attitude towards reality is a characteristic feature:

> Hence, viper thoughts, that coil around my mind,
> Reality's dark dream!
> I turn from you, and listen to the wind.[1]

The poet endeavours to escape from what is at bottom his own scepticism.

Baker observes that 'the native bias' of Coleridge's temperament was 'platonic, mystical, and mythologizing'.[2] There can be no argument as to the justice of this description, but its implications may usefully be considered.

Baker's juxtaposition of the terms 'platonic' and 'mystical' suggests that he is thinking of Plato primarily as the type of those who regard the physical universe as a mere *superficies* and take a transcendental view of ultimate reality; furthermore, the observation that 'the native bias of his temperament' was 'platonic' implies that such a transcendental attitude, in the case of Coleridge—and presumably of Plato—at least, is fundamentally an emotional or intuitive one.

Bertrand Russell finds fault with the philosophy of St. Thomas Aquinas for a similar bias:

> He is not engaged in an inquiry, the result of which it is impossible to know in advance. Before he begins to philosophize, he already knows the truth; it is declared in the Catholic faith. If he can find apparently rational arguments for some parts of the faith, so much the better; if not, he need only fall back on revelation. The finding of arguments for a conclusion given in advance is not philosophy, but special pleading.[3]

Emotionally, Coleridge is drawn towards the idea of a transcendental reality as strongly as Plato or St. Thomas; to employ Jung's term, the regressive aspect of his mind is dominant:

> For all that meets the bodily sense I deem
> Symbolical, one mighty alphabet
> For infant minds; and we in this low world
> Placed with our backs to bright Reality
> That we may learn with young unwounded ken
> The substance from its shadow.[4]

[1] cf. Coleridge, 'Dejection: An Ode' (1802). (Poetical Works ed. E. H. Coleridge, O.U.P., 1912, vol. 1, p. 367, stanza vii).
[2] cf. Baker, op. cit., p. 17.
[3] cf. Russell, *Hist. Western Philosophy*, pp. 484–5.
[4] cf. Coleridge, *The Destiny of Nations: A Vision* (1796, publ. 1817), ll. 18–23 (O.U.P. ed. (1912), vol. I, p. 132). The lines contain an obvious reference to bk. VII of *The Republic*.

Intellectually, however, he lacks both the confidence of Plato in reason as a means of attaining truth, and the firm religious convictions of St. Thomas, whose soul is 'in a safe bank'. Nevertheless, he is impelled to employ reason in the endeavour to 'prove' to himself the validity of his intuition of the divine; this is the obvious difference between Coleridge and Blake, a true mystic who feels no compulsion to verify the truth of his intuitions rationally:

God forbid that Truth should be confined to Mathematical Demonstration![1]

He who does not Know Truth at Sight is unworthy of Her Notice.[2]

To follow the development of Coleridge's philosophical ideas is to conclude that, in Russell's words, 'before he begins to philosophize, he already knows the truth'. The significant thing is his need to have that truth, the reality of the divine, so formulated as to satisfy his reason. In his search for such a formulation, he evolved, under the influence of Priestley and Hartley, a pantheistic view which conflicted with his more orthodox religious beliefs and played an important role in developing his exalted view of the imagination, and perhaps in inhibiting his creative powers. This assertion requires to be enlarged upon, particularly as the conflict referred to is apparent in 'The Ancient Mariner'.

'I regard every experiment that Priestley made in Chemistry, as giving wings to his more sublime theological works.'[3] Apart from his abandoning of the conception of the Trinity in becoming a Unitarian, the most important idea which Coleridge derived from Priestley was that of the affinity between the physical forces of the universe and forces ordinarily thought of as being of a spiritual nature. It is truer to say in Coleridge's case that his study of the ideas set forth in Priestley's *Disquisition on Matter and Spirit* led him to regard the properties of matter as a kind of extension of the spiritual into the physical world, than that it led to a sceptical attitude regarding the reality of the divine.

In his early enthusiasm for Hartley's theory of association, he does indeed speak as a confirmed materialist: 'I am a complete necessitarian and understand the subject as well almost as Hartley

---

[1] cf. Blake, Marginalia to Reynold's *Discourses*, p. 201 (cf. Nonesuch ed. of Blake's *Poetry and Prose* (ed. G. Keynes), 1946, p. 806).

[2] ibid.

[3] cf. Baker, op. cit., p. 10 (quoted from *Unpublished Letters of Coleridge*, ed. E. L. Griggs (New Haven, 1933), vol. i, pp. 94–95).

himself, but I go further than Hartley, and believe the corporeality of thought, namely, that it is motion.'[1] It is perhaps significant, however, that the above remark occurs in a letter written on the day when his sonnet to Priestley as the liberator of religion appeared in the *Morning Chronicle* (11 Dec. 1794); Coleridge's equation of thought with motion implies that he has found logically convincing grounds for regarding the properties of matter as having a divine function. At all events this is unquestionably the outcome of his study of Priestley and Hartley, that 'Properties are God'.[2] The first 126 lines of 'The Destiny of Nations' (1796) are a valuable statement of his pre-Kantian *Weltanschauung*. He maintains a dualistic position, distinguishing between 'mass', wholly inert by nature,

> the naked mass
> (If mass there be, fantastic guess or ghost)
> Acts only by its inactivity[3]

and—borrowing Leibniz's term—'monads', which at once constitute and are controlled by 'one all-conscious Spirit', the vital principle which activates the universe.

The two most important features of Coleridge's view as seen in this poem are its near-pantheism (his hesitant postulation of the existence of 'mass', 'fantastic guess or ghost', prevents it from being wholly pantheistic) and its necessitarianism.

The conflict between Coleridge's Christian persuasions and the view of the divine outlined in 'The Destiny of Nations' appears first in his poetry in 'The Eolian Harp' (1795):

> And what if all of animated nature
> Be but organic Harps diversely fram'd,
> That tremble into thought, as o'er them sweeps
> Plastic and vast, one intellectual breeze,
> At once the Soul of each, and God of all?
>
> But thy more serious eye a mild reproof
> Darts, O belovéd Woman! nor such thoughts
> Dim and unhallow'd dost thou not reject,
> And biddest me walk humbly with my God,
> Meek daughter in the family of Christ!
> Well hast thou said and holily disprais'd

[1] cf. Baker, op. cit., p. 16 (cf. *Letters of S. T. Coleridge*, ed. E. H. Coleridge (Houghton Mifflin Co., Boston, 1895), vol. 1, p. 113).
[2] cf. 'The Destiny of Nations', l. 36 (O.U.P. ed. (1912), p. 133).
[3] ibid. (ll. 36–38).

> These shapings of the unregenerate mind;
> Bubbles that glitter as they rise and break
> On vain Philosophy's aye-babbling spring.
> For never guiltless may I speak of him,
> The Incomprehensible! save when with awe
> I praise him, and with Faith that inly feels;
> Who with his saving mercies healéd me,
> A sinful and most miserable man,[1]

These lines clearly establish that Coleridge's intellectual development away from orthodox Christianity—specifically in his Unitarian rejection of the divinity of Christ—aroused in him feelings of guilt. This ambiguous attitude is evident in 'The Destiny of Nations'. After asserting that 'Properties are God' which can obviously be understood in the 'harmless' sense that God's hand is to be seen in the forces of nature, Coleridge writes:

> Here we pause humbly. Others boldlier think

> .　　.　　.

He then proceeds to outline the view that

> Infinite myriads of self-conscious minds
> Are one all-conscious Spirit.[2]

having dissociated himself, so to speak, from the idea. Significantly, in a note appended to the manuscript of 'The Destiny of Nations', Coleridge remarks of the lines:

> Glory to Thee, Father of Earth and Heaven!
> All-conscious Presence of the Universe!
> Nature's vast ever-acting Energy![3]

Tho' these Lines may bear a sane sense, yet they are easily, and more naturally interpreted with a very false and dangerous one. But I was at that time one of the *Mongrels*, the Josephidites, a proper name of distinction from those who believe *in*, as well as believe Christ the only begotten Son of the Living God before all Time.[4]

The general tenor of Coleridge's thought having been established, it is possible to read his earlier poem 'Religious Musings: A Desultory Poem, Written On The Christmas Eve Of 1794' with fuller understanding. A detailed examination of this work is not to our purpose

---

[1] cf. 'The Eolian Harp', ll. 44–62 (O.U.P. ed., vol. I, p. 102).
[2] cf. 'The Destiny of Nations', ll. 43–44 (O.U.P. ed., vol. I, p. 133).
[3] ibid., ii. 459–61.
[4] cf. O.U.P. ed., vol. I, p. 147.

here. It is probably best described as an attempt to reconcile the religious ideas which derive from Priestley and Hartley (both of whom are lauded in the poem) with the imagery, at least, of orthodox Christianity. God is 'our universal Sire', but it is apparent that Coleridge does not regard Him as being, in the strict Christian sense, separate from the universe; in particular, all human minds are part of God, though the individual is able to introduce a discordant note into the prevailing harmony:

> . . . in His vast family no Cain
> Injures uninjured (in her best-aimed blow
> Victorious Murder a blind Suicide) . . .
> . . . 'Tis the sublime of man,
> Our noontide Majesty, to know ourselves
> Parts and proportions of one wondrous whole![1]

Christ is praised as the first Unitarian:

> Lovely was the death
> Of Him whose life was Love! Holy with power
> He on the thought-benighted Sceptic beamed
> Manifest Godhead, melting into day
> What floating mists of dark idolatry
> Broke and misshaped the omnipresent Sire.[2]

Christ is indeed the Son of God, but only in a sense to which all men may aspire.

We know that Coleridge was contemplating the composition of a poem dealing with guilt for some time before 'The Ancient Mariner' was written. Wordsworth's account, as given by Lady Richardson, is as follows: 'We agreed to write jointly a poem, the subject of which Coleridge took from a dream which a friend of his once dreamt, concerning a person suffering under a dire curse from the commission of some crime.'[3] Such an attempt had, in fact, already been made in the form of a prose narrative, *The Wanderings of Cain* (1798), of which only Coleridge's contribution, the second book or canto, is extant. It is surely significant, in view of the religious dilemma which we have remarked in Coleridge's earlier work, that this prose fragment deals with the temptation of Cain by an evil spirit, which, having assumed the likeness of Abel, confuses Cain with the idea that there are two Gods, the God of the Living and the God of the Dead.

---

[1] cf. ll. 119–28 (O.U.P. ed., vol. I, pp. 113–14).
[2] cf. ll. 28–33 (O.U.P. ed., vol. I, p. 110).
[3] cf. *Reminiscences of The Hon. Mr Justice Coleridge*, Grosart iii, p. 442.

G.E.L.—M

The ideas involved in *The Wanderings of Cain* are illumined by a rough draft found among Coleridge's papers.[1] From this we learn that in this alternative version Cain was to have been persuaded to burn out his eyes by an evil spirit, as a reward for which sign of penitence he would be 'gratified with the most delicious sights and feelings'. Cain at first refuses, saying that 'God himself who had inflicted his punishment upon him, had done it because he neglected to make a proper use of his senses, etc.' This passage is almost certainly a vindication of Coleridge's anticlericalism—the theme of the prose *Allegoric Vision* (1795). The 'Fiends of Superstition' are denounced in 'Religious Musings' as follows:

> I will raise up a mourning, O ye Fiends!
> And curse your spells, that film the eye of Faith,
> Hiding the present God; whose presence lost,
> The moral world's cohesion, we become
> An Anarchy of Spirits! Toy-bewitched,
> Made blind by lusts, disherited of soul,
> No common centre Man, no common sire,
> Knoweth! A sordid solitary thing,
> Mid countless brethren with a lonely heart
> Through courts and cities the smooth savage roams
> Feeling himself, his own low self the whole;
> When he by sacred sympathy might make
> The whole one Self![2]

The connexion between the passage above and the ethical aspect of 'The Ancient Mariner' is obvious; it is clear also that in *The Wanderings of Cain* we are to identify the false 'God of the Dead' whose evil messenger—if we take the rough draft referred to above into consideration—counsels Cain to blind himself, with the God of Christian dogma.

'THE RIME OF THE ANCIENT MARINER'

37. We may now apply the evidence of Coleridge's religious attitude examined above to his most important poem, 'The Rime of the Ancient Mariner', in which Coleridge attempts to make ethical and explicit what is at bottom a mystical intuition of the essential oneness of reality.

Professor Baker observes of the mariner's crime:

[1] cf. O.U.P. ed., vol. I, p. 285 (footnote).
[2] cf. 'Religious Musings', ll. 142–54 (O.U.P. ed. vol. I, pp. 114–15).

The shooting of the albatross with a crossbow is a highly symbolic action, a fact which literal-minded critics, who find the poem a tract on 'the prevention of cruelty to albatrosses', have ludicrously missed. It is a Dostoevskian poem of crime and punishment, of outrage and redemption . . . The entire voyage-poem is a myth whose symbols have universal relevance.[1]

The ethical problem referred to in this passage requires to be considered in connexion with the examination of Coleridge's use of grotesque imagery, because the poet's treatment of the problem serves to emphasize the great difference between 'The Ancient Mariner' and the myth.

Baker cautions us against adopting too literal-minded an attitude towards the mariner's crime. The shooting of the albatross, scarcely an evil deed when taken 'at face value', becomes more culpable when it is seen symbolically.

It is perhaps somewhat misleading, therefore, to describe the work as 'a Dostoevskian poem of crime and punishment'; Raskolnikov, in *Crime and Punishment*, is after all guilty of a bloody murder. One might even go so far as to say that the two works are in an important sense antithetical; whereas Coleridge is concerned to increase the gravity of the mariner's crime by suggesting its wider implications, Dostoevsky is concerned to demonstrate that even so brutal a crime as Raskolnikov's, seen in its full psychological and social context, may arouse sympathy and forgiveness for its perpetrator. This, however, is incidental to our present purpose. It is more to the point to emphasize that the opposition which Baker's passage suggests between the *literal* and the *symbolic* understanding of the narrative— specifically, of the shooting of the albatross—is scarcely to be found in a genuinely symbolic—as distinct from allegorical—narrative. Thus the struggles of Hercules with the Nemean lion or the Hydra of Lerna, typifying man's struggle with death, are both literally and symbolically arduous; a terrible reality is expressed in a terrible image.

Coleridge himself, in his profound distinction between allegory and symbol, stresses the point that whereas in allegory the literal level of the action is comparatively unimportant, in symbolic writing it is an essential part of the reality of the whole:

Allegory is nothing but a translation of abstract notions into a picture-language which is itself nothing but an abstraction from objects of the senses; the principal being more worthless even than its phantom proxy,

[1] cf. Baker, op. cit., pp. 208–9.

both alike unsubstantial and the latter worthless to boot. On the other hand a symbol . . . always partakes of the reality which it renders intelligible; and while it enunciates the whole, abides itself as a living part in that unity, of which it is the representative.[1]

Coleridge makes it abundantly clear that he regards the literal level in symbolic writing as being of vital importance in its own right; indeed, he implies unmistakably that in such writing—as distinct from allegory—there are no separable 'levels of meaning'; we murder to dissect.

The question arises whether, in 'The Ancient Mariner', Coleridge has been able to create a symbolic work which is in harmony with his own requirements of symbolism, one, that is, in which the imagery can be accepted by the reader as true; or whether he has not rather, despite his endeavours, produced a moral allegory. The answer is that a symbol can only be real in the deepest sense when it is not regarded as a mere symbol, when it is accepted by the writer or his audience as literally true; religious symbolism such as the fall of Lucifer or the Trinity is real in this sense to the Christian. In fiction the closest approximation that can be made to this fusion of image and reality is immeasurably inferior in so far as it involves a conscious and deliberate organization of ideas; myth becomes fable, parable, allegory; symbol becomes cypher. We have already seen that surrealistic art is at bottom an attempt to express emotional or intuitive realities in symbolic form by some method ('free' association, spontaneous creation, &c.) which will keep the sceptical, 'meddling intellect' at bay.[2] The visionary Blake appears to have achieved this aim in the grand, naïve confidence of his 'Auguries of Innocence', a poem with strong affinities to 'The Ancient Mariner':

> He who shall hurt the little Wren
> Shall never be belov'd by Men.
> He who the Ox to wrath has mov'd
> Shall never be by Woman lov'd.
> The wanton Boy that kills the Fly
> Shall feel the Spider's enmity.
> He who torments the Chafer's sprite
> Weaves a Bower in endless Night.[3]

[1] cf. Coleridge, *Statesman's Manual* (complete works, ed. W. T. G. Shedd, Harper and Brothers, New York, 1884, vol. I, p. 437). cf. Baker, op. cit., p. 204.
[2] See pp. 92 ff.
[3] cf. Blake, *Poetry and Prose*, p. 119.

Blake's continual emphasis on the need to believe, the evils of scepticism, and so on, suggests a sophistication, an objectivity towards his own symbols, which is scarcely to be found in the genuine religious vision; but he makes no compromise with the 'meddling intellect'. His images are presented as realities, not as a 'picture-language' or parable, though his prophetic works have frequently been subjected to analysis as though they were a kind of confused allegory.

'The Ancient Mariner', unlike the works of Blake, which are presented to the reader as matters of fact, is a work of fiction, requiring for its proper appreciation 'that willing suspension of disbelief for the moment which constitutes poetic faith'. Ornamented with archaisms, dealing with preternatural events removed from the immediate world in space and time, the poem seems to be at once too sophisticated for a vision and insufficiently credible for a parable; instead of a man who fell among thieves, we are confronted with a man who fell among spirits and spectres. Nevertheless, it is in its simplest aspect, that of the uncanny story, that the poem comes closest to the naïve myth or religious vision.

In writing a ballad Coleridge expresses, and endeavours to communicate, his belief in the supernatural, the state of emotion induced in him by such ballads as 'The Wife of Usher's Well'. He is attempting to put himself in the place of 'the polar ancient' he mentions in 'The Destiny of Nations', thrilling his 'uncouth throng' with terrible legends:[1]

> For Fancy is the power
> That first unsensualises the dark mind,
> Giving it new delights; and bids it swell
> With wild activity; and peopling air,
> By obscure fears of Beings invisible,
> Emancipates it from the grosser thrall
> Of the present impulse, teaching Self-control,
> Till Superstition with unconscious hand
> Seat Reason on her throne.[2]

Seen in this light, 'The Ancient Mariner' may fairly be described as a symbolic poem; the mariner and his fatal deed, the grotesque elements —the spectre-bark, the 'thousand thousand slimy things', the rising of the dead men, and so on—are meant to affect us like the *revenants* of 'The Wife of Usher's Well'. They are not cyphers, they do not 'stand for something'; they simply *are*, appealing to our emotions, not to our reason, and, allowing for the fact that they are deliberate

[1] cf. 'The Destiny of Nations' (O.U.P. ed. (1912), vol. I, p. 134).   [2] ibid.

fiction, expressing Coleridge's sense of the unknown, the weird, the infinite. If we are to appreciate this aspect of the poem to the full, therefore, as far as possible we should endeavour to read it, if not entirely naïvely and 'uncouthly' (an attitude which it is the whole purpose of the magnificent touches of realism to induce in us), then at least as we read 'The Wife of Usher's Well' or 'The Demon Lover', as an infectious declaration of the reality of the supernatural.

There remains a second aspect of the poem to be considered, the theological. In examining the intellectual structure which subserves the narrative, however, we should be careful to distinguish between the expressive and the representative sides of the work. Clearly, a great deal of intellectual scaffolding may have been employed in the construction of a work, the development of a style, &c., which the writer does not intend to appear in the finished product at all. This is particularly true of work in which the writer's aim is to produce an effect of mystery, of *naïveté*, or of antiquity. Our awareness of the actual conditions of creation may be an aesthetic loss as well as a scholastic gain. Thus the 'Rowley' poems are now read in a very different frame of mind from that intended by Chatterton. The mere knowledge that 'The Ancient Mariner' is a 'bogus' ballad partly vitiates the response Coleridge wished to produce, inducing reservations we do not have in the case of 'The Wife of Usher's Well'.

It is obvious enough from a comparison of 'Religious Musings' and 'The Destiny of Nations' with 'The Ancient Mariner' that in the latter poem Coleridge is largely versifying theological notions derived originally from Priestley; but how much of the philosophy which he ploughed into the poem was meant to be dug up again in its pristine form?

We know that the slaying of the albatross and its consequences exemplify in 'picture-language' a discord amongst the 'Monads of the infinite mind' (though the necessitarian and near-pantheistic merges into the Christian ethos). Strictly speaking, such knowledge, like the fact that the central incident was suggested by Shelvocke's *Voyages*, is extraneous to the proper appreciation of the work, and its possession and application raises difficulties similar to the 'faults' which Johnson discovered in *A Midsummer Night's Dream*: 'We need not wonder to find Hector quoting Aristotle, when we see the loves of Theseus and Hippolyta combined with the Gothick mythology of fairies.'[1] We are

[1] cf. Johnson, *Preface to Shakespeare* (1765) (*Shakespeare Criticism; A Selection*, ed. D. Nichol Smith (World's Classics ed., O.U.P., 1942, p. 103)).

analysing 'something rich and strange', a synthesis, back into its component parts when we consider the poem in terms of ideas rather than in terms of events.

Why should the Ancient Mariner be inflicted with great suffering, and his shipmates die, because of such a trivial act as the shooting of a bird? The question, and the various answers, are concerned not with the nature of the supernatural, but with Coleridge's ethical views. If we read the poem as a naïve ballad, as Coleridge intended we should, the question scarcely arises. Thus in 'The Wife of Usher's Well', one of the ghostly brothers says:

> The cock doth craw, the day doth daw,
> The channerin' worm doth chide;
> Gin we be missed out of our place,
> A sair pain we maun bide.

We accept this as we accept the whole poem, as a matter of fact.

Such a literal acceptance of 'The Ancient Mariner' as a story of the supernatural, properly shrouded in mystery, cannot, of course, satisfy the 'meddling intellect'; the critical intelligence, aware in the present instance of the theoretical scaffolding of the work, demands to know what the various events and images *mean*. The marginal glosses added later (1815–16) are evidence of Coleridge's own anxiety to make the workings of the spiritual machinery clearer to the reader—and to himself, to 'explain', for example, the position of the Polar Spirit in what becomes an increasingly Christian hierarchy:

The bodies of the ship's crew are inspirited and the ship moves on; . . . But not by the souls of the men, nor by dæmons of earth or middle air, but by a blessed troop of angelic spirits, *sent down by the invocation of the guardian saint.*

The lonesome Spirit from the south-pole carries on the ship as far as the Line, *in obedience to the angelic troop*, but still requireth vengeance.

The Polar Spirit's fellow-dæmons, the invisible inhabitants of the element, take part in his wrong; and two of them relate, one to the other, that penance long and heavy for the ancient Mariner *hath been accorded to the Polar Spirit*, who returneth southward.[1]

The interpretation of the poem in terms of theological ideas is complicated, however, by Coleridge's hesitation between two systems, remarked above in 'The Eolian Harp'.[2] Baker observes:

The mariner's crime of shooting the albatross is a crime against the

[1] The italics are mine.   [2] See pp. 163–4.

seamless robe of God's love, the unity of all nature and all creatures, a wanton act, a gratuitous act, to use Gide's term; underlying the concept of violation is the Plotinian doctrine of the One and the Many.[1]

Considered as an exposition of the (near) pantheistic ideas of 'Religious Musings' and 'The Destiny of Nations', the fate of the Ancient Mariner is the automatic result of his deed. The slaying of the albatross sets in motion a series of misfortunes which his affection for the water-snakes, an act of re-identification with the universal spirit, helps to avert. Upon this pantheistic background, however, Coleridge superimposes the Christian ethos; thus the mariner makes amends for his deed both by his act of re-identification, and by being shrived by the hermit, when his agony disappears—to return, of course, periodically.

No doubt the mariner's punishment can be justified with some ingenuity in Christian terms; it may be argued that the slaying of the albatross may fairly be regarded as a grave sin on the grounds that wickedness is a subjective condition which is not to be estimated merely by the way in which it manifests itself, for example. It might also be argued that the Christian imagery is merely 'ornamental', that the mariner's natural propensity to think of his plight in Christian fashion and the encounter with the hermit do not really have any effect upon the inexorable working out of his destiny, the glosses being no part of the original scheme. A careful reading of the poem with the ethical aspect in mind, however, clearly shows a transition from a pantheistic to a Christian attitude of mind on the part of the poet. Still with the ethical aspect of the poem in mind, we may ask whether it is not the impression of the reader that the continued sufferings of the mariner, acceptable as the inexorable consequences of an act of dissociation from the scheme of things, are far less so as a just penance imposed deliberately by the 'great Father', the Christian God. Is it not significant that Baker should feel it necessary to emphasize the *symbolic* nature of the act for which such heavy punishment is meted out? The legend of the Wandering Jew is symbolic, and has a universal relevance; the legend of Cain is symbolic, and has a universal relevance. In neither case is it necessary to append a warning against taking too literal a view of the heinous nature of the crime committed. The simple fact is that in ethical terms an act which by its very 'triviality' impressively suggests the unity of all things, or more precisely of all living things, and is thus highly appropriate to

[1] cf. Baker, op. cit., p. 178.

the exposition of an ethical system of a pantheistic nature, is far less appropriate to the Christian ethos, which does not emphasize the bond between man and the universe, but rather that between man and his Maker, and between man and his human neighbour. The explicit attempt to reconcile the two systems at the end of the poem shows Coleridge's awareness of the difficulty:

> He prayeth well, who loveth well
> Both man and bird and beast.
>
> He prayeth best, who loveth best
> All things both great and small;
> For the dear God who loveth us,
> He made and loveth all.

The stanzas disarmingly imply it is our duty to love all things equally, that there is no difference in the sight of God *in kind* between love of man and love of bird or beast.

Ultimately the critic must recognize that the ethical-theological aspect of the work, however much in evidence, is, so to speak, parasitic upon its real nature. Coleridge himself came to regard his encouragement of this parasitic growth as a blemish:

Mrs Barbauld once told me that she admired the Ancient Mariner very much, but that there were two faults in it,—it was improbable, and had no moral. As for the probability, I owned that that might admit some question; but as to the want of a moral, I told her that in my own judgment the poem had too much, and that the only, or chief fault, if I might say so, was the obtrusion of the moral sentiment so openly on the reader as a principle or cause of action in a work of such pure imagination. It ought to have had no more moral than the Arabian Nights' tale of the merchant's sitting down to eat dates by the side of a well, and throwing the shells aside, and lo! a genie starts up, and says he *must* kill the aforesaid merchant, *because* one of the date shells had, it seems, put out the eye of the genie's son.[1]

Dr. Tillyard comments: 'Probably Coleridge was stung to perversity by Mrs Barbauld's being so stupid, and did not mean what he said.'[2]

It would seem to be a sufficient objection to this view, however, to note that we are not here confronted with a Boswellian report of

[1] cf. *Table Talk* (1822–1834), 31 May 1830 (cf. *Passages from the Prose and Table Talk of Coleridge*, ed. W. H. Dircks, Walter Scott Ltd., London, 1894, p. 211).

[2] cf. Tillyard, *Poetry and its Background* (Chatto and Windus, London, 1955), p. 67.

words spoken in the heat of the moment, but with Coleridge's subsequent recollection of the conversation; if he did not mean what he said, he would scarcely repeat his words without qualification at a later juncture. It is important to establish that Coleridge is in earnest in his insistence that 'The Ancient Mariner' ought to have been more like an Arabian Nights' tale, because the remark throws light upon the significance of the exotic setting and the strange imagery of the poem.

COLERIDGE'S CREATIVE PROBLEMS

38. We have already seen, in the case of Virginia Woolf, the difficulties experienced by the sophisticated artist who is not merely aware of the strangeness and mystery of life, but is also intensely aware of her own awareness, so to speak, in satisfactorily objectifying her feelings:

> I have a great and astonishing sense of something there, which is 'it'. It is not exactly beauty that I mean . . . A sense of my own strangeness, walking on the earth is there too: of the infinite oddity of the human position.[1]
> One sees a fin passing far out. What image can I reach to convey what I mean? Really there is none, I think . . . Life is, soberly and accurately, the oddest affair; has in it the essence of reality. I used to feel this as a child—couldn't step across a puddle, once, I remember, for thinking how strange . . .[2]

The primitive mind expresses its sense of the mysterious and divine by means of rituals, myths, taboos, and so on. Virginia Woolf expressed her sense of the mysterious by describing the mystical experience itself, 'the moment of illumination'.

Both Coleridge and Wordsworth were, of course, consciously aware of the mystical experience. The great difference between them lies in the fact that Wordsworth regarded it as a thoroughly normal feature of life, however interesting. It is illuminating to contrast with Mrs. Woolf's emphasis on the sense of strangeness, of 'infinite oddity', which accompanies the mystical experience, such passages of Wordsworth's as:

> Then, sometimes, in that silence, while he hung
> Listening, a gentle shock of mild surprise
> Has carried far into his heart the voice
> Of mountain torrents[3]

[1] and [2] See p. 90.
[3] cf. 'There Was A Boy', ll. 18–21.

or: Thanks to the human heart by which we live,
       Thanks to its tenderness, its joys and fears,
       To me the meanest flower that blows can give
       Thoughts that do often lie too deep for tears.[1]

If we take the imagery employed by the two poets, Wordsworth and Coleridge, in their attempts to express their mystical intuitions or feelings as being in some sense indicative of their respective attitudes towards the mystical experience, it is clear that Coleridge's attitude more closely resembles that of Mrs. Woolf than it does that of Wordsworth. The question arises whether this concomitant sense of strangeness is something inherent in the actual impulse, or is an effect produced by that impulse. It is, of course, possible to assert that Coleridge's 'moments of illumination' were more intense than Wordsworth's, but mere assertion is of little value. It is far more likely that the difference in imagery is the consequence of a difference in emotional—and intellectual—orientation. Wordsworth associated the mystical experience with the influence of natural objects. He inured himself to an attitude of childlike receptiveness and regarded the moments of illumination, when they came, as being an intensification of the pleasure and spiritual benefit which he derived continuously from nature. They did not, therefore, upset his emotional equilibrium. 'Peter Bell', Wordsworth's 'Ancient Mariner', is characteristically a story of repentance brought about by the influence of natural objects; the only spirits in it are those of the mind.

Unlike Wordsworth, Coleridge regarded the mystical experience as deriving from an inner source. In 'The Destiny of Nations' he speaks of the natural world as a symbolic alphabet by means of which we may learn of the existence of God:

> For all that meets the bodily sense I deem
> Symbolical, one mighty alphabet
> For infant minds; and we in this low world
> Placed with our backs to bright Reality,
> That we may learn with young unwounded ken
> The substance from its shadow.[2]

It is, however, an alphabet which he prefers not to employ in his poetry as Wordsworth does. A more accurate description of his attitude towards nature is to be found in *Anima Poetae*:

[1] cf. 'Ode; Intimations of Immortality from Recollections of Early Childhood', ll. 204–7.
[2] See p. 161.

In looking at objects of Nature while I am thinking, as at yonder moon dim-glimmering through the dewy window pane, I seem rather to be seeking, as it were *asking* for, a symbolic language for something within me that always and for ever exists, than observing anything new. Even when that latter is the case, yet still I have always an obscure feeling as if that new phenomenon were the dim awaking of a forgotten or hidden truth of my inner nature. It is still interesting as a word—a symbol.[1]

It is thoroughly characteristic of Coleridge to see natural objects as possible symbols primarily of an *internal* principle. Needless to say, there is no *logical* difficulty in reconciling the views expressed in the two passages above; orthodox Christian theology depends on the recognition of two eternal principles, an inner and an outer. Emotionally, however, the two attitudes are quite distinct, and the difference manifests itself in the respective imagery of Wordsworth's and Coleridge's work. The former, regarding natural objects as forms by which spiritual reality impresses itself upon the mind, feels that he can best express his intuitions of that reality with reference to the same 'alphabet'. Coleridge, on the other hand, rejects Wordsworth's axiom: 'Let Nature be your Teacher.'[2] When he writes, in 'Dejection: An Ode' (1802):

> I may not hope from outward forms to win
> The passion and the life, whose fountains are within,[3]

he is merely expressing a state of mind which has long been habitual. The sense of the infinite is not, in his view, something impressed on the mind 'in a wise passiveness'[4] from outside, but an impulse from the depths of the unconscious. In seeking to express it, therefore, he naturally employs the kind of images with which he associates the impulse, in his case 'transcendental' ones, a symbolic alphabet of figures which do *not* 'meet the bodily sense'. It is enlightening to compare and contrast Coleridge's attitude with that of Blake, who remarks of Wordsworth's title 'Influence of Natural Objects In calling forth and strengthening the Imagination in Boyhood and early Youth': 'Natural Objects always did & now do weaken, deaden & obliterate Imagination in Me. Wordsworth must know that what he Writes Valuable is Not to be found in Nature.'[5]

Coleridge, like Blake, attempts to look *through*, rather than *at*, 'the

---

[1] cf. Baker, op. cit., p. 203.   [2] cf. 'The Tables Turned', l. 16.
[3] cf. stanza III, ll. 45–46 (O.U.P. ed., 1912, vol. I, p. 365).
[4] cf. Wordsworth, 'Expostulation and Reply'. l. 24.
[5] cf. Blake, Annotations to Wordsworth's *Poems* (1815) (cf. Nonesuch Blake (1946), p. 821).

vegetable glass of Nature'. Blake, however, insists on regarding his images as a direct and accurate description of ultimate reality, in which one must believe as one believes in the Trinity or the literalness of Scripture. Coleridge, whilst he obviously feels that this is the proper way to write symbolic poetry, lacks both the mysticism and the *panache* which Blake exhibits in presenting his work as a direct revelation of the divine. Coleridge certainly regards his works of imagination as having an affinity with eternal reality, but, deeply conscious of the fictitious aspect of these works, he regards the relationship as an indirect one. It will be useful at this point to quote the famous passage in chapter XIII of *Biographia Literaria*:

> The IMAGINATION then I consider as either primary, or secondary. The primary IMAGINATION I hold to be the living Power and prime Agent of all human Perception, and as a repetition in the finite mind of the eternal act of creation in the infinite I AM. The secondary Imagination I consider as an echo of the former, co-existing with the conscious will, yet still as identical with the primary in the *kind* of its agency, and differing only in *degree*, and in the *mode* of its operation. It dissolves, diffuses, dissipates, in order to re-create; or where this process is rendered impossible, yet still at all events it struggles to idealize and to unify. It is essentially *vital*, even as all objects (as objects) are essentially fixed and dead.
>
> FANCY, on the contrary, has no other counters to play with, but fixities and definites. The Fancy is indeed no other than a mode of Memory emancipated from the order of time and space; while it is blended with, and modified by that empirical phenomenon of the will, which we express by the word CHOICE. But equally with the ordinary memory, the Fancy must receive all its materials ready made from the law of association.[1]

The concept of the 'secondary imagination' is clearly a rationalization of Coleridge's desire to have his cake and eat it, to dissolve, diffuse, dissipate, and reorganize his material artistically, whilst still expressing eternal reality. The secondary imagination has a foot in both worlds, so to speak, the transcendental and the physical. What is particularly significant about the attitude of mind revealed in the passage above, for our purposes, is the implication that in so far as the imagery of a poem is merely derived from experience, whether or not that experience has been manipulated for artistic purposes, it cannot express eternal reality; one criterion of genuinely symbolic imagery is therefore its non-empirical quality—it must suggest the preternatural or supernatural. In this Coleridge's attitude is much

[1] cf. *Biographia Literaria* (1817) (ed. J. Shawcross, O.U.P., 1907, repr. 1958), vol. I, ch. XIII, p. 202.

like that of Blake: 'Imagination is the Divine Vision not of The World, or of Man, nor from Man as he is a Natural Man, but only as he is a Spiritual Man. Imagination has nothing to do with Memory.'[1]

It will be noted that Coleridge significantly glosses over the fact that the material which the 'secondary imagination' dissolves, diffuses, and dissipates in order to re-create must be derived from experience, no less than the material of fancy.

The Arabian Nights' story which Coleridge describes in connexion with 'The Ancient Mariner' well exemplifies what Coleridge understands by a work of (secondary) imagination. A work of primary imagination would presumably be a direct expression of the supernatural; the fairy story or ballad contains an echo of the supernatural.

Coleridge's views on imagery may briefly be stated as follows; natural objects, 'essentially fixed and dead' of themselves, may be pressed into service as symbols, but since 'in our life alone does Nature live,'[2] the more *objective* the imagery, the more external it is to our 'shaping spirit of Imagination,'[3] the less effectively it echoes the 'something within . . . that always and forever exists'.[4] As we have seen, this view is one which Coleridge shares with Blake: 'Natural Objects always did & now do weaken, deaden & obliterate Imagination in Me. Wordsworth must know that what he Writes Valuable is Not to be found in Nature.' If the artist must inevitably make use of the mere stuff of sensory experience, then it needs to be re-created, associated with the infinite, the divine, qualities which Coleridge finds most in evidence in the mind itself.

The process of giving expression to the sense of the eternal is thus carried on by Coleridge in a thoroughly deliberate fashion. The *naïveté* of his belief in a body of imagery which he continued to regard as an objectively real vehicle of the divine, the imagery of Christianity, was impaired by his theological speculations, with the result that such imagery, with its intellectual associations, made no abiding appeal to him emotionally as a means of expressing the 'something within . . . that always and forever exists', apart from 'peripheral' images which had escaped the theological net—the Virgin Mary, the mark of Cain, the Wandering Jew.

In endeavouring to 'echo' rather than to depict eternal reality, Coleridge naturally gravitates towards traditional images of the un-

---

[1] cf. Blake, Annotations to Wordsworth's *Poems* (1815) (Nonesuch ed., p. 822).
[2] cf. 'Dejection: An Ode', stanza IV.   [3] ibid., stanza VI.
[4] See p. 176.

canny, a compromise between the visions of Blake and the Wordsworthian description of 'dead' objects. The 'invisible inhabitants of this planet', the lamia, the demon-lover, are, so to speak, 'half real', ageless extrusions of the unconscious mind with precisely the subjective validity at which Coleridge aims.

Apart from preternatural imagery, and the supernatural imagery of Christianity, the natural imagery employed by Coleridge consists largely of phenomena which suggest the unbounded—the 'wide wide sea' of 'The Ancient Mariner', the 'caverns measureless to man' of 'Kubla Khan'; the spiritual—the bird, the sun and moon, the wind; the mysterious—mist and cloud, the forest at night, the underground river, &c. The use of exotic and archaic names and images, the ballad metre and archaic diction, serve the same purpose of expressing, and inducing, a feeling for the unknown and mysterious.

Coleridge is too accomplished an artist not to be aware of the value of homely touches to set off the prevailing mood of his work. The return to a more familiar setting at the end of 'The Ancient Mariner' serves to emphasize the strangeness of the mariner's experiences and the abiding strangeness of his lonely destiny. The 'silly buckets on the deck' contrast exquisitely with the gorgeous alien spectacle of the water-snakes on the one hand and the storm on the other. The reassuring nature of the 'sweet sounds' which come from the lips of the dead men is conveyed by comfortingly familiar imagery:

> Sometimes a-dropping from the sky
> I heard the sky-lark sing;
> Sometimes all little birds that are,
> How they seemed to fill the sea and air,
> With their sweet jargoning!

The function of these images in Coleridge's work, however, is very different from that of the homely images of Wordsworth. They do not, so to speak, 'carry the air', but have a contrapuntal role.

Nothing shows the predilection of Coleridge for the odd, the extraordinary, more than the images which he uses to add realism to 'The Ancient Mariner'. The famous description of Lucy:

> A violet by a mossy stone
> Half hidden from the eye!
> —Fair as a star, when only one
> Is shining in the sky

is a triumph of normalcy; much of the strength of the lines derives from their obviousness—or apparent obviousness. Coleridge, even where he endeavours to convince, to produce a realistic effect, endeavours also to surprise, or, what comes to the same thing, to pass on to the reader the details which had particularly appealed to him in his reading. The icebergs are 'as green as emerald'; the sun is 'like God's own head'; the mariner faints with thirst in the midst of a vast expanse of water; he is as incapable of speech as though he had been 'choked with soot', and in order to shout he sucks his own blood; the sun peers through the ribs of the phantom ship like a prisoner through the bars of a dungeon; the souls of the dead *whizz* past the mariner. The point need scarcely be laboured that Coleridge delighted in the exotic and the extraordinary—a point made with relish and abundance of detail in the first chapter of *The Road to Xanadu*—but it is important to emphasize that in employing such images to express his sense of the supernatural he is revealing the fact that he regards the sense of the supernatural as something exotic and extraordinary in itself. We have already seen that the regressive side of Coleridge's nature, 'the native bias of his temperament', impels the ratiocinative side of his mind to devise arguments for the reality of the super-natural. In Russell's words, 'before he begins to philosophize, he already knows the truth'. Nevertheless, however much he was con-vinced intellectually of the transcendental nature of reality, the ratiocinative habit of mind so deeply ingrained in him profoundly influences his imaginative work in three ways.

First, unlike Blake, he has a strong impulsion towards logical coherence and system, which persists even in work which is primarily an attempt to express and communicate a mystical intuition, as in 'The Ancient Mariner'. Despite his brilliant distinction between symbolic writing and allegorical writing, which makes it perfectly clear that he regards suggestion, not exposition, as the proper method of poetry, Keats's famous remark remains substantially true:

. . . *Negative Capability*, that is, when a man is capable of being in uncertainties, mysteries, doubts, without any irritable reaching after fact and reason—Coleridge, for example, would let go by a fine isolated veri-similitude caught from the Penetralium of mystery, from being incapable of remaining content with half-knowledge.[1]

Second, the attitude of mind which accompanies this ingrained habit of rational thinking, of 'directed thought', naturally leads him to regard the powerful promptings of the unconscious, the sense of the eternal, as something abidingly strange, something which

[1] See p. 73.

disturbs his 'normal' outlook. He therefore chooses appropriately strange, non-normal imagery to express such feelings.

Third, Coleridge was convinced that a ratiocinative attitude of mind was the wrong one for a poet, and had an injurious effect upon his imaginative work:

> Well would it have been for me, perhaps, had I never relapsed into the same mental disease; if I had continued to pluck the flower and reap the harvest from the cultivated surface, instead of delving in the unwholesome quicksilver mines of metaphysic lore.[1]

> But now afflictions bow me down to earth;
> Nor care I that they rob me of my mirth;
> But oh! each visitation
> Suspends what nature gave me at my birth,
> My shaping spirit of Imagination.
> For not to think of what I needs must feel,
> But to be still and patient, all I can;
> And haply by abstruse research to steal
> From my own nature all the natural man—
> This was my sole resource, my only plan:
> Till that which suits a part infects the whole,
> And now is almost grown the habit of my soul.[2]

Whilst it is true that this idea of the opposition between imagination and speculation is fully and explicitly developed by Coleridge at a later period, his great imaginative works must to some extent be regarded as the manifestation of a reaction against ratiocinative thought, specifically against philosophical speculation: 'At a very premature age, even before my fifteenth year, I had bewildered myself in metaphysics, and in theological controversy.'[3] One is reminded of the intellectual frustration of Faust:

> Alas! I have explored
> Philosophy, and Law, and Medicine;
> And over deep Divinity have pored,
> Studying with ardent and laborious zeal,
> And here I am at last, a very fool,
> With useless learning cursed,
> No wiser than at first![4]

[1] cf. Introduction to *Biographia Literaria* (1817) (cf. *Coleridge: Poetry and Prose* (1925, repr. 1954), p. 154).
[2] cf. 'Dejection: An Ode' (1802), stanza VI.
[3] cf. Introduction to *Biographia Literaria* (Garrod ed., p. 154).
[4] cf. Goethe, *Faust I* (cf. O.U.P. (World's Classics) ed. (1907, repr. 1955) of John Anster's trans., p. 73).

Like Faust, Coleridge turns to the preternatural

> That from some Spirit I might hear
> Deep truths . . .[1]

The spirit which he conjures up is the shaping spirit of imagination.

The natural consequence is that the imagery which Coleridge chooses to express this non-rational spirit bears the marks of his reaction. If this imagery has a positive quality, giving significant form to feelings which Coleridge regards as emanating from an eternal source, it has also a negative side. Its strangeness, deliberately fostered, expresses Coleridge's rejection of both the 'dead' world of nature and of systematic thought. The fact that systematic thought is in evidence in the work which contains this imagery—in the ethical content of 'The Ancient Mariner', for example—indicates the ineradicable polarity of the human mind; Coleridge could no more dispense with directed thinking than he could be wholly satisfied with it.

'Our literature', wrote Hazlitt, 'is Gothic and grotesque.'[2] The juxtaposition of the two adjectives, though we can still feel their relationship to be more than merely alliterative, is less immediately comprehensible than it was in 1820. The idea of 'the Gothic' can be distinguished from that of 'the grotesque' much more readily today. In the Romantic period the Gothic tale had a double incongruity; it was seen to be incongruous both with 'the natural conditions of organisation', and with the common-sense attitude of mind which we associate with the eighteenth century. In examining, say, the Gothic novel for examples of the grotesque, it is primarily the first kind of incongruity which we tend to have in mind—the physically abnormal, the unnatural. It is, however, important that we should not overlook the second kind of incongruity, the conflict of 'Gothic' art with the standards of the immediate past; the satisfaction which the artist derived from seeing his work as the expression of a revolutionary attitude. In Coleridge's case the standards which are rejected in his poems of the preternatural are not merely those of classicism, but those of an attitude of mind to which he was himself prone and with which he was deeply dissatisfied.

CHRISTABEL

39. Santayana defines the grotesque as 'the half-formed, the per-plexed, and the suggestively monstrous', a phrase which might

[1] ibid., p. 74.   [2] See p. 11.

almost have been coined with 'Christabel' in mind. Coleridge tells
us that in 'Christabel' he hoped to achieve what he had failed to do in
'The Ancient Mariner':

> With this view (i.e. effective representation of the supernatural) I wrote
> the Ancient Mariner, and was preparing, among other poems, the Dark
> Ladie and the Christabel, in which I should have more nearly realised my
> ideal than I had done in my first attempt.[1]

His retort to Mrs. Barbauld's criticism of 'The Ancient Mariner'[2] is an
indication of the nature of that ideal; the ineffable, the endlessly
suggestive, imagery which should proliferate in the mind of the reader
and defy rational analysis. It is, I think, essential to a proper understanding of 'Christabel' to bear in mind Coleridge's criticism of 'The
Ancient Mariner' on the grounds that there was too obvious an
'obtrusion of the moral sentiment'. The consequence is that
'Christabel', whilst it is a powerful expression of Coleridge's sense of
the supernatural, has its integrity as an 'echo' of the eternally real
impaired to some extent by the poet's determination to eschew
didacticism. He is convinced that the echo will be all the more effective if it is muffled and mysterious.

There is a shift of emphasis. 'The Ancient Mariner' and 'Christabel'
have, of course, a great deal in common. Both belong to the kind of art
which has been described above as regressive-negative.[3] But whereas
in the former work Coleridge is primarily concerned with 'rendering
reality intelligible',[4] in the latter he attempts to disturb the reader
rather than to enlighten him.[5]

It is because of Coleridge's determination that 'Christabel' shall
be strange, bewildering, and nebulously significant that it is a less
positive expression of the supernatural than 'The Ancient Mariner',
sophisticated though the latter poem undoubtedly is in comparison
with a real myth; it leads him to concentrate upon the communication of the uncanny rather than of truth, upon mystery rather than

---

[1] cf. *Biographia Literaria*, ch. XIV (*On the Poetical Tenets and Poetry of
Wordsworth*).

[2] See p. 173.   [3] See p. 88 (§25).   [4] See note 1, p. 168.

[5] One might compare Coleridge's attempt, in 'Christabel', to convey a
mood rather than a 'message' with Shelley's remarks in the Preface to
'Prometheus Unbound': 'Didactic poetry is my abhorrence . . . My purpose
has hitherto been simply to familiarise the highly refined imagination of the
more select classes of poetical readers with beautiful idealisms of moral
excellence, &c.' (cf. O.U.P. ed. of *Shelley's Works* (1907, repr. 1943), p. 203).
It is perhaps ironic that Shelley greatly admired 'The Ancient Mariner'.

myth. The true visionary is like a man baldly relating a dream. He is concerned with the significance of his experience, not with its strangeness.[1] On balance, it may be said that in 'The Ancient Mariner', whilst Coleridge clearly regards both aspects of his imagery as important, its significance matters to him more than its mystery; its truth as a picture of reality is the prime consideration, its uncanniness is secondary.

In 'Christabel', for Coleridge, the most significant thing about the imagery and the incidents is their strangeness, their divergence from the 'superficial' norm of common sense and the matter-of-fact, rather than what Santayana calls 'inward possibility'. The very fact that in the second part of the poem Coleridge *does* begin to develop the 'inward possibility' of the imagery and the situation seems to me to bear out rather than to contradict this view, because it is precisely at the juncture where the action of the narrative begins to 'come into focus', with the ousting of Christabel from her father's affections by Geraldine, that the poem is broken off.

The term grotesque, as we have seen, leads us to expect an immediacy of impact—in particular, the physically monstrous—which is not characteristic of 'Christabel'. In part, the emotional enervation of the 'Gothic', its loss of the power and freshness which it had in the late eighteenth century, accounts for this lack of impact. Fundamentally, however, the grotesqueness of the poem does not lie in the physically strange—the beautiful witch with the withered bosom is, of course, one example of this—so much as in the psychologically strange. If we take Santayana's phrase 'the suggestively monstrous' as a criterion of the grotesque, it may be said that whereas we tend to put the emphasis on 'monstrous', with regard to 'Christabel' the important word is 'suggestively'. One might perhaps clarify this point by reference to two of Kafka's narratives. In *The Metamorphosis* (*Die Verwandlung*), a commercial traveller turns into a gigantic cockroach; the physically monstrous plays an important part in the story. *The Trial* (*Das Urteil*), in which a man is arrested, tried, and sentenced without the precise nature of his offence ever coming to light, is grotesque in a different way, at least in so far as the method is concerned. It takes the reader into a world where nothing is certain, where 'all melts under our feet'. The grotesqueness of 'Christabel', particularly in the first part of the poem, is chiefly of this latter kind.

The central incident of Part One, Geraldine's lying with Christabel,

[1] See pp. 81, 160.

darkly suggests some kind of temptation. We are told that Geraldine
has her will with Christabel for one hour:

> Off, woman, off! this hour is mine—
> Though thou her guardian spirit be,
> Off, woman, off! 'tis given to me.[1]

Christabel is put into a trance in which she has fearful dreams:

> With open eyes (ah woe is me!)
> Asleep, and dreaming fearfully,
> Fearfully dreaming, yet, I wis,
> Dreaming that alone which is—
> O sorrow and shame! Can this be she,
> The lady who knelt at the old oak tree?[2]

The attempt to corrupt Christabel's innocence, presumably through
the medium of these wild dreams, is unsuccessful:

> A star hath set, a star hath risen,
> O Geraldine! since arms of thine
> Have been the lovely lady's prison.
> O Geraldine! one hour was thine—
> Thou hadst thy will! By tairn and rill,
> The night-birds all that hour were still.
> But now they are jubilant anew[3]

Christabel relaxes, 'gathers herself from out her trance', and is
apparently in no way the worse for her ordeal except that she is placed
under a spell which prevents her from revealing what she now knows
about Geraldine, who goes on in Part Two to harm Christabel in
another way by ousting her from her father's affections.

Ernest Hartley Coleridge describes the assault on Christabel's
innocence as follows:

Once again the demon is half quelled by the light, and shudders[4] even

---

[1] cf. 'Christabel', part I, ll. 211–13.
[2] ibid., Conclusion to part I, ll. 292–7.
[3] ibid., ll. 301–8.
[4] The actual lines: Then drawing in her breath aloud,
                Like one that shuddered, she unbound
                The cincture from beneath her breast
(I. 247–9), are a particularly brilliant example of association. The deep
breath Geraldine takes *in order to unfasten* the tight cincture—a touch of
realism—suggests an agonized gasp or shudder, which might perhaps be
referred to her horror of the brand she is about to reveal rather than to fear
of the lamplight.

as she triumphs. But her hour is come, and she will leave with the innocent the mark of guilt and shame with which some higher spirit of evil has signed and sealed her bosom and half her side. It is the sacrament of Hell, the unholy communion of the mystery of sin.[1]

It would seem more likely, perhaps, that Geraldine's mark of shame is a species of punishment set on her by 'some higher spirit' of justice and goodness rather than of evil; in any case, such a mark implies that she is something more complex than a mere 'demon'. This may also be suggested by her apparent misgivings about harming Christabel:

> Yet Geraldine nor speaks nor stirs;
> Ah! what a stricken look was hers!
> Deep from within she seems half-way
> To lift some weight with sick assay,
> And eyes the maid and seeks delay
> Then suddenly, as one defied,
> Collects herself in scorn and pride,
> And lay down at the maiden's side.[2]

It is, of course, possible that this hesitation is due not to the pangs of conscience but to the restraining influence of Christabel's guardian spirit or dead mother. The uncertainty is of a piece with the vagueness of the whole, which incurred such adverse criticism as the following:

The manuscript runs thus, or nearly thus:—
> Behold her bosom and half her side,
> Hidden, deformed and pale of hue.[3]

This [latter] line is necessary to make common sense of the first and second part. 'It is the key stone that makes up the arch.' For that reason Mr Coleridge left it out. Now this is a greater psychological curiosity than even the fragment of Kubla Khan . . .

There is something disgusting at the bottom of his subject which is but ill glossed over by a veil of Della Cruscan sentiment and fine writing, like moonbeams playing on a charnel house, or flowers strewed on a dead body.[4]

[1] cf. E. H. Coleridge, Facsimile ed. of 'Christabel' (Frowde, London, 1907), p. 8.
[2] cf. 'Christabel', I. ll. 255–62.
[3] The omitted line (between ll. 252 and 253) runs:
> 'Are lean and old and foul of hue.'
(cf. O.U.P. (E. H. Coleridge) ed. (1912), p. 224.)
[4] cf. The Examiner, 2 June 1816 (quoted E. H. Coleridge, Facsimile ed. of 'Christabel', pp. 75–76).

Conceivably the reviewer's insistence that the omitted line makes 'common sense' of the poem is due to his subscribing to a widespread idea that Geraldine is, in fact, a man in disguise.[1]

E. H. Coleridge ably defends the omission:

Both editor and reviewer must have known perfectly well that the omission of the line had nothing whatever to do with delicacy or indelicacy, and that its retention would have removed the remotest possibility of there being 'anything disgusting at the bottom of the subject'. It was left out on the principle of '*omne ignotum pro* MYSTERIO'. Hence the effect of this passage on Shelley. 'Towards midnight on the 18th of July [1816] Byron recited the lines in *Christabel* about the lady's breast; when Shelley suddenly started up, shrieked and fled from the room. He had seen a vision of a woman with eyes instead of nipples.' (*Shelley* by J. A. Symonds, 1878, pp. 90, 91.)[2]

It is obvious that the 'disgust' of the reviewer was not occasioned by this line alone, but by the morbidness of the whole. The point he makes, however, regarding the 'psychological curiosity' of the omission, and E. H. Coleridge's defence of the omission as a deliberate and justifiable piece of 'negative suggestion', are both highly relevant to the general thesis that in contrast to the naïve myth, to the kind of work which has been termed regressive-positive, Christabel is not so much an 'explanation' of the mysterious—as, say, the figure of the witch was originally developed to 'explain' various phenomena (night fears, misfortunes, &c.)—as it is an evocation of the mysterious, a reaction against the philosophy which seeks to 'conquer all mysteries by rule and line.'[3]

In the poem as we have it[4] Christabel is predominantly a passive figure, wronged first by Geraldine and then by her father, and seems involuntarily destined for a great deal of suffering. It is perhaps in keeping with the strangeness of the poem that Coleridge later remarked that whilst writing 'Christabel' he had Crashaw's lines on

---

[1] cf. E. H. Coleridge, Facsimile ed., for Rossetti's suggestion that it was because of this rumour that Coleridge altered l. 254 from 'And she is to sleep with Christabel' to : 'O shield her! shield sweet Christabel!'

[2] ibid., p. 76.

[3] cf. Keats, 'Lamia', l. 235.

[4] Although the poem consists of only 677 lines, Coleridge speaks of it as running to 1,300 lines in a letter to Davy, the Bristol printer, in October 1800. Chambers surmises that Coleridge may have composed 1,300 lines without writing them down (cf. E. K. Chambers, *Samuel Taylor Coleridge: A Biographical Study*, O.U.P., 1938, pp. 134–7).

St. Theresa's thirst for martyrdom continually in mind:

> Since 'tis not to be had at home
> She'll travel to a martyrdom.
> No home for hers confesses she
> But where she may a martyr be.
>   She'll to the Moors; and trade with them
> For this unvalued diadem:
> She'll offer them her dearest breath,
> With Christ's name in't, in change for death:
> She'll bargain with them, and will give
> Them God, teach them how to live
> In Him; or, if they this deny,
> For Him she'll teach them how to die.
> So shall she leave amongst them sown
> Her Lord's blood, or at least her own.
>   Farewell then, all the World adieu;
> Teresa is no more for you.
> Farewell, all pleasures, sports, and joys
> (Never till now esteemèd toys).
> Farewell, whatever dear may be,
> Mother's arms or father's knee:
> Farewell house, and farewell home!
> She's for the Moors, and martyrdom.

These verses were ever present to my mind whilst writing the second part of Christabel; if, indeed, by some subtle process of the mind they did not suggest the first thought of the whole poem.[1]

There is nothing of St. Teresa's zeal for suffering in Coleridge's poem; Christabel is not a martyr but a victim. Her situation is, in fact, the reverse of Teresa's as described by Crashaw:

> Since 'tis not to be found at home
> She'll *travel* to a martyrdom.

So far as the two existing parts of 'Christabel' are concerned, any influence from Crashaw's poem could scarcely amount to more than the general idea of innocence victimized by evil. Moreover, whereas Teresa's role is an active one, not only is Christabel a passive figure, but even as such she is not the true centre of human interest until late in Part Two. Geraldine, who, as has been remarked, is far more than a mere demon in Part One, becomes a still more complex figure

---

[1] cf. Thomas Allsop (ed.), *Letters, Conversations, and Recollections of S. T. Coleridge* (Moxon and Co., London, 1836), I, pp. 194–6.

as the daughter of Sir Leoline's old friend and enemy; the motives for her mysterious wickedness become potentially more complicated. Only with Geraldine's reduction to a simple creature of evil, a mere lamia,[1] and Christabel's fall from favour is there a shift of human interest towards the heroine of the poem, and even then our attention is diverted to some extent by curiosity regarding the fate of Sir Leoline.

Whilst the transformation of Geraldine into a mere monster undoubtedly clears the ground for Coleridge to develop the figure of Christabel more fully, and helps to establish the lines of the narrative, it damages the 'suggestively monstrous' quality of the work. The beautiful creature blasted with the mark of guilt and shame, bent on some mysteriously evil purpose and hesitating even as she makes her attempt on Christabel's virtue, is the keystone of the mystery; with her transformation into a lamia with 'shrunken serpent eyes' we emerge from the shadows into a world of comparative black and white.

E. H. Coleridge comments on the transformation as follows: 'The half mythical, half pathological conception of the *witch* Geraldine as a human snake denotes a "transition to another kind", a development of the idea. What suggested or determined this departure?'[2]

If anything is to be learned from Coleridge's reference to the influence of Crashaw's poem on St. Teresa on 'Christabel', it is that, as the title implies, he intended Christabel to be the central figure of the work. To this end it was obviously necessary that the figure of Geraldine, dominating the poem because of her hold on the reader's curiosity, should be brought more into focus or dismissed from the story altogether. Coleridge adopts the former and clearly preferable alternative. The significant thing is that, as the poem thus comes into perspective, it comes to an end. The reason, surely, was that Coleridge saw 'the obtrusion of the moral sentiment', the development of a story with a point to it, to have become inevitable. In actual fact such an outcome was inevitable from the beginning, given Coleridge's

---

[1] The first identification of Geraldine with the serpent occurs in Bracy's account of his dream (part 2, ll. 524 ff.). There is, however, an earlier introduction of the human-serpent motif in Sir Leoline's words:

> . . . let the recreant traitors seek
> My tourney-court—that there and then
> I may dislodge their reptile souls
> From the bodies and forms of men.

(Part 2, ll. 440-3.)

[2] cf. E. H. Coleridge, Facsimile ed. of 'Christabel', pp. 28-29.

habit of mind: '. . . I can assert, upon my long and intimate knowledge of Coleridge's mind, that logic the most severe was as inalienable from his modes of thinking as grammar from his language.'[1]

Coleridge was an incorrigible interpreter of his own dark symbols, 'incapable of remaining content with half-knowledge', as Keats put it. Whereas in 'The Ancient Mariner', however, the moral is actually drawn, 'Christabel' is abandoned on the point of becoming a story with a moral, perhaps a very great one, like the former poem. The fact that Christabel is a fragment is at once evidence that Coleridge lacked the 'negative capability' of such a writer as Blake, and an indication that, in attempting to resist his natural tendency to intellectualize his 'intimations of immortality', he inhibited his creative powers.

The natural pattern of Coleridge's imaginative work is the expression of his sense of the eternally real in symbolic fashion, followed by (or accompanied by, for the two processes are intimately connected) an interpretative development of that symbolism. The fact that 'Christabel' is a fragment is equally evidence of Coleridge's inability to continue the narrative in the same vein of subterranean suggestion, and of his reluctance to 'let in daylight' through the inevitable didactic development.

In *Table Talk*, Coleridge refers to the unfinished state of 'Christabel' as follows:

> The reason of my not finishing Christabel is not, that I don't know how to do it—for I have, as I always had, the whole plan entire from beginning to end in my mind; but I fear I could not carry on with equal success the execution of the idea, an extremely subtle and difficult one. . . .[2]

Two comments may be made: first, that Coleridge is clearly speaking the truth in attributing his abandonment of the poem to lack of energy or enthusiasm rather than to lack of a plan; second, that this lack of enthusiasm largely derived from the fact that he had already with considerable success completed that part of the work which really interested him, in his endeavour to avoid merely rationalistic 'picture-language' poetry.

'KUBLA KHAN'

40. 'Kubla Khan', composed in a darkly conscious state of mind similar to that in which, according to Tatham,[3] Blake composed a

[1] cf. De Quincey, *Reminiscences of the English Lake Poets* (Everyman's Library ed., 1907, repr. 1911, p. 15).
[2] cf. *Table Talk* (1822–1834) (W. H. Dircks ed.).   [3] See note 3, p. 77.

considerable part of his prophetic books, is a work apart, because of
the difficulty of assessing the role of deliberate purpose in the poem.
In *The Sacred River*, Baker comments as follows upon T. S.
Eliot's objection to the poem's lack of 'organization':

> Coleridge himself thought the poem merely 'a psychological curiosity'
> and Eliot, speaking of its 'exaggerated repute', complains that
> 'the imagery of that fragment, certainly, whatever its origin in Cole-
> ridge's reading, sank to the depths of Coleridge's feeling, was saturated,
> transformed there—'those are pearls that were his eyes'—and brought up
> into daylight again. But it is not *used*: the poem has not been written . . .
> Organization is necessary as well as "inspiration".'
> Actually, however, although the poem may not measure up to Eliot's
> standards, there is more organization to it, albeit the organization of a
> dream or the logic of the imagination, than a cursory examination would
> suggest.
> 'The sunny dome' that the poet would create is the heaven of art . . .
> The sunny dome has caves of ice inside; just so, Keats's urn is a 'cold
> pastoral', for the significant moment of art is eternally frozen. The view of
> the poet's power here expressed is at the opposite pole to the mechanistic
> view . . .[1]

Lowes, in a long note on the metre of the poem, maintains that
the labour involved earlier in perfecting the ballad metre had so impressed its rhythms upon Coleridge's mind that he had acquired a
kind of mechanical virtuosity:

> When, then, images like those upon whose rhythmical expression
> Coleridge had expended infinite time and pains poured suddenly up in the
> unconsciousness of sleep, is it incredible that a craftsmanship which had
> itself become through rigorous discipline more than half unconscious,
> should respond, in a glorious *tour de force*, to a familiar stimulus?[2]

The idea is a perfectly credible one; something of the kind must
have happened. Indeed, with some qualification, the idea may surely
be applied to the poem in broader fashion.

We have already seen that problems normally requiring much
conscious effort may be solved in sleep:

> There is no doubt in my mind that all the activities ordinarily taking
> place in consciousness can also run their course in the unconscious. There
> are many examples of an intellectual problem attaining no solution during
> the waking state, but being solved in a dream.[3]

[1] cf. Baker, op. cit., pp. 181–2.
[2] cf. Lowes, op. cit., pp. 598–9 (note 11 to ch. XX).   [3] See pp. 76–77.

It is as well to bear in mind, in view of Lowes's phrase 'the unconsciousness of sleep', that in dreaming we are, in fact, in a 'darkly conscious' state; otherwise the dream could not be experienced. This, clearly, was Coleridge's state of mind:

> The Author continued for about three hours in a profound sleep, at least of the external senses, during which time he has the most vivid confidence, that he could not have composed less than from two to three hundred lines; if that indeed can be called composition in which all the images rose up before him as *things*, with a parallel production of the correspondent expressions, without any sensation or consciousness of effort.[1]

It is pertinent to ask what was the nature of Coleridge's 'intellectual problem', and whether it was actually solved in a darkly conscious state.

Coleridge was convinced that literature should make its effects by suggestion, by employing symbols of a deeply emotive rather than of an intellectual significance:

> . . . Coleridge so valued the quality of suggestion of infinite and unexplored depths that he thought:
> 'the grandest effects of poetry are where the imagination is called forth, not to produce a distinct form, but a strong working of the mind . . .; the result being what the poet wishes to impress, namely, the substitution of a sublime feeling of the unimaginable for a mere image'.[2]

For one for whom 'logic the most severe was as inalienable from his modes of thinking as grammar from his language' to produce work of this kind wholly deliberately necessarily required immense self-discipline. To Coleridge, an exciting image presented itself as a potential metaphor or simile. It was rapidly assimilated to an idea; there was an all but inevitable 'obtrusion of the moral sentiment'.

Coleridge's problem, then, lay in the composition of a poem which should produce in the reader 'a strong working of the mind' without conveying any exact or rational meaning, to shield the creation of an image from his habit of interpretation.

However extraordinary the manner in which 'Kubla Khan' was

---

[1] cf. Introduction to 'Kubla Khan' (1816) (E. H. Coleridge ed. (O.U.P., 1912), vol. I, pp. 295 ff.).

[2] cf. Baker, op. cit., p. 198. The quotation is from Lecture VII of Coleridge's lectures on Shakespeare and Milton, 1811–12 (cf. *Lectures and Notes on Shakespeare and Other English Poets*, ed. T. Ashe, Bell and Sons, London, 1888, p. 91).

composed, the poem is clearly consistent with the above artistic aim. The strange imagery, the mysterious transitions, come as close to communicating that 'sublime feeling of the unimaginable' which frequently accompanies a dream as anything in literature. It is all too easy to ignore the evidence of artistic control—the metre, the diction, the judgement apparent in the selection of images. The poem cannot, however, seriously be regarded as possessing only formal coherence. What is obviously true of the metre and diction is true also of the choice and juxtaposition of images; they are subordinated to the significance of the whole. The crucial point is the kind of significance which Coleridge desired to achieve; the mysteriousness of the poem, the uncertainty of interpretation, cannot merely be attributed to lack of art. It must be borne in mind that, whether in a darkly conscious state or not, Coleridge was *composing*, composing in accordance with a deeply considered view of literature. 'Kubla Khan' is thus treacherous ground for the amateur psychologist who chooses to regard it as an unpremeditated outpouring of images in 'free association'. Exclusion, selection, discrimination, mental processes normally occurring in consciousness and associated with deliberate purpose, are clearly at work here by the species of transference referred to above.

So much requires to be said as a corrective to the idea that the poem is lacking in 'organization'. What it really lacks is explicitness, an omission which, aesthetically speaking, no one could deplore. In 'Kubla Khan', Coleridge has produced, for one short flight, a kind of poetry which answers to almost all his theoretical requirements; curiously, the 'submerged' subject of the poem—I do not mean to imply that the poem is an allegory—is the nature and interaction of those requirements.

No man was ever yet a great poet, without being at the same time a profound philosopher . . . In Shakespeare's *poems* the creative power and the intellectual energy wrestle as in a war embrace. Each in its excess of strength seems to threaten the extinction of the other.[1]

These words, written with Shakespeare's poems in mind, apply to no poetry more than to that of Coleridge. It is, however, vital to an understanding of Coleridge's views to note how he continues the above passage:

What then shall we say? even this; that Shakespeare, no mere child of

[1] cf. *Biographia Literaria* (1817), ch. XV (cf. O.U.P. ed. (1958), vol. II, p. 19).

nature; no automaton of genius; no passive, vehicle of inspiration possessed by the spirit, not possessing it; first studied patiently, meditated deeply, understood minutely, *till knowledge, become habitual and intuitive, wedded itself to his habitual feelings*, and at length gave birth to that stupendous power, by which he stands alone . . .[1]

Coleridge insists, then, that the fruits of conscious thought enter great poetry indirectly, so to speak, through their effect upon the poet's feelings, without breaking its flow or lowering its emotional warmth by open didacticism, systematic argument, and so on.

In 'Kubla Khan' the imagery comes close to Coleridge's ideal of the 'symbol', which should not merely be a thought expressed in picture-language, but should have an autonomous quality, existing in its own right; it retains its suggestiveness in the face of all the interpretations to which it has been subjected, and clearly cannot be 'exhausted' by an interpretation in terms of the creative process. However, some attempt may be made to demonstrate the coherence of the imagery on the latter level.

Briefly, the first section of the poem suggests the planning of a work of art. The artist (Kubla Khan) decides upon the nature of his work, its situation, and its setting ('so (i.e. 'therefore') twice five miles of fertile ground/With walls and towers were girdled round').

The second section, dealing with the source of the sacred river and its sudden, discontinuous emergences, may reasonably be regarded as symbolizing the abrupt, wayward nature of poetic genius, inspiration. In *Biographia Literaria*, Coleridge tells us that without 'depth, and energy of thought', poetic genius 'would give promises only of transitory flashes and a meteoric power'.[2] In Shakespeare's poems these two forces conflict, but are reconciled in the drama when the knowledge gained by conscious thought has become 'habitual and intuitive':

. . . like two rapid streams, that, at their first meeting within narrow and rocky banks, mutually strive to repel each other and intermix reluctantly and in tumult; but soon finding a wider channel and more yielding shores blend, and dilate, and flow on in one current and with one voice.[3]

---

[1] ibid., pp. 19–20. The italics are mine. (cf. Wordsworth's Preface to the Lyrical Ballads: 'Not that I always began to write with a distinct purpose formally conceived; but habits of meditation have, I trust, so prompted and regulated my feelings, that my descriptions of such objects as strongly excite those feelings, will be found to carry along with them a *purpose*, &c.).
[2] cf. *Biographia Literaria*, ch. XV (O.U.P. ed. (1958), vol. II, p. 19).
[3] ibid.

One might tentatively suggest that the lines:

> And 'mid this tumult Kubla heard from far
> Ancestral voices prophesying war!

might be construed as a reference to the conflict described above: 'In Shakespeare's *poems* the creative power and the intellectual energy wrestle as in a war embrace.'[1]

At the end of the section we hear of the 'caves of ice' in the pleasure dome; I take this as a representation of Coleridge's ideal of a work of literature with a 'submerged' intellectual content, knowledge which has become habitual and intuitive.

It is surely significant that between the prophecy of war, the suggestion of conflict between the two powers, conscious and unconscious, and the final image of

> A sunny pleasure-dome with caves of ice!

occur lines suggesting the reconciliation of the two which Coleridge found in the greatest art, specifically in Shakespeare's drama:

> The shadow of the dome of pleasure
> Floated midway on the waves;
> Where was heard the mingled measure
> From the fountain and the caves.

The final section introduces a third factor in successful composition, on a more personal level; genius and the intuitive influence of profound thought are the necessary equipment of the great poet, but without *joy*, that delight in the universe and in poetic creation of which Coleridge laments the loss in 'Dejection; An Ode', the poet can produce nothing. The final image of himself as a man possessed clearly conveys Coleridge's conviction that, however much it may be influenced by the absorption of ideas arrived at by profound meditation, great poetry is, to employ Wordsworth's great phrase, 'the spontaneous overflow of powerful feelings'. Of the appositeness of this phrase to 'Kubla Khan' there can be no doubt, but equally, whether one considers the poem in terms of its form or of its content, it would be mistaken to deny its internal coherence or to regard it as a fragment, in spite of Coleridge's own assertion that he 'could not have composed less than from two to three hundred lines' whilst he was asleep.

[1] ibid.

CONCLUDING REMARKS

41. The above examination of one of the levels of significance of 'Kubla Khan' does not take into account the chief function of poetic symbolism as seen by Coleridge, that of expressing—and conveying—the poet's sense of the eternal. A 'work of secondary imagination', however much it 'dissolves, diffuses, dissipates, in order to re-create', is an echo, at one remove, of 'the eternal act of creation in the infinite I AM'. The poem thus symbolizes at a deeper level 'the eternal act of creation'.

Here, as in his other poems of the imagination, Coleridge selects exotic, bizarre, and elusive imagery to suggest that 'something within me that always and for ever exists'.[1] His 'Abyssinian maid', as a source of inspiration, stands in contrast to Wordsworth's homely 'Highland lass', as the Ancient Mariner, Geraldine, Kubla Khan stand in contrast to Peter Bell, Goody Blake, Michael, &c.; the contrasting lists of imagery may be extended much further, of course, to illustrate the same point, that for Coleridge, unlike Wordsworth, the expression of the eternally real through symbolism involved a rejection or 're-creation' of the world immediately present to the senses.

In the case of the visionary, whose symbolism, however contrary to 'the natural conditions of organisation', does not so much defy or run deliberately counter to those conditions as ignore them, grotesqueness is 'accidental'; to regard such symbolism as grotesque is to be out of sympathy with the writer.

Coleridge, on the other hand, clearly intends us to feel the strangeness of his poems, the conflict between their imagery and atmosphere and the physical world, the deliberate incongruity which we have seen to be a fundamental feature of grotesque art. Nevertheless, though we are clearly in the territory of the grotesque in these poems, grotesque imagery of the most palpable kind—physical deformity, for example—is little in evidence.

In part, the absence of the 'shock effect' we look for in grotesque art is due to time and change, as we remarked in the case of 'Gothic' imagery. Thus the exotic imagery of 'The Ancient Mariner' no longer has the same impact on the better-informed reader of today. We have supped full of wonders. The green icebergs, the growling pack-ice, the raging thirst of the mariner surrounded by water, even the iridescent sea and the terrific speed of the vessel which makes the

[1] See p. 176.

mariner faint, all have extraneous 'everyday' associations for the modern reader—the *Titanic*, perhaps, Shackleton and Scott, or the latest Polar expedition; accounts of the survivors of torpedoed vessels, descriptions of luminous plankton, reports of the effects of supersonic speeds on the human body, &c. 'Abyssinian' is a geographical term, less homely in its associations than 'Highland', perhaps, but no longer suggesting the infinitely remote and mysterious. The point need not be laboured.

In part, too, the effect of grotesqueness in these poems is softened by Coleridge's evocation of traditional rather than novel images of the preternatural; one perceives in these images and in the narrative tone an affinity with the ballad and the folk-tale. Kayser insists that the imagery of the folk-tale cannot be termed grotesque, isolated as it is from the world of every day,[1] and whilst this assertion is too sweeping to be accepted in its entirety, it is obviously true that we tolerate such 'isolated' imagery, however extravagant, more readily than, say, Kafka's juxtaposition of the unnatural and the natural.

Above all we must recognize, however, that strangeness, incongruity with the physical order, is not all that Coleridge intends his imagery to suggest. The function of his images is not the anarchic one of surrealistic inventions, symptoms of spiritual claustrophobia; whilst they can only suggest to us something of the nature of the eternal indirectly, in doing so they acquire a degree of positive significance. They are, so to speak, the shapes produced by the spiritual in its attempts to materialize itself through the none too tractable ectoplasm of physical objects and events—at once a distortion of the latter, the ephemeral world of the senses, and a distorted representation of the nature of the real, 'the infinite I AM'. It is the latter aspect of his imagery with which Coleridge is primarily concerned, its 'inward possibility': 'We call these (suggestively monstrous) inventions comic and grotesque when we are considering their divergence from the natural rather than their inward possibility.'[2]

If the incongruity of Coleridge's imagery with 'the natural conditions of organisation' continually produces an effect of strangeness and often of grotesqueness—the spectre-bark, the witch with the withered breast, the woman wailing for her demon-lover—Coleridge's chief concern is nevertheless not how far he can deviate from the natural, but how closely he can approximate to, and arouse in his reader some awareness of, supernatural reality.

[1] See p. 64.   [2] See p. 16.

G.E.L.—O

NOTES TO CHAPTER 7

(i) In my remarks on 'Kubla Khan' I have emphasized that the poem must be regarded primarily as a composition, not as an outpouring of disorganized fragments. This is in agreement with the remarks about the effects of opium made by Miss Elisabeth Schneider in *Coleridge, Opium and Kubla Khan* (University of Chicago Press, 1953). My use of the phrase 'darkly conscious' to describe Coleridge's probable state of mind during the composition of the poem is intended to describe much the same condition of mind as that suggested by Miss Schneider:

> Coleridge may have been in a sort of 'reverie' . . . perhaps a somewhat deeper reverie than that of a reader or spectator enthralled by a novel or play, as he described the state of 'dramatic illusion'. No doubt he had been taking opium; perhaps, too, the euphoric effect of opium rendered his process of composition more nearly effortless than usual.[1]

I have compared this 'reverie' of Coleridge's to the state of mind in which Blake was accustomed to compose during the night. It may well be that the effect of opium on the poem was the indirect one of deepening the sleep to which Coleridge refers in his introduction of 1816 and adding to the mildly comatose mood in which he composed. The details of the brief 'alternative' account of the composition of the poem 'in a sort of Reverie brought on by two grains of Opium, taken to check a dysentery'[2] are similar, though the 'profound sleep' of the 1816 introduction is not mentioned in it.

It is one thing to minimize the effects of opium and sleep upon the process of composition, in opposition to the more extreme views of 'Kubla Khan' as an opium dream; it is another thing to dismiss Coleridge's assertions that the poem was written in an unusual state of mind altogether, as irrelevant to the criticism of the poem, as Mr. House does: 'Coleridge played, out of modesty, straight into the hands of critics'.[3]

Like House, I regard 'Kubla Khan' as a poem dealing with the problems of artistic creation, though the suggested interpretation given above differs considerably from his. The chief point of difference

[1] cf. Schneider, op. cit., p. 90.

[2] In a note appended to a MS. version of 'Kubla Khan', to which attention was first drawn by Miss A. Snyder (*Times Lit. Supp.*, 2 Aug. 1934, p. 541). cf. Schneider, op. cit., pp. 24–25.

[3] cf. Humphry House, *Coleridge: The Clark Lectures 1951–52* (Rupert Hart-Davis, London, 1953), p. 114.

is that, whereas House regards the poem as being 'a poem about the act of poetic creation',[1] I have been concerned to argue that in the first part of the poem at least Coleridge has gone far towards realizing his aim of producing a poem in which the symbols have an autonomous quality and cannot be 'exhausted' by a consistent interpretation on any one level.

(ii) Miss Schneider refers to Coleridge's distinction between symbolism and allegory (p. 257), but does not regard it, as I do, as central to an understanding of Coleridge's work. In criticizing Mr. Wilson Knight's interpretation of 'Kubla Khan', she observes: '. . . his habit was to expound his interior meanings outright. Often enough he conferred upon images of nature some deep significance, but he regularly made that explicit.'[2] Whilst this was undeniably Coleridge's habit, it was one which he was much concerned to rid himself of: the great problem for Coleridge as a poet was to communicate to the reader a regressive mood, to suggest the supernatural, without the fertilizing suggestiveness of his symbols becoming too explicit and turning into the bald statements of moral allegory.

It is with this view of Coleridge's work in mind that I understand his remark to Mrs. Barbauld about 'The Ancient Mariner' to mean that the poem, 'a work of . . . pure imagination', should have the suggestive qualities of a myth or an ancient ballad, not the effect of a cut and dried tract. House insists that since Coleridge did not explicitly distinguish between symbolism and allegory until much later, the distinction has no bearing on the poem:

It is tempting to use Coleridge's later distinctions between allegory and symbol in interpreting 'The Ancient Mariner'; but they had not been expressed in 1797–8. In fact, we may be misled if we start the critique of the 'Mariner' and 'Kubla Khan' with this disjunction of allegory from symbol in mind. For all allegory involves symbolism, and in proportion as symbolism becomes developed and coherent it tends towards allegory.[3]

House goes on to criticize Mr. Robert Penn Warren's detailed analysis of 'The Ancient Mariner'[4] on the grounds that his supposedly symbolical interpretation is, in fact, an allegorical one. What House says about symbolism tending towards allegory is certainly

[1] ibid., p. 115.
[2] cf. Schneider, op. cit., p. 254.
[3] cf. House, op. cit., p. 93.
[4] cf. *The Rime of The Ancient Mariner* . . . with an essay by Robert Penn Warren (Reynal and Hitchcock, New York, 1946).

true; it was precisely this difficulty with which Coleridge was concerned. I have tried to show, with reference to Coleridge's earlier work, that the distinction between symbolism and allegory, far from being a mere critical subtlety elaborated by Coleridge after his greatest work had been created, has its roots deep in his personality, and plays an essential role in determining the development of 'The Ancient Mariner', 'Christabel', and 'Kubla Khan'.[1]

[1] If Coleridge's own account of his speculations at Cambridge in *Biographia Literaria* is accepted, the distinction was already taking shape in his mind at that time, and is implicit in his rejection of 'an amphibious something, made up, half of image, and half of abstract meaning'. cf. *Biographia Literaria* (O.U.P. ed., vol. I, ch. I, p. 15).

8

DICKENS: A CIRCLE OF STAGE FIRE

'CELESTIAL CARICATURES'

42. Alice Meynell says of Dickens:

> . . . his public was as present to him as an actor's audience is to the actor, and I cannot think that this immediate response was good for his art. Assuredly he is not solitary. We should not wish him to be solitary as a poet is, but we may wish that now and again, even while standing applauded and acclaimed, he had appraised the applause more coolly and more justly, and within his inner mind.[1]

The comparison of Dickens to an actor, modulating his tones and adapting his 'business' in accordance with public reaction, is an apt one in many ways. He was intensely alive to the attitude of his audience—he speaks of 'that particular relation (personally affectionate, and like no other man's) which subsists between me and the public'[2]—and was perfectly prepared to develop or curtail the roles of various characters in his serially published novels according to whether they found favour or not with his readers. He was an astute businessman, to whom his vast sales and his position as a national institution were factors of great importance; and this naturally militated against artistic experimentation or the expression of unorthodox ideas. The effects can be seen in Dickens's tentative query to Forster as to whether in Forster's opinion he could 'trace a gradual deterioration' in the character of Walter Gay, the hero of *Dombey and Son*, 'without making people angry'. The much-criticized happy ending of *Great Expectations*, like that of *The Return of the Native*, was obviously written in defiance of the author's aesthetic intuition, for reasons of expediency. Bulwer Lytton's success in persuading Dickens to end the novel happily was due rather to Dickens being

---

[1] cf. A. Meynell, *Dickens as a Man of Letters* (1917) *English Critical Essays* (20th Century), O.U.P., 1933, repr. 1947, pp. 56–57).
[2] cf. H. Kingsmill, *The Sentimental Journey/A Life of Charles Dickens* (Wishart and Co., 1934), p. 187.

brought to perceive that the original ending was likely to be unpopular than to doubts about its artistic appropriateness or its moral significance.

Such cases of aesthetic cowardice were not entirely due to Dickens's fears for his circulation. He came to regard his relationship with the public in an almost religious light and himself as the apostle of cheerfulness and loving-kindness, to promote which he was prepared to ignore with a clear conscience both probability and 'good taste' in the narrow sense.

His description of a projected weekly periodical, *The Cricket*, in a letter to John Forster illustrates both the 'evangelical' and the commercial aspects of this relationship. The contents of the weekly were to be as follows:

> Carol philosophy, cheerful views, sharp anatomization of humbug, jolly good temper; papers always in season, pat to the time of year; and in a vein of glowing, hearty, generous, mirthful, beaming reference in everything to Home and Fireside . . . and I would chirp, chirp, chirp away in every number until I chirped it up to—well, you shall say how many hundred thousand![1]

Is there not, one well might ask, a tincture of unanatomized humbug in the concluding lines?

Kingsmill contends that Dickens was incapable of examining his own emotions critically, so that they tend to lose touch with reality and become exaggerated:

> Thackeray . . . was alternately cynical and sentimental, and oscillating between the two made the worst of both. In Dickens, on the other hand, there was hardly a trace of cynicism, his emotions being so sacred to him that he refused to expose them to dissection by his critical faculty, which had to content itself with playing on the surface of life. The division between comedy and sentimentality in Dickens's novels corresponds exactly to the division between his perceptive faculties and his emotionalism. In later life this division in him, both as a man and a writer, became less rigid, more precarious, but in his earlier years he could pass without any backward glance of uneasiness straight from Smike or the Cheeryble brothers to such a scene as that in which two of the members of Vincent Crummles's company [cynically] discuss a play which Nicholas is translating from the French.[2]

Kingsmill's separation of Dickens's comedy from his 'emotionalism', together with his assertion that Dickens remained emotionally

---

[1] cf. Kingsmill, op. cit., pp. 127–8.
[2] cf. Kingsmill, op. cit., p. 70.

immature, clearly requires some examination. It rests primarily on the assumption that 'psychological realism' is the best criterion of an artist's emotional maturity:

False sentiment is produced by the deliberate or instinctive suppression of those elements in a situation which complicate its emotional appeal, and therefore make it for most persons disturbing instead of soothing. It is a substitution of the part for the whole. There are just and even generous employers of labour, but no successful business man, or indeed human being, is as free from cunning and self-interest as the Cheeryble brothers. The raptures of Dickens's young lovers are real, but Dickens's assumption that these raptures form a solid foundation for married happiness is untrue to his and everyone's experience. The relief of Smike at the prospect of death is reasonable, but to bring out the true pathos of his death it would be necessary to show that his relief was shared by Nicholas.[1]

Mrs. Meynell points out that the very 'substitution of the part for the whole' to which Kingsmill objects in Dickens's sentimental passages is an essential part of his comic technique:

The advice which M. Rodin received in his youth from Constant— 'Learn to see the other side; never look at forms only in extent; learn to see them always in relief'—is the contrary of the counsel proper for a reader of Dickens. That counsel should be, 'Do not insist upon seeing the immortal figures of comedy "in the round". You are to be satisfied with their face value, the face of two dimensions. It is not necessary that you should seize Mr Pecksniff from beyond, and grasp the whole man and his destinies.' The hypocrite is a figure dreadful and tragic, a shape of horror; and Mr Pecksniff is a hypocrite, and a bright image of heart-easing comedy. For comic fiction cannot exist without some such paradox.[2]

It is obvious enough that the unrelieved goodness of Little Dorrit or Tom Pinch, the interminable pompousness of Mr. Chadband, the absolute inertia of the Circumlocution Office, are all equally far from being true to experience. The notorious description of the death of Little Nell is no more exaggeratedly pathetic than the description of the death of Mr. Gamp is exaggeratedly ludicrous: 'And as to husbands, there's a wooden leg gone likeways home to its account, which in its constancy of walkin' into wine vaults, and never comin' out again 'till fetched by force, was quite as weak as flesh, if not weaker.'[3] There can be few more compelling examples of synecdoche,

---

[1] ibid., pp. 69–70.
[2] cf. Meynell, op. cit. p. 44.
[3] cf. *Martin Chuzzlewit*, ch. XL (O.U.P. ed. (1951), p. 625).

the substitution of the part for the whole, than Mrs. Gamp's substitution of a wooden leg for a husband.

Alice Meynell boldly applies the term 'caricature' to both types of exaggeration, the sentimental and the comic:

> . . . readers have been taught to praise the work of him who makes none perfect; one does not meet perfect people in trains or at dinner, and this seemed good cause that the novelist should be praised for his moderation; it seemed to imitate the usual measure and moderation of nature.
>
> But Charles Dickens closed with a divine purpose divinely different. He consented to the counsels of perfection. And thus he made Joe Gargery, not a man one might easily find in a forge; and Esther Summerson, not a girl one may easily meet at a dance; and Little Dorrit, who does not come to do a day's sewing; not that the man and the woman are inconceivable, but that they are unfortunately improbable. They are creatures created through a creating mind that worked its six days for the love of good, and never rested until the seventh, the final Sabbath, But granting that they are the counterpart, the heavenly side, of caricature, this is not to condemn them. Since when has caricature ceased to be an art good for man—an honest game between him and nature? It is a tenable opinion that frank caricature is a better incident of art than the mere exaggeration which is the more modern practice. The words mean the same thing in their origin —an overloading. But as we now generally delimit the words they differ. Caricature, when it has the grotesque inspiration, makes for laughter, and when it has the celestial, makes for admiration; in either case there is a good understanding between the author and the reader, or between the draughtsman and the spectator . . . perhaps no girl ever went through life without harbouring a thought of self, but it is very good for us to know that such a girl was thought of by Dickens, that he loved his thought, and that she is ultimately to be traced, through Dickens, to God.[1]

It is not necessary to approve of the extended sense in which Alice Meynell employs the term caricature to appreciate her point: so far as mere truth to experience is concerned, if we can tolerate Mr. Chadband or Mrs. Jellyby, why not the Cheeryble brothers or Tom Pinch?

The reason is, in part, that the 'good understanding between the author and the reader' which still obtains with regard to Dickens's grotesque exaggeration has broken down in the case of his sentimental or 'celestial' exaggeration. The twentieth-century reader finds such things as the impregnable good nature of the Cheerybles, the self-sacrifice of Little Dorrit or Marion Jeddler (in *The Battle of Life*), the

---

[1] cf. Meynell, op. cit., pp. 39–41.

dark wanderings of Little Em'ly, and the Christmas cheer of *Pickwick Papers* uncongenial even as fantasies in various aesthetic and ethical respects, of which not the least important is an impression of superficiality, even of actual insincerity, on the part of the author.

Where the distortion, whether of situation or character, appears to the reader to tend in the right direction, he is generally prepared to neglect 'realism of presentation' as less important than 'realism of assessment'.[1] Shaw, for example, comments as follows on the Dickens of *Hard Times*, bracketing him with 'Karl Marx, Carlyle, Ruskin, Morris, Carpenter':

> . . . here he begins at last to exercise quite recklessly his power of presenting a character to you in the most fantastic and outrageous terms, putting into its mouth from one end of the book to the other hardly a word which could conceivably have been uttered by any sane human being, and yet leaving you with an unmistakable and exactly truthful portrait of a character that you recognize at once as not only real but typical.[2]

Aesthetic enjoyment is another factor which may induce the reader to abandon the critical test of realism. George Saintsbury, whilst remarking that Little Dorrit suffers from the 'curse of fundamental unreality', describes the grotesque 'Mr F's aunt' (*Little Dorrit*, ch. XIII.) as 'one of those pure extravaganzas of the author who justify themselves offhand'.[3]

To a great extent, criticism of Dickens for his vulgarity, triteness, exaggerated pathos, superficiality, and insincerity stems from a lack of sympathy with his attitude to his 'serious' characters and to such things as Christmas, marriage, and the home. Whilst this lack of sympathy, strikingly in contrast with the universal appreciation of his genius for the grotesque and the fantastic, can to some extent be justified, Dickens's attitude towards what Alice Meynell calls his 'celestial' caricatures should at least be properly understood. Such a passage as the following betrays a lack of understanding:

> Little Dorrit . . . consecrates herself to the care of her selfish father, and when he comes into his fortune and travels in state with his family over the Continent, she is miserable because he no longer needs her. There was

[1] I am indebted for these phrases to Mr. Ian Watt's *The Rise of the Novel* (Chatto and Windus, London, 1957).
[2] cf. G. B. Shaw, Introduction to *Hard Times* (cf. Edgar Johnson, *Charles Dickens: His Tragedy and Triumph* (Gollancz Ltd., London, 1953), vol. 2, pp. 806-7).
[3] cf. *Camb. Hist. Eng. Lit.* (repr. 1953), vol. XIII, ch. x, p. 331.

a chance here for a fine study in the disguised selfishness of the self-effacing type, had Dickens realized that Little Dorrit's wretchedness at her father being no longer immured in the Marshalsea was not entirely praiseworthy.[1]

Little Dorrit's reality, however, is not of the order of psychological realism; she is, for Dickens, something closely approximating to a religious symbol. In fact such a 'study' as Kingsmill suggests would have the effect of altering the perspective of the whole and confusing the reader. Her significance is well brought out by Professor Butt and Mrs. Tillotson:

[The rejected title] 'Nobody's Fault' represents the 'one idea and design' of social criticism of which 'Society, the Circumlocution Office and Mr. Gowan' are 'three parts' : *Little Dorrit*, the optimism about humanity which sets the rest in perspective. In her Dickens repeats, more subtly, a leading idea of *Oliver Twist* and *The Old Curiosity Shop*: that of the strength and indestructibility of natural, innocent virtue. As with Oliver and Nell, her goodness, with such an upbringing, may be thought implausible; but it must be seen as expressing what still survived of Dickens's own indestructible faith—expressing it almost allegorically, with the validity of fairy tale.[2]

If we are to come anywhere near a satisfactory account of the significance of the grotesque in Dickens's work, it is necessary to consider it in relation to such ideal figures as Little Nell and Little Dorrit. First, however, in order to bring out the character of Dickens's manner of representing reality as he sees it, it will be as well to note the deeper significance of Ruskin's famous comment:

The essential value and truth of Dickens's writings have been unwisely lost sight of by many thoughtful persons, merely because he presents his truth with some colour of caricature. Unwisely, because Dickens's caricature, though often gross, is never mistaken . . . let us not lose the use of Dickens's wit and insight, because he chooses to speak in a circle of stage fire.[3]

It is nothing new to describe Dickens as above all a dramatist. His connexion with the theatre was a very close one, and his novels, as he himself pre-eminently demonstrated, are highly suitable for

[1] cf. Kingsmill, op. cit., p. 160.
[2] cf. J. Butt and K. Tillotson, *Dickens at Work* (Methuen and Co., 1957), pp. 230–1.
[3] In *Unto This Last*. cf. John Forster, *The Life of Charles Dickens*, ed. J. W. T. Ley (Cecil Palmer, 1928), pp. 565–6.

dramatic performance. In particular, however, it is vital to note that
Dickens employs the fundamentally dramatic method of depicting
the interplay of both social and spiritual principles symbolically
through the relationships of deliberately simplified characters.

Obviously, the term 'simplified' is a relative one. Compared with
the virtues and vices of the Morality Play, Dickens's characters are
realistically complex: compared with the characters of a psychological realist like Henry James, they are mere personifications or
'humour' characters. One ought perhaps to note the exceptions to
this generalization. There are minor examples of psychological
realism in every Dickens novel; the chief characters of *Great Expectations* are much more complex than those of earlier novels, and so on.
On the whole, however, it is true to say that for Dickens the introduction of a new aspect of human nature means the introduction of a
new character, and the conflict of good and evil is thus expressed by
the interaction of characters, externally. It is an interesting question
whether the loss in subtlety is or is not outweighed by the opportunities for dramatic situation afforded by Dickens's *modus operandi*,[1]
but in deploring Dickens's failure to make of Little Dorrit 'a fine
study in the disguised selfishness of the self-effacing type', Kingsmill would appear to be regarding Dickens as a kind of unsuccessful
George Meredith.

The difficulty of appreciating such figures as Little Nell and Little
Dorrit properly in the dramatic context of the works in which they
appear cannot, however, be explained away. It is due, more than to
any other single thing, to the fact that, as suggested above, they are
neither pure personifications or symbols like the figures of the Morality Play or the Faerie Queene, nor sufficiently complex to be quite
credible as human beings, falling, so to speak, between two stools.
The question of context is all-important. Where there is a direct
contrast between the idealized figure or setting and some opposing
element we can appreciate its significance most readily. Thus, Little
Dorrit appears to best advantage in the Marshalsea scenes with her
selfish father; and the significance of the figure of Little Nell is
clearest in the following 'kind of allegory':

I sat down in my easy-chair, and falling back upon its ample cushions,

[1] cf. E. M. Forster's distinction between 'flat' and 'round' characters
(*Aspects of the Novel*, Edward Arnold, London, 1927, repr. 1958, pp. 65 ff.).
Of Dickens, Mr. Forster remarks that 'his immense success with types sug-
gests that there may be more in flatness than severer critics admit'.

pictured to myself the child in her bed: alone, unwatched, uncared for, (save by angels,) yet sleeping peacefully. So very young, so spiritual, so slight and fairy-like a creature passing the long dull nights in such an uncongenial place! I could not dismiss it from my thoughts.

We are so much in the habit of allowing impressions to be made upon us by external objects, which should be produced by reflection alone, but which, without such invisible aids, often escape us, that I am not sure I should have been so thoroughly possessed by this one subject, but for the heaps of fantastic things I had seen huddled together in the curiosity-dealer's warehouse. These, crowding on my mind, in connection with the child, and gathering round her, as it were, brought her condition palpably before me. I had her image, without any effort of imagination, surrounded and beset by everything that was foreign to its nature, and farthest removed from the sympathies of her sex and age. If these helps to my fancy had all been wanting, and I had been forced to imagine her in a common chamber, with nothing unusual or uncouth in its appearance, it is very probable that I should have been less impressed with her strange and solitary state. As it was, she seemed to exist in a kind of allegory; and, having these shapes about her, claimed my interest so strongly, that (as I have already remarked), I could not dismiss her from my recollection, do what I would.

'It would be a curious speculation,' said I, after some restless turns across and across the room, 'to imagine her in her future life, holding her solitary way among a crowd of wild grotesque companions; the only pure, fresh, youthful object in the throng.[1]

Here, where Nell is a lay figure in a scene which echoes in modified fashion a commonplace of Platonic and Christian thought, the image of the still untarnished soul in the prison house of an alien world, there is little room for objections of the kind which are raised to what Lord David Cecil calls 'the sweet and sunshiny' scenes in Dickens, or to those pathetic scenes, of which the death of Little Nell is the most 'notorious', where the ideal figure is surrounded, not

---

[1] cf. *The Old Curiosity Shop*, ch. I (Cassell and Co., Special Authorized ed., p. 11). This passage seems to me to give added weight to Professor Butt's and Mrs. Tillotson's remark about the 'almost allegorical' significance of Little Dorrit. The sense of the symbolic or allegorical is strong in Dickens: 'In a broken down gallery at the back of a row of these, there was a wan child looking over at a starved old white horse who was making a meal of oyster shells. The sun was going down and flaring out like an angry fire at the child —and the child, and I, and the pale horse, stared at one another in silence for some five minutes as if we were so many figures in a dismal allegory.' (*The Heart of Charles Dickens: As Revealed In His Letters To Angela Burdett-Coutts* (New York, 1952). (cf. Monroe Engel, *The Maturity of Charles Dickens* (O.U.P., 1959), p. 13).

by the fantastic and discordant, but by 'appropriate', conventional imagery and diction:

One would have thought the death of an innocent and virtuous child should be allowed to carry its own emotion; but Dickens cannot trust us to be moved by Little Nell's departure from the world unassisted by church bells, falling snow at the window, and every other ready-made device for extracting our tears that a cheap rhetoric can provide.[1]

Dickens's poetic imagination is not stimulated by the sweet and the sunshiny. If he does write about them, he falls into the same error as when he writes about sweet and sunshiny characters; he becomes sentimental and a little vulgar; the cottages where Oliver Twist finds rest and David meets Dora are altogether too rose-embowered. The Christmas festivities of *The Cricket on the Hearth* and *Pickwick* are twopenny Christmas cards complete with snow and robins and trite benevolence. Dickens' genius needed something harsh to bite its powerful teeth on; it grinds the tender and delicate to atoms.[2]

Among other objections, Lord David Cecil criticizes the conventional nature of such settings and characters; they are full of 'ready-made' devices; the tone is 'a little vulgar' and 'trite'.

The significance of Dickens's ideal settings and figures is most clearly apparent where there is a strong contrast. Where the ideal is seen in immediate juxtaposition with the grotesque or the evil, the resultant 'compound' has a kind of balance which, so to speak, justifies its component elements. It is more difficult, but important, to read those passages which are wholly idealized with regard to the characters, the circumstances which surround them, and the language in which they are described, in the context of the work as a whole. Just as Little Nell or Oliver Twist requires to be seen as symbolizing one element in a rounded vision of reality rather than as a rounded portrait of a human being, so, too, the death of Little Nell, idealized into a 'celestial caricature' and carefully shielded from the ironic, the ugly, and the incongruous, ought to be read in relation to the rest of the work, to other scenes in which there is a superabundance of the ironic, the ugly, and the incongruous. Thus the morally fruitful death of Little Nell and the barren and wolfish death of Quilp, both scenes equally touched with 'stage fire', give each other the balance

---

[1] cf. Lord David Cecil, *Early Victorian Novelists* (Pelican Books, A. 190), p. 29.

[2] cf. Lord David Cecil, op. cit., pp. 40–41.

which both lack when judged in isolation from a realistic point of view.[1]

In such passages, the idealized death-bed scenes and visions of genteel happiness, Dickens gives us glimpses of the rewards of moral goodness. The fact that the death-bed scenes which best exemplify this involve children (the contemporary reader would perhaps see Little Nell as something more than a child) reflects both Dickens's conception of moral goodness as something innate (Scrooge's redemption, significantly, makes a 'baby' of him)[2] and that relish for the naturally affecting or dramatic situation which in the last analysis is the chief reason for his widespread popularity.

The entry of these saints amongst Dickens's characters upon their well-deserved state of lasting happiness, whether in this world or the next, involves Dickens, with his peculiar merits of style, in a position where he feels obliged to dispense with most of the qualities which we associate with his genius: his mastery of the 'conceit', the witty, hyperbolical, and frequently elaborate comparison; his mock-heroic use of Latinate phraseology to describe trivial incidents; his perception of the ironic or grotesque detail. The 'violent chiaroscuro'[3] of his style gives place to unremarkable, deliberately conventional imagery, and a 'simple, unaffected' tone which is coloured, however,

---

[1] cf. *The Old Curiosity Shop*, ch. LXXII: 'Oh! it is hard to take to heart the lesson that such deaths will teach, but let no man reject it, for it is a mighty, universal Truth. When Death strikes down the innocent and young, for every fragile form from which he lets the panting spirit free, a hundred virtues rise, in shapes of mercy, charity and love, to walk the world, and bless it. Of every tear that sorrowing mortals shed on such green graves, some good is born, some gentler nature comes. In the Destroyer's steps there spring up bright creations that defy his power, and his dark path becomes a way of light to Heaven.' Mr. Jack Lindsay stresses the symbolic aspect of Little Nell, and the importance of appreciating her significance 'in terms of the whole story': 'This wide response shows that we must beware of reducing her to the personal neurosis of Dickens. The image evoked something fundamental and general in the contemporary soul. . . . Nell in isolation was indeed a mere smear of white and a monster; but in terms of the whole story she was a powerful image of something ghastly in its suffering which men must face if they were to keep their souls alive. She was not a character and not a mere guilt-smear, but she was a symbol of universal suffering, of a spiritual state which the book helped to focus.' cf. *Charles Dickens: A Biographical and Critical Study* (Andrew Dakers Ltd., London, 1950), p. 199.

[2] cf. *A Christmas Carol*, stave 5 ('The End Of It'): 'I don't know anything. I'm quite a baby. Never mind. I don't care. I'd rather be a baby.'

[3] cf. Cecil, op. cit., p. 32: 'Bathed in the violent chiaroscuro of his fancy, London and its butchers and bakers show transformed and distorted, so that eyes gleam from black caverns, noses depend enormous and legs stretch to grotesque spindles.'

still, by rhetorical apostrophe and commentary—all the more blatantly, to present-day tastes, for the omission of the above elements.

The 'principle of decorum' which he brings to bear in such passages, by robbing them of an element frequently found in successful pathos which is native to Dickens's cast of mind, namely ironic disproportion,[1] perhaps makes the deaths of Little Nell, Paul Dombey, Smike, less poignant than they might otherwise have been. It is, however, obvious that the pathetic is only part of the effect which Dickens aims at in such scenes. We are meant to be impressed by the power of ideal goodness, the equanimity with which his ideal characters face death, a phenomenon which 'a religion in a state of transition from supernatural belief to humanism is very poorly equipped to face'.[2] We are meant to admire and to be inspired, to feel pity perhaps, but scarcely a tragic sense of waste.

In general, then, the chief reason for the aesthetic failure of Dickens's idealized scenes is that the pure white light which he endeavours to shed upon them, lacking the dramatic relief of either realism or fantasy, tends to strike the reader as trite and unimaginative. For our purposes, the significant thing about these scenes is the omission of the grotesque and fantastic. Dickens associates the grotesque with the imperfect, as does Swift, though it is necessary to qualify this generalization by adding that, as used here, the term imperfect does not by any means invariably imply real disapproval; Mr. Dick, for example, in *David Copperfield*, is an 'imperfect' being whose grotesqueness is certainly not intended to excite disapproval. The more closely a Dickensian character approximates to the ideal or the divine, or a locality to perfection, the more decorous and formal it tends to become.

43. Ruskin, in his examination of grotesque art in *The Stones of Venice*, speaks of 'the noble grotesque', in which the artist employs the grotesque in the attempt to symbolize the divine:

It cannot but have been sometimes a subject of wonder with thoughtful men . . . that a calf, a lion, an eagle, and a beast with a man's face, should in all ages have been preferred by the Christian world, as expressive of Evangelistic power and inspiration, to the majesty of human form.[3]

It may be asked whether Dickens employs the grotesque to symbolize the divine, and to what extent the preternatural figures of the

---

[1] 'Understatement' and the succinctness we associate with it are clearly aspects of this incongruity, generally implying the inability of the sufferer to express the immensity of his loss, as in Lear's 'Undo this button'.
[2] cf. House, *The Dickens World* (O.U.P., 1941), p. 132.   [3] See p. 41.

Christmas Books (*A Christmas Carol, The Chimes, The Cricket on the Hearth, The Battle of Life,*[1] and *The Haunted Man*) serve such a purpose.

Dickens describes the general tone of these works as follows: 'My purpose was, *in a whimsical kind of masque which the good-humour of the season justified*, to awaken some loving and forbearing thoughts, never out of season in a Christian land.'[2]

It is no reflection upon Dickens's sincerity to describe the *Christmas Books* as moral fairy stories of which the form as distinct from the moral content is not intended to be taken too seriously. There is a clear implication in this passage from Dickens's preface to the collected edition of the *Christmas Books* that the ghosts and goblins permissible in a 'Christmas entertainment' would be too trivial for more ambitious work. Significantly, apart from an occasional fleeting and highly decorous reference, the 'Christmas books' do not employ Christian imagery, supernatural imagery of a serious kind. There is certainly no intermingling of the ghosts and goblins with the Christ Child and associated imagery. Dickens and his contemporaries would have found the idea blasphemous.[3]

It is equally significant that, within the 'profane' body of preternatural images employed in these books, it is generally true that the more solemn and rarified the figure the less grotesque it tends to be in appearance. The *speech* of these apparitions, though often highly rhetorical, is always good prose.

The preternatural figures of *A Christmas Carol* thus show a diminishing degree of grotesqueness as the solemnity of their relationship with Scrooge increases. The figure of Jacob Marley, at the lower end of the preternatural scale, with a large number of earthly characteristics and occurring in a scene which is by no means unrelievedly solemn, is highly grotesque. The tassels on his boots bristle as he enters the room; Scrooge, looking through his waistcoat, sees the two buttons on his coat behind. When he removes the wrapper bound about his chin 'as if it were too warm to wear indoors', his lower jaw drops on to his breast; when he binds it on again, 'Scrooge knew . . . by the smart sound its teeth made, when the jaws were

---

[1] *The Battle of Life* has no preternatural content.

[2] *Christmas Books*, The New Oxford Illustrated ed. (O.U.P. 1954), p. xv. The italics are mine.

[3] The fondness of many *fin de siècle* writers for the 'profane' use of Christian imagery—e.g. Oscar Wilde's story 'The Selfish Giant' (*The Happy Prince*, 1888) is largely due to an awareness of this effect of blasphemy and the desire to 'shock' the reader.

brought together by the bandage'. Although the actual utterances of the ghost are solemn enough, the *dialogue* is largely humorous, and this, together with such details as those given above, lead us to remember Marley's ghost as a semi-comic figure; one which, though preternatural, is very far from being divine. The same may be said of the 'old ghost, in a white waistcoat, with a monstrous iron safe attached to its ankle' which Scrooge sees wandering by his window.

The Ghost of Christmas Past owes its grotesqueness of appearance to its being an allegorical representation of memory. It has the white hair of age, but the unwrinkled face of eternal youth; its arms and hands are muscular 'as if its hold were of uncommon strength'; it is adorned with summer flowers but carries an 'evergreen' branch of holly:

But the strangest thing about it was, that from the crown of its head there sprung a bright clear jet of light, by which all this was visible; and which was doubtless the occasion of its using, in its duller moments, a great extinguisher for a cap, which it now held under its arm.[1]

Significantly, Scrooge requests the ghost to put on its cap, suggesting the desire to obliterate the past which Dickens employs later as the theme of *The Haunted Man*.

The figure is thus a grotesque one; as Scrooge looks at it its outline fluctuates, 'being now a thing with one arm, now with one leg, now with twenty legs, now a pair of legs without a head, now a head without a body', in allegorical reference to the indistinctness of memory. The most grotesque of the three Christmas Spirits, it is also the most 'finite' of the three:

'I am the Ghost of Christmas Past.'
'Long Past?' inquired Scrooge: observant of its dwarfish stature.
'No. Your past.'

Moreover, its meeting with Scrooge is in part a humorous one, compared with the visitations of the later spirits, though the effect is less comic than in the case of Marley's Ghost; Scrooge's remarks to the ghost are given in the more subdued form of indirect speech.

The two remaining spirits, 'a jolly giant, glorious to see', and 'a solemn Phantom, draped and hooded', are much closer to being symbols of divine power and are not treated humorously. Neither is a grotesque figure except in the technical sense in which all giants and phantoms can be described as grotesque.

[1] cf. *A Christmas Carol*, stave 2.
G.E.L.—P

The preternatural figures which, in *A Christmas Carol*, come closest to exhibiting the use of the grotesque in a solemn fashion are the two children, Ignorance and Want, which the Ghost of Christmas Present shows to Scrooge just before leaving him. Their significance does not so much lie in the fact that they are themselves particularly bizarre, for they are not, as in Dickens's own insistence on their monstrousness:

They were a boy and a girl. Yellow, meagre, ragged, scowling, wolfish; but prostrate, too, in their humility. Where graceful youth should have filled their features out, and touched them with its freshest tints, a stale and shrivelled hand, like that of age, had pinched, and twisted them, and pulled them into shreds. Where angels might have sat enthroned, devils lurked; and glared out menacing. No change, no degradation, no perversion of humanity, in any grade, through all the mysteries of wonderful creation, has monsters half so horrible and dread.[1]

The dreadfulness of these children, whilst it represents an important aspect of Dickens's use of the grotesque for satirical purposes, is not of a preternatural order, and is obviously very different from Ruskin's conception of the 'noble grotesque'.

The Chimes: A Goblin Story of some Bells, etc. (1844) comes nearer, perhaps, than any other work by Dickens to a 'noble grotesque', i.e. to imagery which is at once grotesque and a serious symbol of divine power, in the Goblins of the Bells. This assertion, however, requires considerable qualification. First, Dickens prepares us for the 'Goblin Sight' which Trotty Veck 'sees' in his swoon by emphasizing the inchoate, 'imperfect' nature of dream imagery:

Black are the brooding clouds and troubled the deep waters, when the Sea of Thought, first heaving for a calm, gives up its Dead. Monsters uncouth and wild, arise in premature, imperfect resurrection; the several parts and shapes of different things are joined and mixed by chance; and when, and how, and by what wonderful degrees, each separates from each, and every sense and object of the mind resumes its usual form and lives again, no man—though every man is every day the casket of this type of the Great Mystery—can tell.[2]

---

[1] cf. *A Christmas Carol*, stave 3.

[2] cf. *The Chimes*: The Third Quarter. Cf. *The Uncommercial Traveller* (Journey 12, paragraph on the inmates of Bedlam): 'Do we not nightly jumble events and personages and times and places, as these do daily? Are we not sometimes troubled by our own sleeping inconsistencies, and do we not vexedly try to account for them or excuse them, just as these do sometimes in respect of their waking delusions? . . . I wonder that the great master who knew everything, when he called Sleep the death of each day's life, did not call Dreams the insanity of each day's sanity.'

Second, the images which follow this passage (which seemingly contradicts their significance by stressing their fortuitous nature) are, for a nightmare vision, drawn in restrained fashion. The swarms of tiny figures which stream from the bells are remarkable for their activity rather than for their appearance; in any case, such grotesqueness as they possess has a human source: 'They take such shapes and occupations as the hopes and thoughts of mortals, and the recollections they have stored up, give them.'[1] The 'bearded figures', apart from a single reference to their 'goblin' mouths ('each with its muffled hand upon its goblin mouth'), are more or less 'conventional' phantoms, 'draped and hooded' like the Ghost of Christmas Yet To Come in *A Christmas Carol.*

The spectre of *The Haunted Man* is 'an awful likeness' of Redlaw, the chief character. The effect of its awfulness is somewhat mitigated by the equanimity with which Redlaw, who has already grown accustomed to being haunted by the beginning of the story, receives it:

At length he spoke; without moving or lifting up his face.
'Here again!' he said.
'Here again!' replied the Phantom.[2]

A more remarkable figure than Redlaw's ghostly *Doppelgänger* for the purpose of the present examination is the 'baby savage' which rushes 'like a wildcat' into Redlaw's room:

A bundle of tatters, held together by a hand, in size and form almost an infant's, but, in its greedy, desperate little clutch, a bad old man's. A face rounded and smoothed by some half-dozen years, but pinched and twisted by the experiences of a life. Bright eyes, but not youthful. Naked feet, beautiful in their childish delicacy,—ugly in the blood and dirt that cracked upon them. A baby savage, a young monster, a child who had never been a child, a creature who might live to take the outward form of man, but who, within, would live and perish a mere beast.[3]

Although this child, unlike the corresponding figures in *A Christmas Carol*, plays a considerable role in the story, it is perhaps more accurate to describe him—like them—as potentially rather than actually grotesque; he is described as possessing the incongruous attributes which elsewhere (in the Artful Dodger, for example, or Jo the crossing-sweeper) are developed in grotesque fashion, principally by emphasizing the oddness of the character's appearance—an

[1] cf. *The Chimes*: The Third Quarter.
[2] cf. *The Haunted Man*, ch. I.
[3] cf. *The Haunted Man*, ch. I (O.U.P. ed. (1954), p. 337).

activity in which Dickens makes great use of his genius for the fantastic metaphor or simile[1]—and by the use of speech (odd turns of phrase, lack of grammar and logic, mispronunciations, malapropisms, &c.) to suggest an inner deformity; it may be noted that the 'baby savage' speaks a good brand of English, apart from the occasional 'ain't', &c.

ECCENTRIC CHARACTERS

44. We have seen that Dickens associates grotesqueness with imperfection, using the latter term in a broad sense which does not necessarily imply strong disapproval. In many cases strong disapproval of the character, institution, or object which is associated with the grotesque is very much in evidence; in such cases Dickens is the classic satirist, identifying his victim with the absurd:

> He perceives with astonishment, that supposing the present Government to be overthrown, the limited choice of the Crown, in the formation of a new Ministry, would lie between Lord Coodle and Sir Thomas Doodle— supposing it to be impossible for the Duke of Foodle to act with Goodle, which may be the case in consequence of the breach arising out of that affair with Hoodle. Then, giving the Home Department and the Leadership of the House of Commons to Joodle, the Exchequer to Koodle, the Colonies to Loodle and the Foreign Office to Moodle, what are you to do with Noodle?[2]

Dickens's works abound, however, with characters whose dress, speech, behaviour are grotesque when judged by the social standard epitomized by Nicholas Nickleby, Arthur Clennam, Esther Summerson, and so on, but who can scarcely be described as objects of satire: Pickwick and his clubmates, Joe Gargery, Captain Cuttle, Doctor Strong, Dick Swiveller, 'lovable innocents' and others whose oddities would have received short shrift from Pope.

---

[1] cf. *Little Dorrit*, ch. IX (Cassell, Special Authorized ed., vol. XII, p. 82): 'A great white cap, with a quantity of opaque frilling that was always flapping about, apologised for Maggy's baldness, and made it so very difficult for her old black bonnet to retain its place upon her head, that it held on round her neck like a gipsy's baby. A commission of haberdashers could alone have reported what the rest of her poor dress was made of; but it had a strong general resemblance to seaweed, with here and there a gigantic tea-leaf. Her shawl looked particularly like a tea-leaf, after long infusion.' Maggy, of course, who describes her history as 'Gin . . . Broom-handles and pokers' (op. cit., p. 83), is a grotesque version of the neglected child.
[2] cf. *Bleak House*, ch. XII (Cassell, Special Authorized ed., vol. XI p. 129).

It is customary to regard Sir Roger de Coverley as the first of the 'lovable innocents'. Without entering into detail, we may regard him as a key figure in an emotional transition. The first stage is that in which the figure is employed to counteract too formal and superficial a view of socially acceptable behaviour, suggesting that small blemishes matter little when weighed against sterling virtues. The second stage is that in which the figure's eccentricities appear less as excusable peculiarities than as desirable symptoms of an unblemished, because unsophisticated, character: '. . . the general good sense and worthiness of his character make his friends observe these little singularities as foils that rather set off than blemish his good qualities.'[1] Sir Roger is represented as a fount of good sense and benevolence with only the mildest of foibles; he is a far cry from Uncle Toby or Mr. Micawber. Nevertheless, there is a subtle ambivalence about him, inasmuch as we are invited to laugh at his oddities and admire his virtues at the same time: 'The whim of narrowly escaping by having been within a day of danger, with other matters above-mentioned, mixed with good sense, left me at a loss whether I was more delighted with my friend's wisdom or simplicity.'[2]

The two extremes of the 'lovable innocent' character may be exemplified by Sheridan's Sir Peter Teazle and Mr. Micawber. Sir Peter, though he is a classic butt—an elderly man with a young wife —is presented in a wholly favourable light, in exemplary contrast to the despicable world of Sneerwell and Backbite. If we judge him by even the strictest standards of social or moral correctness, we shall find him sufficiently unexceptionable. By such standards, the ideals of morality and gentility symbolized by Little Nell, Little Dorrit, Esther Summerson, Nicholas Nickleby, and others, Mr. Micawber comes off badly. The fact is, however, that Micawber arouses a feeling of affection, not in spite of his imperfections, which are far from being of a narrowly moral character, but largely because of them. A. O. J. Cockshut, in *The Imagination of Charles Dickens*, remarks of Micawber: 'To read of Mr. Micawber is, as Chesterton said, like receiving a blow in the face. It is a deeply-felt experience, but it is not susceptible of analytic description.'[3]

It is at all events clear that we do not indulge in moral analysis of

[1] cf. Addison, *Sir Roger At Church* (*Spectator*, no. 112). (cf. *Coverley Papers from The Spectator*, ed. K. Deighton (Macmillan, London, 1947), p. 31.
[2] ibid., pp. 25–26 (Steele, *Sir Roger's Ancestors: Spectator*, no. 109).
[3] cf. A. O. J. Cockshut, *The Imagination of Charles Dickens* (Collins, 1961), p. 114.

Micawber's character as we experience it, but rather accept him *in toto* as we accept the Falstaff of Henry IV (I). It is not that we are blind to Micawber's faults, but that they are, so to speak, beside the point. The significance of Maurice Morgann's defence of Falstaff, the most manful attempt in English letters at just such an 'analytic description' as Mr. Cockshut discountenances, lies in Morgann's feeling that Falstaff must be considered in terms of his total impact, and that condemnation on moral grounds is a kind of post-mortem which has little to do with the actual experiencing of Falstaff. Unfortunately, he resorts to argument, and tabulates Falstaff's virtues as painstakingly as his imaginary opponent lists Falstaff's vices. We need not attempt anything so absurd as to deny that Micawber is a pompous old cadger: much the same can be said of his faults as Cockshut says of Mrs. Gamp's:

> Florence Nightingale, one might say, spent her life in displacing and defeating Mrs Gamp. But all this, undeniable though it is, seems curiously irrelevant to the actual literary quality of the woman. Her voice stills all questionings and puts all general values out of account.[1]

Just though this remark certainly is in its assertion that Mrs. Gamp cannot be explained away as a satirical figure—as August Moddle cannot be *fairly* described, in Taine's myopic phrase, as 'a gloomy maniac'[2]—the guarded adjective 'literary' requires some comment. If Cockshut means that the Florence Nightingale aspect would not have seemed so irrelevant to one who met Sairey Gamp in the flesh, the adjective is clearly justified. There is, however, an implication, or so it seems to me, that the appealing side of Mrs. Gamp is wholly literary and cannot be related to the world of fact in the same way as the satirical aspect of the figure can; that though we might find the oddities of a real-life Gamp amusing, we should scarcely 'warm to her' as we do to the fictitious Gamp.[3]

While it would be pointless to argue such a matter, it is important to insist that the appeal of Mrs. Gamp has its roots in something deeper than Dickens's sense of humour. This is not to imply that the latter is in any way superficial, but simply to say that one cannot account for Mrs. Gamp altogether by describing her as (*a*) a satirical

---

[1] ibid., p. 21.

[2] Forster, *The Life of Charles Dickens*, p. 324.

[3] Thus Alice Meynell (op. cit., p. 44) remarks of Pecksniff (who amuses, both as a satirical and as an 'absurd' figure, but who arouses no sympathy in the reader): 'The hypocrite is a figure dreadful and tragic, a shape of horror; and Mr Pecksniff is a hypocrite and a bright image of heart-easing comedy.'

figure and (*b*) a humorous figure. She is also, like Micawber, a very human figure.

Cockshut observes: 'Dickens's . . . great comic creations, Crummles, Mrs. Gamp, Mr. Micawber, present forms of absurdity not to be found in human nature, and therefore hardly amenable to moral categories.'[1] It is presumably for this reason that 'her voice stills all questionings and puts all general values out of account'. Such a view, which implies that in enjoying Mrs. Gamp's grotesque utterances we lose touch with reality altogether, seems to me inadequate, though it needs to be pointed out that Cockshut is dealing primarily with these utterances as nonsense pure and simple, i.e. with her language in itself rather than as an aspect of her character.

The 'Florence Nightingale' side of Mrs. Gamp and the absurd side, whilst they are both continuous aspects, tend to predominate in turn. Thus the absurd side of her character is predominant for the first half of chapter XXV, shading off into a more satirical representation later in the chapter where her indifference to suffering is emphasized. It is, of course, chiefly in those contexts in which the satirical side of the figure seems 'curiously irrelevant' that we feel most cordial towards her, as in her hilarious conversation with the Pinches on the wharf in chapter XL:

'Our calcilations, ma'am,' I says, 'respectin' wot the number of a family will be comes most times within one, and oftener than you would suppoge exact.' 'Sairey,' says Mrs Harris, in an awful way, 'tell me wot is my indiwidgle number.' 'No, Mrs Harris,' I says to her, 'excuge me, if you please. My own,' I says, 'has fallen out of three-pair backs, and had damp doorsteps settled on their lungs, and one was turned up smilin' in a bedstead unbeknown. Therefore, ma'am,' I says, 'seek not to proticipate, but take 'em as they come and as they go. Mine,' said Mrs Gamp—'mine is all gone, my dear young chick. And as to husbands, there's a wooden leg gone likeways home to its account, which in its constancy of walkin' into wine vaults, and never comin' out again 'till fetched by force, was quite as weak as flesh, if not weaker.'

In this passage, Mrs. Gamp at her most amusing, we find absurdity both in the form of ridicule and of a kind of droll poetry; but the sheer earthiness of it is a vital element in its effect. In such a passage, however much heightened and coloured, we make contact with a reality which simultaneously repelled and fascinated Dickens, the life of the poor London streets.

[1] op. cit., p. 18.

Hugh Kingsmill put his finger on one of the elements in the Gamp figure which created this earthy appeal, both for Dickens himself and for his readers—more specifically for contemporary readers:

> Mrs Gamp was perhaps the most popular of all Dickens's comic characters, both with his public and with Dickens himself, who refers to her more often in his letters than to any other of his creations. It is easy to understand her charm for the Victorians, for although her talk is not openly lewd, as it would have been in Smollett or Ben Jonson, she exudes with every gin-sodden breath a rankly realistic view of sex which both lessened its seductiveness and eased for the moment the strain of being sentimental about it. While Dickens was writing the first half of *Martin Chuzzlewit*, Mrs Dickens was carrying his fifth child, and Mrs Gamp doubtless came into being to soothe Dickens's nerves, frayed by his wife's incurable addiction to pregnancy.[1]

Now it is not strictly true that Mrs. Gamp 'exudes with every gin-sodden breath a rankly realistic view of sex'; it is not present in the majority of her more memorable sayings ('Rich folk may ride on camels, but it ain't so easy for 'em to see out of a needle's eye'); it is absent in the sick-room scene (chapter XXV):

> 'Ah!' sighed Mrs Gamp, as she meditated over the warm shilling's-worth, 'what a blessed thing it is—living in a wale—to be contented! What a blessed thing it is to make sick people happy in their beds, and never mind one's self as long as one can do a service. I don't believe a finer cowcumber was ever grow'd.'

The 'worm's eye view' of sex which she undoubtedly symbolizes is *one* aspect of a representation of the seamy side of life, the world of the comic postcard which George Orwell analyses so unforgettably in his essay *The Art of Donald McGill*.

The blowsy figure of Mrs. Gamp, like the grotesque figures of the comic postcard, provides a release from the repressions of moral idealism and the canons of respectability; but the release is only a partial one, possible only when compounded for by overt ridicule and disapproval.

Even the grotesque trait for which Mrs. Gamp is perhaps best remembered, her invention of Mrs. Harris, has something elementally human about it. There is a childlike quality about the sense of comfort and prestige which she derives from her imaginary companion[2]

---

[1] cf. Kingsmill, op. cit., p. 115.
[2] For a sentimental but not entirely unrealistic parallel to Mrs. Harris, cf. A. A. Milne's poem 'Binker' (*Now We Are Six*).

which makes her not simply more fantastic but more attractive as a person.

Like Mr. Micawber, Mrs. Gamp is grotesque. The grotesqueness of both characters, however, like that of a great number of Dickensian figures, has two sides to it. On the one hand it is satirically intended. Such satire may be specific—it may make some point about nursing conditions, pretentious behaviour, and so on—or it may merely draw attention to eccentricities of appearance, speech, behaviour, which are absurd by polite standards. Whilst it may not be true of all satirical humour that we laugh because we feel superior to the victim—after all, we may be intensely aware that the satire is aimed at ourselves and still be amused—it is peculiarly characteristic of Dickens's humour that the reader is flattered into feeling an effortless sense of superiority. From an Olympian height we watch with amusement, conscious of the gulf which yawns between ourselves and the Cratchits or Peggottys. Such satire need not necessarily entail disapproval of the character in question; the grotesqueness of the Artful Dodger or Jo the crossing-sweeper is intended to excite disapproval of social conditions.

On the other hand, we must also take into account the 'lovable innocent' aspect of many grotesque characteristics, those foibles and oddities which give their possessor warmth and colour and are intended to awaken our sympathy, however humorously. If at the one extreme we have figures of impeccable gentility and virtue, Little Nell, Esther Summerson, Florence Dombey, Arthur Clennam, in whom inward grace is reflected in the outward signs of perfect manners, youth, and good looks, figures beside which Dickens's grotesques appear all the more imperfect and inferior, at the other extreme are those soulless institutions and theories, the workhouse, the law, the factory, commercialism, Benthamism, and so on, which aim at reducing human beings to ciphers and crushing individuality. The attitude of mind which led Dickens to attack these things is in large measure related to his intense awareness and appreciation of the *peculiarities* of human nature as they manifest themselves in appearance, behaviour, and speech.

There are certainly many grotesque figures in Dickens's works, Quilp, Fagin, Uriah Heep, and others, of whom we are meant to disapprove entirely; their grotesqueness is all of a piece, wholly pejorative. Significantly, Dickens's villains are often characterized by some grotesquely *inhuman* feature: Carker's much-mentioned smile 'has something in it like the snarl of a cat',[1] Quilp is utterly monstrous, Heep is a 'red-headed animal'.[2]

Such figures, symbols of incorrigible evil, are the true antitheses of Dickens's 'celestial caricatures'; as such, they are treated melodramatically rather than satirically.

45. It may be useful to indicate the chief kinds of grotesqueness to be found in Dickens's characters by listing the main kinds of incongruity with which he deals. In the following brief list the 'standard' is given first, then the type of deviation, and finally examples of figures which evince such incongruity. Many figures listed below might be placed in more than one category.

(i) Gentility: uncouthness of language, appearance, &c., clumsiness: Sam Weller, Clemency Newcome (*The Battle of Life*).

(ii) The ideally romantic: the absurdly romantic: Flora Finching, John Chivery.

(iii) The heroic, the historic: the trivial, the pretentious: mock-heroic description, Little Swills (*Bleak House*), Mr. Chadband.

(iv) The everyday, the normal: the extravagant, 'pure' grotesqueness: Mr. Dick, Flora Finching's aunt, Miss Havisham.

(v) Humanity: inhumanity: Squeers, Bounderby, Chancery.

(vi) The natural: the unnatural: the Artful Dodger, Jo, Tom-all-Alone's, Coketown.

(vii) Unselfishness, fellow-feeling: various forms of egotism, selfishness, moral myopia: Harold Skimpole, Mrs. Jellyby, Pecksniff.

These categories, which are meant to be representative rather than exhaustive and which could obviously be subdivided almost indefinitely, will serve to indicate in simple fashion where the milder varieties of grotesqueness are to be found. The three last categories are those to which the purely satirical figures belong (though it may be repeated that such grotesque figures as the Artful Dodger, Jo, and Maggy (*Little Dorrit*) are not themselves denounced).

Of the remaining categories, though the 'deviations' have been given pejorative names for the most part, it should be remarked that the standards are by no means rigid, as they are in the later categories where we find examples of Dickens at his most adamant. Above all, in the case of group (iv), the grotesques can scarcely be regarded as

---

[1] cf. *Dombey and Son*, ch. XIII.

[2] Cockshut, op. cit., draws attention to the inhuman aspect of Heep (p. 119) and observes of Fagin: 'Cruickshank's famous drawing, in which the condemned Fagin does not look human at all, is entirely in the spirit of the text' (p. 32).

having a satirical side at all; Miss Havisham does indeed play more
than an 'atmospheric' role, but her sheer eccentricity largely justifies
her inclusion in this group, which, of course, interpenetrates the
others. Perhaps the best way of describing Mr. Dick and Flora
Finching's aunt is to call them dramatic grotesques. We are meant to
feel that the world is a more exhilarating place because such characters
exist in it; if we insist on regarding them as impossible creatures like
the Mad Hatter or the Dong, we fail to appreciate their significance.
Lord David Cecil observes: 'Any grotesque feature he noticed in the
world came as grist to Dickens' mill. And such features as were not
grotesque he tried to make so.'[1]

The important phrase here is 'in the world'. The second sentence
seems to imply, somewhat unfortunately, that Dickens set to work to
make characters, events, &c., which he did not regard as grotesque
into characters and events which were. The truth is rather that those
things which Dickens did not regard as grotesque—self-sacrifice, for
example—appear in idealized form. What he endeavoured to do was
to bring out by dramatic exaggeration the potential colour and humour
of everyday life; but, for Dickens, these qualities were already implicit
in his material. It is at least as important to recognize his fantastic
London as London as to appreciate its fantasy. The various strands of
fantasy can be seen fairly clearly in the following passage:

'Chaymaid!' cried the waiter. 'Gelen box num seven wish see room!'
'Stay!' said Clennam, rousing himself. 'I was not thinking of what I
said. I answered mechanically. I am not going to sleep here. I am going
home.'
''Deed sir? Chaymaid! Gelen box num seven, not go sleep here, gome.'[2]

First there is Dickens's pleasure in the bizarre language of the waiter,
a spontaneous pleasure in the odd or eccentric. Second, there is his
pleasure in the actuality of the grotesque (whether it is an accurate or
heightened rendering, we are clearly meant to regard it as representative). Third, there is the satirical aspect, which in the present
instance is not very strong.

Cockshut remarks: 'His prefaces reveal a literal mind, and a determination to prove that his strangest imaginative flights are only sober
reporting.'[3] In dramatizing his experience, Dickens does not intend
to falsify it, though, of course, he oscillates between the world as he

---

[1] cf. Cecil, op. cit., p. 32.
[2] cf. *Little Dorrit*, ch. III (Cassell ed., vol. XII, p. 25).
[3] Cockshut, op. cit., p. 11.

sees it and the world as he wishes it to be. A strong affinity exists between his use of the pure grotesque, i.e. his use of the grotesque for dramatic as distinct from satirical purposes, and his 'sentimentality'. Both, for Dickens, have their roots in reality. Cockshut twice refers us to the preface in which Dickens attempts in 'dully literal' fashion to establish the factual nature of Spontaneous Combustion.[1] Closely parallel to this is Dickens's lengthy insistence, in the preface to *Nicholas Nickleby*, that the Cheeryble brothers, notoriously sentimental as they are, were 'drawn from life . . . and . . . no creations of the Author's brain'. Adolphus Ward cites evidence of this insistence on the reality of his characters from Forster, who observes that

> what he had most to notice in Dickens at the very outset of his career, was his indifference to any praise of his performances on the merely literary side, compared with the higher recognition of them as bits of actual life, with the meaning and purpose, on their part, and the responsibility on his, of realities, rather than creations of fancy.[2]

Ward remarks that 'few great humorists have so persistently sought to efface the line which separates the barely possible from the morally probable'.[3] The fact is that Dickens was himself convinced, and wished to convince his readers, that his view of the world was fundamentally a truthful one; that among other things the world is, and ought to be, full of exhilarating goodness and exciting strangeness which need to be held before the reader's attention.

FACT AND FANCY, MELODRAMA, THE MACABRE

46. Humphry House's reference to the religious convictions of Dickens and his contemporaries as being 'in a state of transition from supernatural belief to humanism' has already been quoted. The implications of such a state of affairs may usefully be considered at this stage in connexion with Dickens's work.

Morality is the progressive aspect of religion. Both by temperament and through the influence of the contemporary attitude, Dickens was a moralist in religion:

> There seemed to be some unlucky inconsistency in the atmosphere that day; for though the proportions of St Paul's Cathedral are very beautiful,

---

[1] Cockshut, op. cit., pp. 132, 183.
[2] cf. A. W. Ward, *Dickens* (English Men of Letters Series (Macmillan and Co., 1908), p. 215).
[3] ibid., p. 219.

it had an air of being somewhat out of drawing, in my eyes. I felt as though the cross were too high up, and perched upon the intervening golden ball too far away.[1]

House remarks, with regard to the sentimental death-beds in Dickens, that a religion which is moving away from supernatural belief 'is very poorly equipped to face death, and must dwell on it for that very reason'.[2] In general, we may inquire what else is lacking in such a religious attitude. The supernatural side of religion provides 'objective equivalents' for that sense of the eternal—Virginia Woolf's 'fin passing far out'[3]—which Jung calls the regressive aspect of mind. Where traditional religious symbols no longer satisfy the individual emotionally, other ways of expressing this sense of the eternal or infinite have to be found, the degree of urgency varying with the individual temperament. The more extroverted and progressive this is, the weaker the sense of the transcendental or transnatural.

Dickens's preoccupation with the world of fact—the merest glance at his pages reveals his appetite for physical reality—is evidence of a predominantly progressive temperament. His religious attitude, his concern with the here and now, with social injustice and inhumanity, reflects the same progressive orientation. The problem of good and evil in his work is conceived of in social terms, rather than in cosmic terms as in Hardy's work. He makes continual use of the characteristic instrument of the progressively inclined artist, satire.

We are accustomed to think of Dickens's work as fantastic, melodramatic, unrealistic, and so on, but this is only relatively true. Ward, as we have seen, remarks that Dickens sought to efface the dividing line between 'the barely possible and the morally probable'; whatever the last vague phrase may mean, it is certain that for Dickens only the possible, as he conceived it, had a serious appeal.

Dickens, then, desires no other world but the one he lives in, but before that world can meet with his entire approval it requires to be modified in two ways. Of these, one kind of modification, demanded rather than depicted in his work—social and political improvement—

---

[1] cf. *The Uncommercial Traveller* (XXXIV: 'On An Amateur Beat').
[2] cf. House, op. cit., p. 132. Mr. K. J. Fielding (*Charles Dickens: A Critical Introduction*, Longmans, London, 1958), whilst admitting that Dickens was 'without a strong personal religious experience' (p. 139), insists that Mr. House's criticism of his religion is 'much too strong'. It is, however, the supernatural rather than the ethical side of Dickens's religion (and of Victorian religion in general) that Mr. House criticizes.
[3] See p. 90.

is advocated in wholly deliberate fashion; the other, an intensification of the strangeness of the world about him and of the heroic conflict of good and evil, is much less conscious. The latter modification is simply impressed upon his narrative as the way he saw things, in two kinds of exaggeration, grotesqueness and sentimentality. Both are outlets for Dickens's sense of the infinite, too weak in Dickens to provoke a rejection of 'this vegetable glass of nature' as in a mystic like Blake, but powerful enough to induce him to pour into the mould of humanitarianism the fervour of religion, 'mouthing formulae from another scheme of values as if they expressed his own',[1] and to throw over the *ordinary* events of life an air of novelty and strangeness.

The peculiarities of Dickens's characters are to be regarded in part as a kind of protest against the tyranny of institutions and theories which aim at reducing people to ciphers and existence to a wholly predictable process. The most noteworthy expression of this rebellion is the educational method of Mr. M'Choakumchild in *Hard Times*:

Fact, fact, fact, everywhere in the material aspect of the town; fact, fact, fact, everywhere in the immaterial. The M'Choakumchild school was all fact, and the school of design was all fact, and the relations between master and man were all fact, and everything was fact between the lying-in hospital and the cemetery, and what you couldn't state in figures, or show to be purchaseable in the cheapest market and saleable in the dearest, was not, and never should be, world without end, Amen.[2]

The opposition of fact and fancy in *Hard Times* ('You must discard the word Fancy altogether. You must have nothing to do with it')[3] requires some comment, particularly in view of Dickens's 'dully literal' insistence on the factual nature of such things as Spontaneous Combustion and his 'obsessive devotion to detail'.[4] *Hard Times* is concerned with social injustice. The Gradgrind-M'Choakum-child philosophy is attacked because of its social repercussions, because it leads to economic oppression and takes the joy out of life for the working people:

Surely, none of us . . . are to be told . . . that . . . there was any Fancy in them demanding to be brought into healthy existence instead of struggling on in convulsions? That exactly in the ratio as they worked long and

[1] cf. House, op. cit., p. 132.
[2] cf. *Hard Times*, bk. I, ch. V (Cassell ed., vol. VIII, p. 368).
[3] ibid., ch. II (Cassell ed., p. 357).
[4] cf. Cockshut, op. cit., p. 183. (cf. Engel, op. cit., 'Dickens had . . . little sympathy with any art which did not make terms with what he considered to be reality' (pp. 10–11).)

monotonously, the craving grew within them for some physical relief—some relaxation, encouraging good humour and good spirits, and giving them a vent . . . which craving must and would be satisfied aright, or must and would, inevitably go wrong, until the laws of Creation were repealed.[1]

Utilitarian economists, skeletons of schoolmasters, Commissioners of Fact, genteel and used-up infidels, gabblers of many little dog's-eared creeds, the poor you will have always with you. Cultivate in them, while there is yet time, the utmost graces of the fancies and affections, to adorn their lives so much in need of ornament; or, in the day of your triumph, when romance is utterly driven out of their souls, and they and a bare existence stand face to face, Reality will take a wolfish turn, and make an end of you.[2]

Here, fancy is conceived of as a valuable safety-valve. The criticism of M'Choakumchild's teaching is similar in tone: 'No little Gradgrind had ever associated a cow in a field with that famous cow with the crumpled horn . . . or with that yet more famous cow who swallowed Tom Thumb . . .'[3] It is the social significance of fancy which is emphasized throughout. M'Choakumchildism is myopic and inadequate, not because it is opposed to a transcendental reality, but because it prevents its victims from taking a romantic view of the real, physical world—a very different thing. The case of Louisa Gradgrind, which is contrasted with the serene attitude to life of Sissy Jupe, requires to be examined in order to bring out Dickens's view of fancy as a vital factor in the development of a proper attitude to the world in which we live. Louisa's passionate avowal of her sense of something other than facts and figures, considered out of context, is a sympathetic representation of the mystical attitude:

. . . if you had known that there lingered in my breast, sensibilities, weaknesses capable of being cherished into strength, defying all the calculations ever made by man, and no more known to his arithmetic than his Creator is,—would you have given me to the husband whom I am now sure that I hate? . . . Would you have robbed me . . . of the immaterial part of my life, the spring and summer of my belief, my refuge from what is sordid and bad in the real things around me, my school in which I should have learned to be more humble and trusting with them, and to hope in my little sphere to make them better? . . . With a hunger and thirst upon me, father, which have never been for a moment appeased; with an ardent impulse towards some region where rules, and figures, and definitions were not quite absolute; I have grown up, battling every inch

[1] cf. *Hard Times*, bk. I, ch. V (Cassell ed., p. 369).
[2] ibid., bk. II, ch. VI (Cassell ed., p. 469).
[3] ibid., bk. I, ch. III (Cassell ed., p. 359).

of my way . . . What I have learned has left me doubting, misbelieving, despising, regretting, what I have not learned.[1]

The significance of this powerful expression of the sense of the spiritual, considered thus in isolation, should not be overlooked; Dickens is clearly describing something which he has himself experienced. Nevertheless, Louisa's frame of mind is meant to be pitied rather than adopted, in the context of the novel; the evil effects of her upbringing have caused her to turn away from the world about her. Robbed of her mental equilibrium, she sacrifices herself in 'visionary' fashion to help her brother: 'I made that wild escape into something visionary, and have slowly found out how wild it was.'[2]

In chapter IX, Dickens speaks of

the dreams of childhood—its airy fables; its graceful, beautiful, humane, impossible adornments of the world beyond: so good to be believed in once, so good to be remembered when outgrown, for then the least among them rises to the stature of a great Charity in the heart . . .[3]

Louisa, frustrated, has never 'outgrown' her fantasies; instead of a playful, nostalgic attitude towards pure fantasy, leavening sound common sense with 'the best influences of old home', and casting a romantic light over reality—the attitude of Sissy Jupe—she has reacted against her upbringing into a kind of barren mysticism:

Her remembrances of home and childhood were remembrances of the drying up of every spring and fountain in her young heart as it gushed out. The golden waters were not there. They were flowing for the fertilization of the land where grapes are gathered from thorns, and figs from thistles.[4]

In *Hard Times* the symbolic opposition of the world of Gradgrind and that of Sleary is a much more profound expression of Dickens's dissatisfaction with the *Weltanschauung* of 'utilitarian economists' than the explicit opposition of fact and fancy remarked above. Unlike the cow which swallowed Tom Thumb, the world of Sleary is undeniably real, but its reality is not of a kind which can be comprehended statistically; it is incontrovertible evidence that there are more things in heaven and earth than are dreamt of in the philosophy of Thomas Gradgrind, things which are at once factual and inexhaustibly strange:

[1] cf. *Hard Times*, bk. II, ch. XII (Cassell ed., p. 507).
[2] ibid., (Cassell ed., p. 508).
[3] ibid., bk. II, ch. IX (Cassell ed., p. 493).
[4] ibid. (Cassell ed., p. 494).

'Emma, thee lotht her huthband. He wath throw'd a heavy back-fall off a Elephant in a thort of a Pagoda thing ath the Thultan of the Indieth, and he never got the better of it; and thee married a thecond time—married a Cheethemonger ath fell in love with her from the front—and he'th a Overtheer and makin' a fortun'.[1]

This gentleman was mentioned in the bills of the day as Mr E. W. B. Childers, so justly celebrated for his daring vaulting act as the Wild Hunts-man of the North American Prairies; in which popular performance, a diminutive boy with an old face, who now accompanied him, assisted as his infant son: being carried upside down over his father's shoulder, by one foot, and held by the crown of his head, heels upwards, in the palm of his father's hand, according to the violent paternal manner in which wild huntsmen may be observed to fondle their offspring. Made up with curls, wreaths, wings, white bismuth, and carmine, this hopeful young person soared into so pleasing a Cupid as to constitute the chief delight of the maternal part of the spectators; but in private, where his characteristics were a precocious cutaway coat and an extremely gruff voice, he became of the Turf, turfy.[2]

Nothing, perhaps, in the whole of Dickens's work illustrates so clearly the significance of the grotesque for Dickens as a window looking on infinity as his choice of Sleary's circus as a counterblast to M'Choakumchildism. The introduction of a supernatural or preter-natural element for the purpose would have struck him as insufficiently realistic; on the other hand, to have contrasted the evils of Coketown with, say, the Utopian conditions of a model industrial community of the Robert Owen type, with plenty of recreation and a good living wage, would have been to leave one of the strongest of his objections to utilitarians *et hoc genus omne* unaired. Sleary's circus is at one and the same time a symbol of the strangeness and richness of life and a solid and permanent reality: 'You *mutht* have uth, Thquire. Do the withe thing and the kind thing too, and make the betht of uth; not the wurtht!'[3]

Although it is the accepted thing to admire the grotesque and deplore the sentimental in Dickens's work, this, however just, is to some extent ironical in view of the close affinity between these two tendencies. Both are properly to be regarded as the resolution of a conflict between Dickens's fundamentally practical and progressive temperament and the stubborn insistence of his religious sense on

---

[1] cf. *Hard Times*, bk. III, ch. VII (Cassell ed., p. 553).
[2] ibid., bk. I, ch. VI (Cassell ed., p. 373).
[3] cf. *Hard Times*, bk. III, ch. VIII (Cassell ed., p. 562).

G.E.L.—Q

making its influence felt. House accuses Dickens of 'mouthing formulae from another scheme of values as if they expressed his own' in such scenes as the death of Jo in *Bleak House*; of bestowing upon his virtuous characters the consolations of an immortal happiness in which he himself had no real belief. In both his sentimental figures and scenes and his dramatic use of the grotesque (his *satirical* use of the grotesque remains to be considered) Dickens attempts a kind of compromise between out-and-out realism and the transcendental symbol. Thus Little Nell, Little Dorrit, &c., are human angels, figures which are meant to bring the breath of heaven into a workaday world. Quilp and Fagin belong to the same category; they are human devils. Quilp, Fagin, Little Nell, Little Dorrit, and Oliver Twist[1] are best described as melodramatic figures, avoiding the slightly confusing term sentimental.

Such figures, with one foot on the plane of symbolic narrative and the other in Victorian London, introduce a black and white simplification characteristic of the myth (or of its more sophisticated ramification, the fairy-tale) into a predominantly realistic context. Little Nell and Quilp complement each other admirably; in a more obviously symbolic setting, Quilp's pursuit of Nell might have been powerfully compelling and full of significance. As it is, both figures are denounced as unrealistic. Lord David Cecil remarks the same conflict of planes in the case of Fagin: 'Fagin . . . is ludicrous considered as a real character; an ogre of a fairy-tale out to entrap little boys. But the horror inspired by his trial scene could not be more terrific if he were drawn with all the criminological insight of Dostoievski.'[2]

The transformation of character frequently castigated in Dickens's work, the development of Little Emily into a kind of female Ancient Mariner, the metamorphosis of Montague Tigg into a 'sinister conspirator', the outrageous transformation of Mr. Micawber into a sterling figure of energy and initiative, stems largely from the same attempt to fuse together different levels of significance. Where good and evil are involved Dickens endeavours to express the immensity of

---

[1] Fielding draws attention to the symbolic side of Oliver Twist: 'In a passage later dropped from his *Preface* Dickens explained that "in little Oliver" he "wished to show . . . the principle of Good surviving through every adverse circumstance and triumphing at last". He is intentionally generalized so that we care little about him as a person, Dickens knew how to turn this sort of convention to account' (op. cit., p. 33).

[2] cf. Cecil, op cit., p. 36.

the issues involved by resorting to extremes. Cockshut comments: 'His innate melodramatic tendency . . . left him very imperfectly aware that good and evil exist together in the same person.'[1] In my opinion it is more accurate to say that what we call Dickens's melodrama, the exaggerated effect of black and white oppositions in realistic narrative, is fundamentally due to the desire to depict the events of ordinary life *sub specie aeternitatis*, to establish the existence in human behaviour of 'another scheme of values', of the supernatural. It is also indisputable that Dickens was a professional writer concerned to give his public the kind of entertainment it wanted. Without ignoring this factor, it remains true to say that Dickens was able to satisfy his public without significantly falsifying his own attitude to life.

47. In what I have called the dramatic use of the grotesque, i.e. the use of bizarre images and characters to impart to the narrative 'something rich and strange', this same regressive factor, best regarded as a secondary influence upon a predominantly practical cast of mind, is to be seen at work. Let us now consider the chief kinds of grotesque image to be found in Dickens's work; arbitrarily we may distinguish three main groups, the dramatic, the satirical, and the 'ambivalent', but the three groups merge into one another.

In that amazing ragbag of journalistic pieces *The Uncommercial Traveller*, Dickens tells us: 'My walking is of two kinds: one, straight on end to a definite goal at a round pace; one objectless, loitering, and purely vagabond. In the latter state, no gipsy on earth is a greater vagabond than myself.'[2] The pieces themselves may be roughly classified into two corresponding groups, some concerned with exposing various social ills, others concerned merely to entertain the reader, vehicles for odd facts and fancies. In the latter group we find the grotesque employed for its own sake. In 'Night Walks' (XIII) we have Dickens's thoughts upon Waterloo Bridge:

> The chopped-up murdered man, had not been lowered with a rope over the parapet when those nights were; he was alive, and slept then quietly enough most likely, and undisturbed by any dream of where he was to come. But the river had an awful look, the buildings on the banks were muffled in black shrouds, and the reflected lights seemed to originate deep in the water, as if the spectres of suicides were holding them to show where they went down. The wild moon and clouds were as restless as an evil

---

[1] Cockshut, op. cit., p. 13.
[2] cf. *The Uncommercial Traveller*, X ('Shy Neighbourhoods') (Cassell ed., p. 439).

conscience in a tumbled bed, and the very shadow of the immensity of London seemed to lie oppressively upon the river.[1]

In two of the pieces we are taken to the morgue. Significantly, he tells us: 'Whenever I am at Paris, I am dragged by invisible force into the Morgue. I never want to go there, but am always pulled there.'[2] He relates how on one occasion he saw the corpse of a 'large dark man' which afterwards haunted his imgination, spoiled his bathing, his dinner, and so on.

For the most part, however, Dickens's use of the grotesque is accompanied by humour, a symptom of detachment. Even the corpse mentioned above is treated jocularly:

> . . . I was forced to see a large dark man whose disfigurement by water was in a frightful manner, comic, and whose expression was that of a prize-fighter who had closed his eyelids under a heavy blow, but was going immediately to open them, shake his head, and 'come up smiling'.[3]

In the macabre grotesque, the expression of that side of his nature which drags him 'by invisible force into the Morgue', we find Dickens at his most regressive, closest to Coleridge and the Romantics, farthest from Swift. But the peculiar grotesqueness which we associate with Dickens at his most characteristic is the product of his combination of the strange and the humorous; like the corpse in the Paris morgue, even such macabre monsters as Quilp and Fagin are 'in a frightful manner, comic'. It is nevertheless important to note that they are not burlesque figures which we are meant to find absurd, but a serious representation of the diabolical. Their 'comic' aspect might perhaps be compared to that of the Witches in *Macbeth* which are also 'in a frightful manner, comic'—though, needless to remark, the frightfulness of the Witches is proportionately far greater than that of Quilp and Fagin. The point is that in the total complex of these characters the comic element is a subordinate one.

As we move further away from the extreme 'Coleridgean' end of Dickens's work, the humorous element in his grotesque imagery increases in importance, and, significantly, the artistic value of his work increases also. The bizarre and extraordinary side of his imagery is more nearly balanced by the humorous element. Thus in 'Night Walks' the macabre image of the 'chopped-up murdered man' is succeeded by the more typically grotesque description of

[1] cf. *The Uncommercial Traveller*, XIII (Cassell ed., pp. 465–6).
[2] ibid. VII (Cassell ed., p. 416).
[3] ibid. (Cassell ed., p. 417).

... a man in a high and long snuff-coloured coat, and shoes, and, to the best of my belief, nothing else but a hat, who took out of his hat a large cold meat pudding; a meat pudding so large that it was a very tight fit, and brought the lining of the hat out with it ... Left to himself in his box, he stood the pudding on the bare table, and, instead of cutting it, stabbed it, overhand, with the knife, like a mortal enemy; then took the knife out, wiped it on his sleeve, tore the pudding asunder with his fingers, and ate it all up. The remembrance of this man with the pudding remains with me as the remembrance of the most spectral person my houselessness encountered.[1]

For the most part the comic grotesque characters in the novels are presented to us in less simple fashion than this; they are labelled for us morally. Such 'pure extravaganzas' as Flora Finching's aunt are the exception. In such figures, however, devoid of either sentimental or satirical modification, we see the fundamental tension in Dickens's use of the grotesque. Coleridge employs the grotesque, in the form of the strange, the exotic, the preternatural, approvingly, as an echo of the infinite. Swift employs the grotesque, in the form of the absurd, the preposterous, the ridiculous, pejoratively, as a symbol of stupidity and vice. Dickens has a foot in both camps, so to speak, and the image of the man with the pudding in his hat reflects the fact. He is simultaneously a 'spectre'—a profound mystery—and a figure of fun:

On the second occasion of my seeing him, he said, huskily to the man of sleep, 'Am I red to-night?' 'You are,' he uncompromisingly answered. 'My mother,' said the spectre, 'was a red-faced woman that liked drink, and I looked at her hard when she lay in her coffin, and I took the complexion.' Somehow the pudding seemed an unwholesome pudding after that, and I put myself in its way no more.[2]

If we ask ourselves whether Dickens approves of the existence of such a figure, the answer is clearly both yes and no. His existence adds to the mystery and the gusto of life. On the other hand, the figure is ridiculous and has something 'unwholesome' about it. It is enlightening to consider what Blake and Coleridge, or Pope and Swift, would have made of such a figure.

48. The connexion between the sentimental aspect of Dickens's work and the non-satirical use of the grotesque may be described in a more explicit way by saying that Dickens's religious sense manifests itself both in his preoccupation with the mysterious, from the macabre

---

[1] cf. *The Uncommercial Traveller*, XIII (Cassell ed., p. 470).
[2] ibid.

to the merely eccentric, and in his melodramatic or sentimental exaggeration of human goodness and 'inhuman' wickedness.

At this point the parallel between these two aspects of Dickens's religious sense in their relation to the prevailing 'factual' current of Dickens's mind may be further developed. There is an obvious connexion between the form of his 'celestial caricatures'—in part principles of good and evil, in part realistic characters—and his views on the social and moral value of the imagination or fancy as expressed in *Hard Times*. These views require further consideration.

For Coleridge, as for Blake and Wordsworth in their different ways, the imagination is an intuitive means of apprehending eternal truth. As Dickens saw religion in the progressive guise of social morality, so he saw the imagination in the guise of 'fancy', and its role as that of softening the outlines of 'grim reality'. Briefly, he regards the *use* of the imagination as vital to the well-being of both the individual and the community. In the absence of some such theory as Coleridge's conception of the 'secondary imagination', by means of which Coleridge is able to regard even the wildest fantasy as an 'echo' of eternal reality, Dickens naturally regards the truth of an imaginative creation as being proportionate to the extent to which it is based on physical reality. Consequently, whilst he considers even the most unreal fantasy to have a moral significance—'. . . the dreams of childhood —its airy fables, its graceful, beautiful, humane, impossible adornments of the world beyond: so good to be believed in once, so good to be remembered when outgrown'[1]—he sees his own proper task as that of encouraging his readers to adopt an imaginative view of the world about them. He speaks of this task both as taking a fanciful view of fact and as bringing out the 'romantic' aspect of reality as though it is something inherent in the physical world. In either case, he is reluctant to admit that 'fanciful treatment' is inconsistent with 'the exact truth':

It does not seem to me to be enough to say of any description that it is the exact truth. The exact truth must be there; but the merit or art in the narrator, is the manner of stating the truth. As to which thing in literature, it always seems to me that there is a world to be done. And in these times, when the tendency is to be frightfully literal and catalogue-like—to make the thing, in short, a sort of sum in reduction that any miserable creature can do in that way—I have an idea . . . that the very holding of popular literature through a kind of popular dark age, may depend on such fanciful treatment.[2]

[1] cf. *Hard Times*, bk. II, ch. IX (Cassell ed., p. 493).
[2] cf. Forster, op. cit., pp. 727–8.

One of the most remarkable of Dickens's statements about the importance of fancy is to be found in his preface to the first number of *Household Words*:

No mere utilitarian spirit, no iron binding of the mind to grim realities, will give a harsh tone to our *Household Words*. In the bosoms of the young and old, of the well-to-do and of the poor, we would tenderly cherish that light of Fancy which is inherent in the human breast; which, according to its nurture, burns with an inspiring flame, or sinks to a sullen glare, but which, (or woe betide that day!) can never be extinguished. To show to all, that in all familiar things, even in those which are repellant on the surface, there is Romance enough, if we will find it out:—to teach the hardest workers at this whirling wheel of toil, that their lot is not necessarily a moody, brutal fact, excluded from the sympathies and graces of imagination; to bring the greater and the lesser in degree together, upon that wide field, and mutually dispose them to a better acquaintance and a kinder understanding—is one main object of our *Household Words*.

The mightier inventions of this age are not, to our thinking, all material, but have a kind of souls in their stupendous bodies which may find expression in *Household Words*. The traveller whom we accompany on his railroad or his steamboat journey, may gain, we hope, some compensation for incidents which these later generations have outlived, in new associations with the Power that bears him onward; with the habitations and the ways of life of crowds of his fellow-creatures among whom he passes like the wind; even with the towering chimneys he may see, spirting out fire and smoke upon the prospect. The Swart giants, Slaves of the Lamp of Knowledge, have their thousand and one tales, no less than the Genii of the East; and these, in all their many phases of endurance, in all their many moving lessons of compassion and consideration, we design to tell.[1]

In the concluding number of *Household Words*, Dickens refers to 'that fusion of the graces of the imagination with the realities of life which is vital to the welfare of any community'.[2]

What emerges from the examination of Dickens's remarks on the significance of fancy may be summarized briefly as follows:

(i) Whilst it is essential to human happiness that fancy, 'inherent in the human breast', should be nurtured and encouraged, in the responsible adult mind it finds its true 'objective correlative', not in 'the land where grapes are gathered from thorns',[3] but in the real

---

[1] cf. *Household Words*, 30 March, 1850 ('A Preliminary Word') (Cassell ed., vol. XIX (Collected Papers), pp. 328–9).

[2] cf. *Household Words*, 28 May 1859 ('Address') (Cassell ed., vol. XIX, p. 331).

[3] cf. *Hard Times*, ch. IX (Cassell ed., p. 494).

world about us, as an ancillary to common sense and a stimulus to benevolence. The human appetite for the wonderful is best satisfied by the conviction that we live in a wonderful world; the fanciful and the factual are complementary, not alternative, attitudes to life.

(ii) Dickens thus sees it as his proper task to show us the ordinary world in a new and exciting way, in all its 'wild, grotesque, and fanciful aspects'; 'In *Bleak House*', he tells us, 'I have purposely dwelt upon the romantic side of familiar things.'

This is by no means the worst of literary programmes; the all-important thing is the manner in which it is carried out.[1] The point which requires to be emphasized in connexion with the opinions set out in the passages quoted from *Household Words* and the views expressed in *Hard Times* is that it is *familiar* things which are to be ornamented with the graces of imagination and presented in a novel and wonderful light. Above all, it is to Dickens's determination to treat the familiar and the commonplace in a romantic and fanciful manner that we must look for the source of the grotesqueness which we associate with his work. It will be as well to note at this juncture that satirical caricature, no less than romantic exaggeration, exhibits the commonplace in a fanciful light.

THE SEMI-EXOTIC, HYPERBOLE AND AMBIVALENCE

49. It is possible to combine the factual and the wonderful in a number of ways, some of which may be listed:

(i) The artist may deal with the exotic or unfamiliar, as say, Melville does in *Moby Dick*, or Scott in *Waverley*.

(ii) He may employ fanciful comparisons, hyperbole, and meta-phor: 'As much mud in the streets, as if the waters had but newly retired from the face of the earth, and it would not be wonderful to meet a Megalosaurus, forty feet long or so, waddling like an elephan-tine lizard up Holborn Hill.'[2]

(iii) He may exaggerate character or incident.

(iv) In less easily definable fashion, the artist may influence our attitude by adopting a highly dramatic or heroic tone, by the use of rhetoric to describe a generous act, a sick-bed, &c.

Dickens uses all these means of making the world of fact seem strange and exciting; but his inclination to think of the wonderful in

---

[1] This is not intended to imply that Dickens worked in accordance with a fixed theory, merely that the summary indicates one of his chief aims.

[2] cf. *Bleak House*, ch. I (Cassell ed., vol. XI, p. 1).

terms of the fanciful or the peculiar results in the reader being confronted not so much with an absorbing and exciting representation of
the world about him as with a caricature of that world which is
fascinating because it is fantastic. It is as if Dickens had little faith in
the 'entertainment value' of unadorned reality. In part, no doubt,
this attitude was imposed by the peculiar demands of serial publication, particularly intense in weekly publication, but obviously
compelling in the monthly instalment system as well. The continual
interruption of the narrative—seen from the reader's rather than the
writer's point of view—naturally led to the neglect of such 'long-
term investments' as the gradual development of character or the
subtle heightening of tension characteristic of Samuel Richardson or
Henry James in favour of bold black and white effects, incidents
dramatic in themselves rather than in relation to the whole; variety
is given precedence over logic, and the curious is employed, in Swift's
phrase, as a 'ring in the nose' to lead the reader from instalment to
instalment.[1] It is no doubt easy to exaggerate this influence. Dickens's
manner of writing is a reflection of his personality, not merely of the
exigencies of serial publication. The 'picaresque' type of plot which
he employs in *Pickwick Papers, The Old Curiosity Shop, Nicholas
Nickleby, Martin Chuzzlewit*, makes long-term planning largely unnecessary. Moreover, as Professor Butt and Mrs. Tillotson have pre-
eminently demonstrated, Dickens's work is by no means without
organization. Nevertheless, serial composition may be said to have
intensified Dickens's natural disposition towards 'violent chiaroscuro',
and this presentation of what we recognize to be fundamentally
realistic characters and incidents, as it were in a continuous state of
excitement, with great fluctuation of tone,[2] is certainly a contributory

[1] cf. Address announcing the termination of *Master Humphrey's Clock*,
Sept. 1841: 'I have often felt cramped and confined in a very irksome and
harrassing degree by the space in which I have been constrained to move. . .
Many passages in a tale of any length, depend materially for their interest
on the intimate relation they bear to what has gone before, or to what is to
follow . . . in the present (weekly) form of publication it is often . . . quite
impossible to preserve [this needful connexion] sufficiently through the
current numbers.' (cf. Cassell ed., vol. XIX, p. 286.) Fielding insists that
serial publication had a beneficial effect on Dickens's work: '*Hard Times* . . .
was the first of Dickens's later novels to have the advantage of being written
for weekly publication. "The difficulty of the space", he wrote, "is CRUSH-
ING"; but it compelled him to write with economy, and forced him to fit
the story into a compact structure' (op. cit., p. 131).
[2] In this respect, Dickens might be contrasted with Somerset Maugham,
whose level, matter-of-fact manner of narration, devoid of rhetoric and
hyperbole, induces a particularly willing 'suspension of disbelief'.

factor in that abnormal effect—as of the familiar seen in a distorting mirror—which is thoroughly characteristic of Dickens, and which Kayser speaks of as one of the chief criteria of grotesque art: 'The grotesque is the alienated world . . . It is our world, which has changed.'[1]

Kayser insists that the world of the fairy-tale is not grotesque because, though alien, it does not conflict with the normal standards of life, having its own conventions. At all events, as we have seen, the interpenetration of the familiar and the fanciful, as in the work of Kafka, produces a particularly grotesque effect.

Something of this may be seen in Dickens's use of what might be termed the semi-exotic, phenomena on the periphery of our everyday experience—slums, wharves, circuses, travelling shows, prisons—things which act as a kind of meeting-place of the strange and the familiar. We are, moreover, continually travelling backwards and forwards between such semi-exotic surroundings and middle-class drawing-rooms, between the world of Bill Sikes and the world of Mr. Brownlow, and witnessing the intercourse of figures from these different worlds—Skimpole and the bailiff, Chadband and Jo, Ruth Pinch and Sairey Gamp. In another writer's work the result of these interconnexions might perhaps have been to normalize the unfamiliar. In Dickens they are contributory to the general effect of alienation, largely because the 'semi-exotic' settings and the outlandish characters associated with them bulk too large, both in dramatic importance and in the sheer amount of space devoted to them, to be absorbed into a predominantly conventional milieu, even if the latter could be said to exist in Dickens, where the drawing-room and its occupants (lawyers, clergymen, businessmen) are frequently no less peculiar than the 'semi-exotic' characters, the guttersnipes, criminals, and strolling players.

The fanciful comparison, of its very nature a 'playful', attributive use of fancy, is exactly suited to Dickens's attitude and is his most characteristic stylistic device; secure from the possibility of any accusation that he is distorting reality (to liken Mr. M'Choakumchild to an ogre does not make him any the less Mr. M'Choakumchild), he ornaments his narrative with metaphors, frequently elaborated into lengthy 'conceits', which for sheer force of wit are not unworthy to be compared with those of *A Tale of a Tub*:

There was nothing about him in the way of decoration but a watch,

[1] cf. Kayser, op. cit., p. 198.

which was lowered into the depths of its proper pocket by an old black ribbon, and had a tarnished copper key moored above it, to show where it was sunk.[1]

... an amazing little old woman, with a face like a staring wooden doll too cheap for expression, and a stiff yellow wig perched unevenly on the top of her head, as if the child who owned the doll had driven a tack through it anywhere, so that it only got fastened on. Another remarkable thing in this little old woman was, that the same child seemed to have damaged her face in two or three places with some blunt instrument in the nature of a spoon; her countenance, and particularly the top of her nose, presenting the phenomena of several dints, generally answering to the bowl of that article.[2]

... a sobbing gaslight in the counting-house window, and a burglarious stream of fog creeping in to strangle it . . .[3]

It would be a mistake to ignore the cumulative effect of the innumerable metaphors and conceits in Dickens's work on the reader's frame of mind. Apart from the immediate effect of each such ornament, the continuous flow of fanciful notions exerts a powerful influence on our emotions. Cockshut, commenting on Dickens's 'marvellous vividness in the presentation of physical objects', remarks that the fog in *Bleak House* is 'at once the most actual and the most symbolical of all fogs'.[4] Lord David Cecil, quoting the famous opening paragraphs of *Bleak House*, points out still more discerningly that the description of the fog is not merely a vividly realistic one, but also a highly fanciful one:

... it is not merely an exact description of reality like one of Mr Arnold Bennett's descriptions of the Five Towns. Its drama and humour and fancy, the 'haggard unwillingness' of the gas lamps, the snow mourning for the death of the sun, the driving insistent rhythm of the prose in which it is written, above all the furious energy which informs every syllable, injects it with a vitality and individuality of its own.[5]

Kayser, remarking the fondness of the grotesque artist for such objects as climbing plants, self-propelled vehicles, puppets, robots, and masks, observes that the mechanical strikes us as alien because it is inanimate matter which has achieved life, and that the human becomes alien when it is dead, inanimate.[6] Dickens is especially fond

[1] cf. *Little Dorrit*, ch. III (Cassell ed., vol. XII, p. 27).
[2] ibid., ch. XIII (Cassell ed., p. 128).
[3] cf. *Our Mutual Friend*, bk. III, ch. I (Cassell ed., vol. XVI, p. 349).
[4] cf. Cockshut, op. cit., p. 128.
[5] cf. Cecil, op. cit., p. 35.   [6] cf. Kayser, op. cit., p. 197.

of representing dead objects as alive and of comparing his characters to inanimate things or to animals. His natural propensity to describe things dramatically, combined with a scarcely less strong compulsion to present things in a humorous light, finds a satisfying outlet in his staple device of personification:

It was a double house, with long, narrow, heavily-framed windows. Many years ago it had had it in its mind to slide down sideways; it had been propped up, however, and was leaning on some half-dozen gigantic crutches.[1]

. . . a maimed table, a crippled wardrobe, a lean set of fire-irons like the skeleton of a set deceased . . .[2]

. . . glimpses were to be caught of a roast leg of pork bursting into tears of sage and onion in a metal reservoir full of gravy, of an unctuous piece of roast beef and blisterous Yorkshire pudding, bubbling hot in a similar receptacle, of a stuffed fillet of veal in rapid cut, of a ham in a perspiration with the pace it was going at.[3]

. . . the engine would blow and heave and perspire, like an engine wiping its forehead and saying what a run it had had . . .[4]

. . . when a ray of sunlight has fallen on the locker in my presence, I have noticed its inexpressive countenance to be deeply marked by a kind of Bramah erysipelas or small-pox.[5]

. . . all the water-pipes in the neighbourhood seemed to have Macbeth's Amen sticking in their throats, and to be trying to get it out.[6]

. . . a treacherous old chair by the fire-place, whose withered arms had hugged many a client and helped to squeeze him dry.[7]

. . . a very hideous church with four towers at the four corners, generally resembling some petrified monster, frightful and gigantic, on its back with its legs in the air.[8]

The list of examples could be extended almost indefinitely. To yield to the temptation to illustrate Dickens's fondness for personification by quoting the more brilliant examples would be to produce a slightly false impression of the whole; but quantity is important as well as quality here, and the cumulative effect of less remarkable personifications than those quoted is an important constituent in the prevailing grotesqueness of Dickens's work.

[1] cf. *Little Dorrit*, bk. I, ch. III (Cassell ed., vol. XII, p. 26).
[2] ibid. (Cassell ed., p. 32).
[3] ibid., bk. I, ch. XX (Cassell ed., p. 194).
[4] cf. *The Uncommercial Traveller*, XIII (Cassell ed., vol. XV, p. 470).
[5] ibid. XIV (Cassell ed., p. 472).
[6] ibid. (Cassell ed., p. 477).
[7] cf. *The Old Curiosity Shop*, ch. XXXIII (Cassell ed., vol. V, p. 205).
[8] cf. *Our Mutual Friend*, Bk. II, ch. I (Cassell ed., vol. XVI, p. 182).

Dickens's delight in the elaborate associative chain which we have seen to be characteristic of the Metaphysicals and Swift, the tenacity with which he pursues a fanciful idea, is very much in evidence in many examples of the opposite process to the above, the representation of human beings as dead objects. Thus Pancks, old Casby's agent in *Little Dorrit*, after first being associated with a mechanical object, '. . . he was in a perspiration, and snorted and sniffed and puffed and blew, like a little labouring steam-engine',[1] is subsequently perceived by Dickens to stand in the same relation to Casby as 'a little coaly steam-tug' stands to 'an unwieldy ship'. The idea is then characteristically repeated with endless variations. Pancks 'steamed out of his little dock at a quarter before six',[2] 'took in his victuals much as if he were coaling',[3] 'shot out these cinders of principles, as if it were done by mechanical revolvency',[4] and so on. Grandfather Smallweed, in *Bleak House*, is a similar case:

The excellent old gentleman being, at these times, a mere clothes-bag with a black skull-cap on top of it, does not present a very animated appearance, until he has undergone the two operations at the hands of his grand-daughter, of being shaken up like a great bottle, and poked and punched like a great bolster.[5]

Again, the idea is developed at length. Twemlow, in *Our Mutual Friend*, is described as follows:

There was an innocent piece of dinner-furniture that went upon easy castors, and was kept over a livery-stable yard in Duke Street, St James's, when not in use, to whom the Veneerings were a source of blind confusion. The name of this article was Twemlow. Being first cousin to Lord Snigsworth, he was in frequent requisition, and at many houses might be said to represent the dining-table in its normal state. Mr and Mrs Veneering, for example, arranging a dinner, habitually started with Twemlow, and then put leaves in him, or added guests to him. Sometimes, the table consisted of Twemlow and half-a-dozen leaves; sometimes, of Twemlow and a dozen leaves; sometimes, Twemlow was pulled out to his utmost extent of twenty leaves.[6]

The lengthy description in *The Uncommercial Traveller* of 'Dry

[1] cf. *Little Dorrit*, bk. I, ch. XIII (Cassell ed., vol. XII, p. 121).
[2] ibid. (Cassell ed., p. 127).
[3] ibid. (Cassell ed., p. 129).
[4] ibid. (Cassell ed., p. 131).
[5] cf. *Bleak House*, ch. XXI (Cassell ed., vol. XI, p. 234).
[6] cf. *Our Mutual Friend*, bk. I, ch. II (Cassell ed., p. 5).

Rot in men',[1] and the spontaneous combustion of the 'old root', Krook, may be cited as further examples of this particularly grotesque type of association.

In metaphor and simile, then, Dickens finds a means of giving fact a further 'fanciful' dimension, enabling him to give vent to the wildest images whilst still in a position to observe that he does not 'wilfully or negligently mislead' his readers in matters of fact.[2]

These figures of speech are, however, merely favourite patterns in the stiff brocade of Dickens's style. If that style can be described in a single word, that word is hyperbolical. His attempts at the macabre and the pathetic—exaggerated drama (or melodrama)—have been referred to. Humorous or ironic exaggeration is still more in evidence, and whilst some varieties of this style, particularly the sentimental-facetious, have, like his melodrama, lost much of their appeal for readers in the present century, their basic feature, that of deliberate disproportion between subject-matter and style—in a word, of incongruity—is too central in Dickens's work to be ignored.

The most obvious form which this stylistic disproportion takes is the highly Latinate and circumlocutory description of the commonplace, frequently punctuated by anticlimax:

> The real name of the little man was Harris, but it had gradually merged into the less euphonious one of Trotters, which, with the prefatory adjective, Short, had been conferred upon him by reason of the small size of his legs.[3]

> It was the anniversary of that happy day on which the church of England as by law established, had bestowed Mrs Kenwigs upon Mr Kenwigs . . .[4]

Of all Dickens's works, *Pickwick Papers* is the one in which this grotesque disproportion between style and subject is most in evidence, the whole being narrated in a facetiously pompous tone:

> . . . the scorbutic youth intimated a burning desire to pull the nose of the gentleman with the emblems of hope; in reply to which that individual expressed his decided unwillingness to accept of any 'sauce' on gratuitous terms, either from the irascible young gentleman with the scorbutic countenance, or any other person who was ornamented with a head.[5]

---

[1] cf. *The Uncommercial Traveller*, XIII (Cassell ed., p. 467).
[2] cf. Preface to *Bleak House*.
[3] cf. *The Old Curiosity Shop*, ch. XVII (Cassell ed., p. 109).
[4] cf. *Nicholas Nickleby*, ch. XIV.
[5] cf. *Pickwick Papers*, ch. XXXII.

The most significant thing about this 'mock-heroic' tone is that it is itself comic, not merely because it is ironically employed, but because it is affected; it is humorous in the way that Mr. Micawber is humorous, though, of course, we are meant to laugh *at* the unconscious affectation of Micawber and to laugh *with* the narrator of Pickwick Papers. Many such passages are thus not merely mock-heroic, but mock-pompous as well. The humour comes from two sources; first, the inability of the subject-matter to measure up to the 'lofty' tone—here it is the figure which is too small for the dress, so to speak; second, the ludicrously unsuitable nature of the style when applied to commonplace and familiar matters—in this case it is the figure which constitutes the 'standard' and the dress which is too big. Significantly, the chapter-heading for the 'inflated' account of the Kenwigs's anniversary party ironically cautions us against assuming that the commonplace is necessarily vulgar: 'Having the misfortune to treat of none but common people, is necessarily of a mean and vulgar nature.' The pompous tone in which the party is described is partly a satirical stab at the determined gentility of the Kenwigses, Mrs. Kenwigs in particular; but it is also, as in *Pickwick Papers*, droll in itself. The total effect is to present the commonplace in an amusing, mildly ironic fashion without seriously implying that it fails to measure up to some 'lofty' standard, because the standard suggested by the tone is altogether *too* lofty. There are plenty of examples in Dickens's work of straightforward irony, where the meanness or moral squalor of the subject is emphasized by way of contrast, by ironic praise, or pretended flippancy of tone. Equally, there are straightforward examples of the satire of the pompous and affected, Buzfuz, Micawber, Chadband, punctured by confrontation with a commonplace figure, Sam Weller, young David Copperfield, Jo. In the kind of humorous incongruity between subject-matter and style described above, however, there is a peculiar ambivalence; the commonplace is at once satirized, or at least treated in ironic fashion, and made the standard to which the over-inflated style is ludicrously inappropriate.

It is chiefly because of his characters that Dickens is considered to be a grotesque writer; certainly, it is primarily through his characters that he endeavours to effect that 'fusion of the graces of the imagination with the realities of life' which he regarded as ideal.

Something has been said about the fondness which Dickens shows for the 'semi-exotic', i.e. settings which, though not entirely alien to the experience of the 'polite reader', were at least unfamiliar.

In contrasting such 'peripheral' characters as turnkeys, strolling players, criminals, &c., with 'drawing-room' characters, lawyers, businessmen, and so on, the eccentricity of many of the latter 'politer' characters was noticed, and in the larger context of a general consideration of Dickens's characters the term 'peripheral' may conveniently be employed a second time to describe the kind of effect which Dickens aimed at producing. Adolphus Ward remarks that Dickens 'sought to efface the line which separates the barely possible from the morally probable'. More sympathetically, but without substantially disagreeing, we might say that he attempted to make his characters as interestingly odd as he could without making them incredible. They are meant to be extreme examples of actual types.

For this reason he continually insisted that his characters had their feet firmly planted in reality, and was especially gratified by remarks about their truth to life. This applies equally to his satirical and to his sentimental characters. In various prefaces he asserted the reality or realism of such characters as Nancy and the Artful Dodger ('the stern and plain truth'),[1] Squeers (a 'faint and feeble' picture of the reality),[2] the Cheeryble brothers ('the Brothers Cheeryble live'),[3] Sairey Gamp ('four-and-twenty years ago, a fair representation of the hired attendant on the poor in sickness'), and Betsy Prig (a 'fair specimen of a Hospital Nurse').[4] To disbelieve in the reality of Pecksniff is a characteristic of the tribe of Pecksniff; Jonas Chuzzlewit is 'the extreme exposition of a direct truth'.[4] Dickens's view, simply stated, is that whilst these characters may not be the unvarnished truth, at all events he is using clear varnish, dramatizing and exaggerating but not falsifying.

It is precisely this underlying realism in Dickens's characters, his flashes of psychological insight, as in the 'Dostoievskian' description of Fagin in the dock, and his incomparable evocation of physical immediacy, as in the initial description of Quilp,[5] which make so many of Dickens's characters grotesque. We see them in relation to a central standard. For the most part they belong to the sphere of the improbable rather than the impossible; they are, so to speak, 'half-real'.

Apart from such *alter egos* as David Copperfield or Pip, which are

---

[1] cf. Preface to *Oliver Twist* (3rd ed, 1841) (Cassell ed., vol. XIX, p. 263).
[2] cf. Preface to *Nicholas Nickleby* (1st ed.) (Cassell ed., vol. XIX, pp. 272–3).
[3] ibid. (Cassell ed., p. 274).
[4] cf. Preface to *Martin Chuzzlewit* ('Charles Dickens' ed.) (Cassell ed., vol. XIX, pp. 297 ff.).
[5] cf. *The Old Curiosity Shop*, ch. III (Cassell ed., vol. V, pp. 17–18).

psychologically more realistic, the vast majority of Dickens's characters are of this 'half-real' nature. They serve two main purposes: (a) a regressive one, that of intensifying the values of the world about us, of making it a satisfactory 'objective correlative' for a sense of the eternal which is 'in a state of transition from supernatural belief to humanism', and (b) a progressive one, that of satirizing various social ills and vices. Whilst certain characters can fairly readily be allotted to each of the two groups corresponding to these functions, there are others where the general classification is less straightforward. Let us, however, first consider the more obvious cases.

Dickens's melodramatic, macabre, and sentimental characters belong to the group in which the first of these functions is the more important. Little Nell, Little Dorrit, Paul Dombey, Oliver Twist, figures which tend to be too bright or good for human nature's daily food, are not customarily considered to be grotesque, a term which we tend to associate with physical deformity or with the wildly grotesque. Nevertheless, the definition of grotesqueness as incongruity perceived with emotion is certainly applicable to such figures judged from the realistic point of view, from which so much adverse comment has been levelled at them. This 'grotesqueness' is not intentional, and its impact is softened by our familiarity with the conventions of melodramatic and sentimental literature.

The figures of evil which complement these virtuous characters, figures which illustrate Dickens's assertion that 'there are in the world some insensible and callous natures that do become, at last, utterly and irredeemably bad'[1] belong to the same group. They are not satirical figures, because the ironical tone of satire is too indirect to convey Dickens's feelings of revulsion. Irredeemable wickedness is a matter for denunciation rather than satire.[2] Many of these villains, as we have seen, have physically grotesque characteristics: Quilp, Fagin, Heep, Carker, Rigaud (*Little Dorrit*),[3] Dennis (*Barnaby Rudge*).[4] They are surrounded by a melodramatic atmosphere,

---

[1] cf. *Preface to Oliver Twist* (Cassell ed., vol. XIX, p. 264).

[2] Squeers, perhaps, is an exception to this generalization; he is both a villain—to a greater extent than, say, Chadband or Pecksniff—and a satirical, not a melodramatic figure.

[3] cf. *Little Dorrit*, bk. I, ch. I: 'When Monsieur Rigaud laughed, . . . [his] moustache went up under his nose, and his nose came down over his moustache, in a very sinister and cruel manner.' This trait is much emphasized.

[4] cf. *Barnaby Rudge*, ch. XXXVI: '. . . a squat, thickset personage, with a low retreating forehead, a coarse shock head of hair, and eyes so small and near together, that his broken nose alone seemed to prevent them meeting and fusing into one of the usual size, &c.'

frequently culminating in a violent or grotesque death, like those of
Sikes, Carker, Tulkinghorn, Bradley Headstone and Rogue Rider-
hood. The 'circle of stage fire' to which Ruskin refers is very much in
evidence throughout the careers of such characters, and they have
almost all been attacked, like the virtuous characters they oppose, for
lack of realism on various grounds. To some extent the familiar
conventions of unnatural villainy in popular literature and drama make
this lack of realism, a serious objection to any character in a basically
realistic narrative, less striking, but as these conventions break down
with the increasing subtlety of characterization, they appear increasingly unnatural, not merely in their inhumanity, as intended, but in
being incredible. Like his virtuous characters, his melodramatic
villains are 'true to life' in a symbolic sense as much as in a realistic
sense, but their presence in a realistic narrative (albeit one written in a
melodramatic convention) naturally leads the reader to see them from
a realistic point of view, with the result described.

The realization of Dickens's second great purpose, that of social
satire, involves exaggeration (or a 'fusion of the graces of the imagination with the realities of life') no less than the realization of his aim of
bringing out 'the romantic side of familiar things'. His attempts to find
symbols for the 'immaterial' are largely vitiated by his practical
and humanistic cast of mind, with the result that he commonly
achieves only the sentimental—a weaker form of the romantic (which
is itself a weaker form of the religious or mystical). In satirical caricature, on the other hand, Dickens is able to put his imagination
uninhibitedly to a progressive, practical purpose which is more in
harmony with his attitude of mind. As in his use of the fanciful
comparison, he can indulge his imagination without losing contact
with the 'realities of life'. The result is a great portrait gallery of
grotesques: Mr. Bumble, Squeers, Mrs. Jellyby, Harold Skimpole,
Buzfuz, Pecksniff, etc.

Such characters are amongst the most 'colourful' in Dickens's
works, but something must be said about the difference between the
vividness of a satirical caricature like Mrs. Jellyby or Mr. Chadband
and that of a romantically individual character like Falstaff or Long
John Silver. First, the satirical figure must be representative of a
class or an idea. Thus it is generally true to say that whereas the more
idiosyncrasies the romantic figure has the better, the satirical figure,
however exaggerated the depiction of those traits which tie it to its
class, loses much of its effect if it becomes too individual, though, of

course, the figure may gain in other ways than the satirical, like Micawber or Sairey Gamp. Second, whereas the characteristics which make a romantically individual figure richly colourful are clearly approved of by the author, at least in a broad sense, in so far as they make the world a more exhilarating place to live in, the characteristics which make a satirical figure vivid and memorable are unpleasant and undesirable ones. This distinction is often glossed over; the statement is often made that the characters we most enjoy in Dickens's works are precisely those whom we should be most reluctant to meet in real life, bores like Chadband, hypocrites like Pecksniff:

> The hypocrite is a figure dreadful and tragic, a shape of horror; and Mr Pecksniff is a hypocrite, and a bright image of heart-easing comedy.[1]
> The very people that we fly to in Dickens are the very people that we fly from in life.[2]

Two points require to be stressed: first, there is a very important basic difference between the pleasure which we derive from clever ridicule of a disagreeable character and the pleasure which we take in the peculiarities of a figure which excites our approval in one way or another. This is sufficiently obvious where the moral turpitude of the satirical figure is marked. Nobody would describe Squeers, for example, as 'a bright image of heart-easing comedy'. Where the satire is of a milder variety, however, arousing amusement rather than indignation, the gap between the satirical caricature and the romantically eccentric figure is correspondingly smaller, and this leads us to the second point to be noticed in connexion with Dickens's satirical figures: in general, his satire is altogether less savage than that of Swift. There is little of *saeva indignatio* about Mrs. Jellyby, Mr. Chadband, Harold Skimpole, effective as these satirical portraits are, and whilst there are fiercer portraits than these in Dickens's work, they are fairly representative. Moreover, there is a strong tendency for a satirical figure to become a humorous figure, by developing in the direction of pure absurdity or by acquiring traits which have little to do with the satirical intention:

> . . . if a Fiery Serpent had proclaimed it from the top of Salisbury Cathedral . . . Such was my faith in Thomas Pinch, that I would have cast the falsehood back into the Serpent's teeth, and would have taken Thomas

[1] cf. Meynell, op. cit., p. 44.
[2] cf. Chesterton, Introduction to Everyman's Library ed. of *Nicholas Nickleby* (1907 repr. 1909), p. xiii.

to my heart. But I am not a Serpent, sir, myself, I grieve to say, and no excuse or hope is left me.[1]

In such utterances, Pecksniff's hypocrisy becomes, quite literally, a laughing matter. Sairey Gamp is the obvious example of a satirical figure in which the satire has become merely one stratum in a mine of humorous eccentricities.

There remains a range of characters which contain elements from both of these categories, the sentimental-melodramatic and the satirical, in varying proportions, figures at once absurd and agreeable, which are more difficult to classify but which are especially typical of Dickens.

The black and white figures of melodrama are, of course, only one means by which Dickens expresses his sense of 'the Great Mystery of Things'; still more compelling is his feeling for the inexhaustible richness and strangeness of human activity, his keen enjoyment of outlandish behaviour, modes of dress, habits of speech, 'all things original, spare, strange' which make nonsense of attempts to 'work sums in men and women'.

The peculiarities of human nature are presented to us by Dickens for the most part humorously, and whilst the 'criticism' implied in such presentation may be of the mildest in many cases, as in Mr. Pickwick and Sam Weller, Joe Gargery, Mr. Dick, Mr. Sleary, it must not be discounted altogether. There is some suggestion of satire, very much in evidence in such characters as Flora Finching or Mr. Micawber, though the predominant feeling is that the world would be a poorer place without such grotesques, a feeling reinforced by their qualities of loyalty, kindness, and so on.

Whereas many such figures, to which may be added middle-class eccentrics like Mr. Grimwig (*Oliver Twist*), Betsy Trotwood, and Dr. Strong, are from the first predominantly 'sentimental', others are initially satirical caricatures which become more sympathetic as the narrative progresses, moving into the sentimental-humorous category without losing in grotesqueness; moreover, whilst such metamorphoses naturally involve some modulation to a less acidulous tone, that tone remains ironic as well as jocular in many cases. Dick Swiveller is a good example. At the outset he is a mere sponger with a 'prevailing greasiness of appearance'. Later we find him a none too scrupulous dupe of Quilp's: 'As the dwarf spoke, Dick's face relaxed into a compliant smile. . . . By the time he had finished, Dick was

[1] cf. *Martin Chuzzlewit*, ch. XXXI.

looking down at Quilp in the same sly manner as Quilp was looking up at him. . . .'[1] It is only with the advent of the Marchioness that Dick's moral salvation is assured. Forster observes: 'Altogether, and because of rather than in spite of his weaknesses, Dick is a captivating person.'[2] In fact, there is a transition, less startling than other more notorious changes of character in Dickens's work (like that of Micawber, for example), but clearly transforming the character from a satirical grotesque into a sentimental one.

Such humorous figures vary considerably in the intensity of the satirical element according to the form which their absurdities take. The humour is least barbed in portraits like Joe Gargery or loyal servants like Sam Weller or Peggotty, or in the 'lovable innocent' eccentricities of middle-class figures like Mr. Pickwick and Betsy Trotwood. Among the more satirical are silly-romantic figures like Flora Finching or John Chivery (*Little Dorrit*).

Flora Finching, a satirical portrait of Maria Beadnell, the early sweetheart whom Dickens re-encountered to his great disillusionment later in life, is quickly developed into a garrulous grotesque, reminiscent of Mistress Quickly, whose silliness is combined with an amiable nature. Flora's chief satirical function is fulfilled in chapter XIII, in the embarrassingly coy renewal of her acquaintance with Clennam, but she remains an effective burlesque of the woman who refuses to grow up. At the same time, she is a richly amusing figure whose goodness strengthens our feeling that life is all the better for her existence.

At the deepest level the ambivalence of Flora Finching's character is due to the ambiguity of Dickens's own attitude towards romantically inclined characters, particularly, though not exclusively, those who arouse class feeling. On the one hand, Flora Finching is ridiculed because she is lacking in common sense, a sober appreciation of the fact that she is no longer a kitten; on the other hand, 'hearts may count in Heaven as high as heads',[3] and her warmth and good nature make her a far more attractive person than her cold-blooded father, Christopher Casby.

John Chivery, the intensely romantic son of the Marshalsea turnkey, is ridiculed and approved in similar fashion. Like Swiveller and Flora Finching, or for that matter Pickwick, he increases in stature as the narrative proceeds, but whereas Swiveller and Flora

[1] cf. *The Old Curiosity Shop*, ch. XXI (Cassell ed., p. 135).
[2] cf. J. Forster, op. cit., ch. VII, p. 149.
[3] cf. *Our Mutual Friend*, ch. XVI (Cassell ed., vol. XVI, p. 162).

have obvious blemishes of character, Chivery is chiefly ridiculous for his poetical cast of mind, a favourite subject for irony,[1] and his presumption in aspiring to be the rival of Arthur Clennam for Little Dorrit's hand. Whilst he is thus too innocuous to be a satirical caricature, but is rather from the first a comic grotesque, he is not simply a humorous figure like Sam Weller or Peggotty, but a ridiculous one like Augustus Moddle of *Martin Chuzzlewit*. The softness of his head is emphasized as well as the softness of his heart, and the class barrier is clearly in evidence:

As she held out her hand to him with these words, the heart that was under the waistcoat of sprigs—mere slop-work, if the truth must be known —swelled to the size of the heart of a gentleman; and the poor common little fellow, having no room to hold it, burst into tears.[2]

In later chapters Chivery becomes a distinctly admirable figure, though he remains a foil to Clennam's altogether superior qualities; but his ridiculously soft head and commendably soft heart give the character a characteristically Dickensian ambiguity.

If, in the process of bringing out the admirable qualities of Chivery's character, there is a certain strengthening of the 'poor common little fellow's' backbone, there is no radical change of personality, as there is in the case of Micawber. Micawber is perhaps the classic example of an ambivalent, satirical-sentimental figure in Dickens's work. Ultimately the figure is slanted heavily in the 'lovable innocent' direction, but the satirical aspect is too pungent to be glossed over lightly; shiftlessness and sponging are rooted as deeply in Micawber's character as in Falstaff's. The grotesqueness of Micawber is thus both markedly satirical and sentimental. No doubt Dickens attempts to strengthen the impression of Micawber as a welcome and colourful addition to society by giving him, late in the narrative, sudden and unconvincing virtues; but the general effect, like that of the early Falstaff, is an ambivalent one.

CONCLUDING REMARKS

50. From a consideration of the various sources of the grotesque in Dickens's work, it appears that it arises in general from the fact that the world he depicts is not merely an alien one, like that of Keats's 'Endymion', for example, but, to employ Kayser's telling phrase, an

[1] cf. 'The Poetical Young Gentleman' (*Sketches of Young Gentlemen*) (Cassell ed., vol. XIX, pp. 38 ff.).
[2] cf. *Little Dorrit*, ch. XVIII (Cassell ed., p. 180).

alienated world. It both is and is not a realistic picture of the world about us. Moreover, the incongruity which Dickens's compounding of the familiar and the fantastic constantly produces is increased because this alienation occurs in two ways: first, melodramatically, by bathing 'London and its butchers and bakers' in a 'violent chiaroscuro'; second, satirically, by deliberate and ironic caricature of all that Dickens regarded as anti-social, whether people, ideas, or institutions.

These two kinds of modification, the sentimental and the satirical, are, then, expressions of tendencies in Dickens's character, itself much influenced by the spiritual state of his time.

Lord David Cecil observes critically: 'When Dickens is not writing about Mrs Crummles he sometimes seems to be writing a play for Crummles.'[1] Satire and sentiment, however, do not always remain distinct in Dickens's work, but modify one another. The characteristically humorous tone, a blend of irony and sympathy, of so much of his description, and the great range of grotesque figures which are at once ridiculous and agreeable, 'unanalysable' figures like Flora Finching, Dick Swiveller, Mr. Micawber, owe something to both satire and sentiment.

Dickens has been described above as a predominantly progressive personality, absorbed in the world about him, but strongly affected by a sense of the mystical aspect of things which leads him to depict that world in exaggeratedly heroic or colourful fashion. His work has thus affinities with that of both Swift and Coleridge. His attitude towards the imagination, relative to theirs, may be fairly regarded as a kind of compromise. He is insufficiently mystical to regard the creations of the imagination as an expression of reality except in so far as they are based on the physically real. Nevertheless, for Dickens, the imagination is an essential element in the proper apprehension of physical reality. To come upon reason 'through the tender light of Fancy' is to see it as 'a beneficent god, deferring to gods as great as itself'.[2] Whilst Swift, then, employs the grotesque in the form of the absurd for purposes of ridicule, and Coleridge uses it to arouse a sense of wonder, to suggest the unfathomable and mysterious, in the grotesque world of Dickens and especially in his portrayal of human eccentricities, there is something of both these aims and achievements.

[1] cf. Cecil, op. cit., p. 28.
[2] cf. *Hard Times*, ch. IX (Cassell ed., vol. VIII, p. 494).

APPENDIX: N.E.D. DEFINITIONS

Grotesque (grote·sk), *sb.* and *a.* Forms: a. 6 crotes(c)que, 7 crotesco, -ko, β. 7–8 grot(t)esc, -k (e, -q, grot(t)esco, -ko, 7- grotesque. [Orig. a. early mod. F. *crotesque* sb. fem., an adaptation (by assimilation to OF. *crote*=It. *grotta*) of It. *grottesca* 'a kinde of rugged vnpolished painters worke, anticke worke' (Florio 1598), 'anticke or landskip worke of Painters' (Florio 1611), an elliptical use (=*opera* or *pittura grottesca*) of the fem. of *grottesco* adj. f. *grotta*; see GROTTO and -ESQUE. (Cf. Sp., Pg. *grutesco*, an alteration of the It. word after Sp. Pg. *gruta*=It. *grotta*.) It is remarkable that Florio in both his Dicts. (1598 and 1611) has *crotesca* as an It. word, explained as 'antique, fretted, or carued worke'; this, if genuine, would seem to be a re-adoption from Fr. Before the end of the 16th c. the Fr. word was occasionally spelt *grotesque*, after the original It.; this form was adopted into Eng. about 1640, and has been the prevailing form ever since. But early in the 17th c. writers acquainted with It. had introduced the masc. form of the adj., *crotesco*, which occurs as late as 1646; the more usual It. form *grotesco* appears as Eng. first in the 1632 edition of Florio's transl. of Montaigne, and did not become obsolete until the 18th c.

The etymological sense of *grottesca* would be 'painting appropriate to grottos'. The special sense is commonly explained by the statement that '*grotte*, 'grottoes', was the popular name in Rome for the chambers of ancient buildings which had been revealed by excavations, and which contained those mural paintings that were the typical examples of 'grotesque'. (See *Voc. della Crusca*, s.v. *Grotta*, §iv.) Although this seems to be only a late conjecture, without any actual evidence, it appears to be intrinsically plausible.)

A. *sb.*

1. A kind of decorative painting or sculpture, consisting of representations of portions of human and animal forms, fantastically combined and interwoven with foliage and flowers.

1561 *Inv. R. Wardrobe* (1815) 130 Item, twa paintit broddis the ane of the muses and the uther of crotescque or conceptis. [1624 WOTTON *Archit*. II. 97 Whether Grotesca (as the Italians) or Antique worke (as wee call it) should be receiued.] 1636 B. JONSON *Discov., De progres.*

picturæ Wks. (1640) 113 He complaines of their painting Chimæras, by the vulgar unaptly called Grottesque. 1645 EVELYN *Mem.* (1857) I. 143 The foliage and grotesque about some of the compartments are admirable. 1658 W. SANDERSON *Graphice* 25, I would confine Grotesco only to Borders and Freezes. 1686 AGLIONBY *Painting Illustr.* Explan. Terms, Grotesk, is properly the Painting that is found under Ground in the Ruines of Rome. 1715 LEONI *Palladio's Archit.* (1742) I. 59 The Chambers . . . are all . . . painted in grotesque of a very fine Invention. 1762–71 H. WALPOLE *Vertue's Anecd. Paint.* (1786) I. 260 Don Julio Clovio, the celebrated limner, whose neatness and taste in grotesque were exquisite. 1823 P. NICHOLSON *Pract. Build.* Gloss. 586 *Grotesque*, the light, gay, and beautiful style of ornament, practised by the antient Romans in the decoration of their palaces, baths, villas, etc.

    attrib. 1711 SHAFTESB. *Charac.* (1737) III. 6 'Tis the perfection of certain grotesque-painters, to keep as far from nature as possible. *a*1744 POPE *Hor. Sat.* II. vi. 192 Grotesco roofs, and Stucco floors.

    b. A work of art in this style. Chiefly *pl.*, figures or designs in grotesque; in popular language, figures or designs characterized by comic distortion or exaggeration.

    1643 Sir. T. BROWNE *Relig. Med.* I. §15 There are no Grotesques in nature. 1691 tr. *Emillianne's Frauds Romish Monks* 333 They expose to public view in the Streets . . . many infamous naked Pictures, and Grotesques, to cause laughter. 1746 W. HORSLEY *Fool* (1748) I. 141 The reigning Taste of the Age for Oddities, Monsters, Grotesques, Caricatura's, etc. 1756 BURKE *Subl. & B.* II. V, All the designs I have chanced to meet of the temptations of St. Anthony were rather a sort of odd, wild grotesques, than any thing capable of producing a serious passion. 1819 BYRON *Juan* I. xlvi, This [missal] all Kinds of grotesques illumined. 1856 RUSKIN *Mod. Paint.* III, IV. viii, §4 A fine grotesque is the expression, in a moment, by a series of symbols thrown together in bold and fearless connection, of truths which it would have taken a long time to express in any verbal way [etc.]. 1865 *Lond. Rev.* 23 Dec. 668/1 The ornamentalists of that period . . . revelled in their grotesques. 1893 LELAND *Mem.* II, 248 Adorned with fifteenth century grotesques.

    c. *fig.*

    1644–7 CLEVELAND *Char. Lond. Diurn.* 28 A strange Grottesco this, the Church and States. 1710 STEELE *Tatler* No. 202 ℙ 2 This indeed is Ambition in Grotesque. 1889 *Spectator* 21 Dec., To Browning, life is a medley of grotesques, with a glowing horizon beyond it.

2. A clown, buffoon, or merry-andrew. [So in mod. Fr. (as masc. sb.).] Cf. ANTIC.

G.E.L.–S

1864 SALA in *Daily Tel.* 18 Nov., The great grotesque himself will be in the grave. 1871 MORLEY *Voltaire* iii. (1872) 120 Some men of true genius seem only to make sure of fame by straining themselves into grotesques.

3. *Printing.* A square-cut letter without ceriph, **THUS**; formerly called *stone-letter*.

1875 SOUTHWARD *Dict. Typogr.*, *Grotesque*, the name of a peculiar fancy jobbing type.

B. *adj.*

1. *Arch.* Having the character of the work described in A. 1. (In some of the early instances the word may be the sb. used *attrib.*)

1603 FLORIO *Montaigne* I. xxvii. 89 Antike Boscage or Crotesko [*so also ed.* 1613; *ed.* 1632 *has* Grotesko] works, which are fantastical pictures, having no grace, but in the variety and strangenes of them. 1610. FOLKINGHAM *Art of Survey* II. vi. 58 Compartiments are Blankes or Figures bordered with Anticke Boscage or Crotesko-woorke. 1646 Sir T. BROWNE *Pseud. Ep.* III, xxiv, 170 As for Sea-horses . . . they are but Crotesco deliniations. 1664 EVELYN tr. *Freart's Parall. Archit.* 128 There are also Voluta's in the Corinthian and Compounded Capitels, but they consist rather of certain large Stalkes after a more Grotesco design. a1668 DAVENANT *Masque* Wks. (1673) 360 And in the midst was placed a large compartiment composed of Groteske work. 1687 BURNET *Trav.* ii. (1750) 100 They have built great Vaults and Porticos along the Rock, which are all made Grotesque. 1695 DRYDEN *Paral. Poet & Paint.* 26 Grotesque painting is the just resemblance of this. 1841-4 EMERSON *Ess., Manners* Wks. (Bohn) I. 215 Let there be grotesque sculpture about the gates and offices of temples.

2. In a wider sense, of designs or forms: Characterized by distortion or unnatural combinations; fantastically extravagant; bizarre, †quaint. Also *transf.* of immaterial things, esp. of literary style.

1653 J. HALL *Paradoxes* 45 They . . . ought to bee accounted one of those Grotesco Maximes . . . that doe so disfigure and misguide the life of man. 1687 DRYDEN *Hind & P.* III. 1044 An hideous figure of their foes they drew, Nor lines, nor looks, nor shades, nor colours true; And this grotesque design expos'd to public view. 1709 STEELE *Tatler* No. 118 ℙ 6 You have employed your self more in Grotesque Figures, than in Beauties. 1718 LADY M. W. MONTAGU *Let. to Lady Rich* 10 Oct., These grotesque daubers give me a still higher esteem of . . . natural charms. 1728 MORGAN *Algiers* I. Pref. 25 Matters of so peregrine and grotesk a Nature as this [History]. 1762–5 H. WALPOLE *Vertue's Anecd. Paint.* (ed. 2) I. 118 Those Grotesque monsters . . . with which the spouts . . . of ancient buildings are decorated. 1820 HAZLITT *Lect. Dram. Lit.* 36 Our literature . . . is Gothic and grotesque.

absol. 1809 MALKIN *Gil Blas* XI. V. (Rtldg.) 404 He preferred the stately, or rather the grotesque in writing. 1851 RUSKIN *Stones Ven.* (1874) I. App. 367 The Northern love of what is called the Grotesque. 1888 *Pall Mall G.* 4 Apr. II/I The grotesque is a branch of the fantastic.

†b. Of landscape: Romantic, picturesquely irregular. *Obs.*

1667 MILTON *P. L.* IV. 136 A steep wilderness, whose hairie sides With thicket overgrown, grottesque and wilde, Access deni'd. *c* 1764 R. DODSLEY *Leasowes*, in *Shenstone's Wks.* II. (1777) 296 The more pleasing parts of this grotesque and hilly country.

3. Ludicrous from incongruity; fantastically absurd.

1747 *Gentl. Mag.* 374 A woman with her head peeping out of a sack, could hardly . . . make a more Grotesque figure. 1829 LYTTON *Devereux* II. V. 46 O'Carroll gave a grotesque sort of signal between a wink and a beckon. 1840 DICKENS *Old C. Shop* iii, But what added most to the grotesque expression of his face, was a ghastly smile. 1849 MACAULAY *Hist. Eng.* ii. I. 163 These peculiarities appeared far more grotesque in a faction which ruled a great empire. 1863 FR. A. KEMBLE *Resid. in Georgia* 58 You can conceive nothing more grotesque than the Sunday trim of the poor people. 1866 G. MACDONALD *Ann. Q. Neighb.* ix. (1878) 154 The most grotesque machine I ever saw that *did* something. 1870 R. W. DALE *Week-day Serm.* xii. 246 The grotesque doctrine that it is good for trade.

4. *Comb.*, as *grotesque-minded* adj.

1822 MOORE *Mem.* (1853) III. 347 Found there Beresford . . . a grotesque-minded person, very amusing.

Hence *Grote·sque v. trans.*, to give a grotesque form or appearance to; to caricature, travesty.

1875 BROWNING *Aristoph. Apol.* 432 After obscenity grotesqued so much It slunk away, revolted at itself. 1891 *Sat. Rev.* 19 Dec. 707/2 This is to grotesque Dante, not to translate him.

Grotesquely (grote·skli), *adv.* [f. GROTESQUE *a.* + -LY²] In a grotesque manner; with incongruous absurdity; fantastically, whimsically.

1740 H. WALPOLE *Ep. fr. Florence* 285 in Dodsley *Coll. Poems* (1755) III. 80 The wearied arms grotesquely deck the wall. 1814 SCOTT

Wav. lxv, His absurdities . . . had appeared grotesquely ludicrous during his prosperity. 1818 FOSTER in *Life & Corr.* (1846) II. 26 Grotesquely-constructed sentences. 1829 LYTTON *Devereux* II. ii, A man of about the middle age, very grotesquely attired.

Grotesqueness (grote·sknes). [f. GROTESQUE + — NESS.] The quality of being grotesque; incongruous absurdity. Also *concr. pl.* Grotesque objects.

1826 MISS MITFORD *Village* Ser. II. (1863) 329 His face, with all its grotesqueness, was infinitely pleasanter to look at than his figure. 1860 *Heads & Hats* 12 The women [temp. Edw. IV] wore absurdly high coiffures; and the men vied with them in their height, if not in their grotesqueness. 1883 J. HAWTHORNE in *Harper's Mag.* Nov. 926/1, I sauntered about the studio, taking note of the various beauties, grotesquenesses, and curiosities that it contained.

Grotesquerie (grote·skəri). Also grotesquery. [as if a. F. **grotesquerie*, f. *grotesque* GROTESQUE.] Grotesque objects collectively; grotesque quality; a piece of grotesqueness.

1654–66 LD. ORRERY *Parthenissa* (1676) 517 In a large Compartiment composed of Groteskery were seen Sphynxes, Harpyes, the Claws of Lyons and Tygers, to evidence that within inhabited Mysteries and Riddles. 1862 B. TAYLOR *Home & Abr.* Ser. II. II. 339 Where so much is beautiful, the occasional anomalies and grotesqueries of taste fail to offend you. 1877 'H. A. PAGE' *De Quincy* I. v. 92 Casting a 'jet' of gentle humour over the grim grotesquerie of the situation. 1878 BAYNE *Purit. Rev.* iii. 59 The incidents . . . of waking existence are therein . . . tossed and heaped together as the materials of a wild grotesquerie. 1880 HOWELLS *Undisc. Country* xiii. 197 She showed her sense of degradation in the brutal grotesquery. 1885 *Manch. Exam.* 22 July 3/2 The inventive grotesquerie of his [Gustave Doré's] later work.

BIBLIOGRAPHY

CHAPTERS I TO 5:

ABERCROMBIE, Lascelles: *Principles of Literary Criticism;* 'An Outline of Modern Knowledge' Series, V. Gollancz Ltd., London, 1931.

ANDERSON, M. D.: *Animal Carvings in British Churches:* Cambridge University Press, 1938.

BAGEHOT, Walter: *Wordsworth, Tennyson and Browning; or Pure, Ornate and Grotesque Art in English Poetry* (1864), *Literary Studies*, Vol. II: Longmans Green & Co., London, 1895.

BLAKE, William: *Poetry & Prose*, ed. Geoffrey Keynes: Nonesuch Press Centenary ed., London, 1946.

BODKIN, Maud: *Archetypal Patterns in Poetry: Psychological Studies of Imagination:* Oxford University Press, 1934 (3rd impr. 1951).

BOSANQUET, B.: *A History of Aesthetic:* Allen & Unwin, London, 1956 (2nd ed.).

BOSWELL, James: *The Life of Samuel Johnson, LL.D.*, with an Introduction by S. C. Roberts: Everyman's Library, Dent, London, 1951–2.

BRANSTON, Brian: *Gods of the North:* Thames & Hudson Ltd., London, 1955.

BURKE, Edmund: *A Philosophical Enquiry into the Origin of our Ideas of the Sublime and Beautiful*, (ed. J. T. Boulton: Routledge & Kegan Paul, London, 1958.

CAMPBELL, Lily Bess: 'The Grotesque in the Poetry of Robert Browning', *Bulletin of the University of Texas*, Apr. 1907 (no. 92), Austin, Texas.

CECIL, Lord David: *The Fine Art of Reading:* Constable & Co. Ltd., London, 1957.

CHESTERTON, G. K.: *Robert Browning:* Macmillan & Co. Ltd., London, 1903.

DRYDEN, John: *Poetry, Prose & Plays*, selected by Douglas Grant: Rupert Hart-Davis, London, 1952.

FLÜGEL, J. C.: *Theories of Psycho-Analysis:* 'An Outline of Modern Knowledge' Series, V. Gollancz Ltd., London, 1931.

FORDHAM, Frieda: *An Introduction to Jung's Psychology:* Penguin Books (rev. ed.), 1959.

FRY, Roger: *The Arts of Painting and Sculpture:* 'An Outline of Modern Knowledge' Series, V. Gollancz Ltd., London, 1931.

GASCOYNE, David: *A Short Survey of Surrealism:* Cobden-Sanderson, London, 1936 (2nd imp.).

—— *Hölderlin's Madness:* J. M. Dent & Sons Ltd., London (no date).

GOLDWATER & TREVES (ed.): *Artists on Art:* Kegan Paul Ltd., London, 1947.

GRAVES, Robert: *Poetic Unreason and Other Studies:* Cecil Palmer, London, 1925.

HALL, Joseph: *Selections from Early Middle English 1130–1250:* Oxford University Press, 1920.

HEGEL, G. W. F.: *The Philosophy of Fine Art*, translated by F. P. B. Osmaston: Bell & Sons, London, 1920.

HOFFMANN, E. T. A.: *Tales from Hoffmann*, ed. J. M. Cohen: Bodley Head, London, 1951.

—— *Der Zauberspiegel: Ausgewählte Erzählungen:* Knaur Volksausgabe; Droemersche Verlagsanstalt, Munich, 1952.

HUGO, Victor: *Préface du 'Cromwell'* (1827), ed. Edmond Wahl: Clarendon Press, Oxford, 1909.

IRELAND, W. H.: *Scribbleomania or The Printer's Devil's Polichronicon:* Printed for Sherwood, Neely & Jones, Paternoster Row, 1815.

JACOBI, Jolande: *Complex, Archetype, Symbol in the Psychology of C. G. Jung*, translated by R. Manheim: Bollingen Series LVII, Pantheon Books Inc., New York, 1959.

JOAD, C. E. M.: *Guide to Modern Thought:* Faber & Faber Ltd., London, 1933 (cheap ed. 1942).

JUNG, C. G.: *Contributions to Analytical Psychology*, translated by H. G. & C. F. Baynes: Kegan Paul Ltd., London, 1928.

—— *The Psychology of the Unconscious*, translated by B. M. Hinkle: Kegan Paul Ltd., London, 1933.

—— *Symbols of Transformation:* Bollingen Series, Pantheon Books Inc., New York, 1956.

—— *The Archetypes and the Collective Unconscious*, translated by R. F. C. Hull: Bollingen Series XX, Pantheon Books Inc., New York, 1959.

—— and KERÉNYI, : *Essays on a Science of Mythology:* Bollingen Series XXII, Pantheon Books Inc., New York, 1949.

KAYSER, Wolfgang: *Das Groteske; seine Gestaltung in Malerei und Dichtung:* Gerhardt Stalling Verlag, Oldenburg & Hamburg Gesamtherstellung, 1957.

KEATS, John: *Poetical Works*, ed. H. Buxton Forman: Oxford University Press, 1908 (repr. 1948).

—— *Letters*, ed. M. B. Forman: Oxford University Press (3rd ed., 2nd impr.), 1948.

KNAAK, P.: 'Über den Gebrauch des Wortes "grotesque" ': Dissertation, Griefswald, 1913.

KRUDEWIG, Beate: 'Das Groteske in der Ästhetik seit Kant': Inaugural Dissertation, Bonn, 1934.

LEGOUIS, Emile, and CAZAMIAN, Louis: *A History of English Literature:* J. M. Dent & Sons Ltd., London, 1945.

LEHMANN, A. G.: *The Symbolist Aesthetic in France, 1885–1895:* Basil Blackwell Ltd., Oxford, 1950.

LUCAS, F. L.: *Decline and Fall of the Romantic Ideal:* Cambridge University Press, 1936.

—— *Literature and Psychology:* Cassell & Co., London, 1951.

McKELLAR, Peter: *Imagination and Thinking: A Psychological Analysis:* Cohen & West, London, 1957.

MURRAY, James H.: *A New English Dictionary on Historical Principles:* Clarendon Press, Oxford, 1888.

POE, Edgar Allan: *Selected Tales of Edgar Allan Poe*, with an Introduction by John Curtis: Penguin Books, 1956.

POPE, Alexander: *Poetical Works*, ed. A. W. Ward: Globe ed., Macmillan & Co. Ltd., London, 1892.

RUSKIN, John: *The Stones of Venice* (1851–1853): New Universal Library ed., Routledge & Sons, London, 1907.

RUSSELL, Bertrand: *History of Western Philosophy:* Allen & Unwin, 1946.

SANTAYANA, George: *The Sense of Beauty:* Adam & Charles Black, London, 1896.

SCOTT, Sir Walter: 'The Novels of Ernest Theodore Hoffmann', *Foreign Review*, 1827; *Miscellaneous Prose Works of Scott*, ed. Robert Cadell, Edinburgh; Whittaker & Co., London, 1834–36, vol. 18 (Periodical Criticism vol. 2 (1835)) Article X.

SISAM, Kenneth: *Fourteenth-Century Verse and Prose:* Oxford University Press, 1948.

STEPHEN, Leslie: *Samuel Johnson:* English Men of Letters Series, Macmillan & Co., 1878.

SYMONDS, J. A.: 'Caricature, The Fantastic, The Grotesque', *Essays Speculative and Suggestive* (1890): Smith, Elder & Co., London, 1907 (3rd ed.).

TILLYARD, E. M. W.: *Poetry and its Background: Illustrated by Five Poems* (1470–1870): Chatto & Windus Ltd., London, 1955.

WILDRIDGE, T. Tyndall: *The Grotesque in Church Art:* Andrews & Co., London, 1899.

WILSON, Mona: *The Life of William Blake:* Peter Davis Ltd., London, 1932.

WOOLF, Virginia: *The Common Reader (First Series):* Hogarth Press Ltd., London, 1923.

—— *A Writer's Diary* (ed. Leonard Woolf): Hogarth Press Ltd., London, 1953.

WRIGHT, Thomas: *A History of Caricature and Grotesque in Literature and Art:* Virtue Brothers & Co., London, 1865.

CHAPTER 6 (SWIFT):

BRYSON, Gladys: *Man and Society: The Scottish Inquiry of the Eighteenth Century:* Princeton University Press, 1945.

BULLITT, John M.: *Jonathan Swift and the Anatomy of Satire:* Harvard University Press, 1953.

CASE, A. E.: *Four Essays on 'Gullivers' Travels':* Princeton University Press, 1945.

CLARK, A. M.: *Studies in Literary Modes:* Oliver & Boyd, Edinburgh, 1946.

DOBRÉE, Bonamy: *English Literature in the Early Eighteenth Century: 1700–1740:* Oxford University Press, 1959.

DONNE, John: *Poetry & Prose,* ed. W. S. Scott: John Westhouse, London, 1946.

EHRENPREIS, Irvin: *The Personality of Jonathan Swift:* Methuen & Co., Ltd., London, 1958.

—— *Swift: The Man, his Works and the Age,* Vol. I: Methuen & Co., Ltd., London, 1962.

EWALD, William Bragg (jun.): *The Masks of Jonathan Swift:* Basil Blackwell Ltd., Oxford, 1954.

JAMES, William: *Psychology: Briefer Course:* Macmillan & Co., Ltd., London (no date).

JOHNSTON, Denis: *In Search of Swift:* Hodges Figgis & Co., Ltd., Dublin, 1959.

LEAVIS, F. R.: 'The Irony of Swift', *The Common Pursuit:* Chatto & Windus, London, 1953.

LOCKE, John: *An Essay Concerning Human Understanding,* abridged and edited by Raymond Wilburn: Everyman's Library, Dent, London, 1947.

LOVEJOY, Arthur O.: *The Great Chain of Being: A Study of the History of an Idea* (1936): Harvard University Press, 1957 (6th pr.).

LUCIAN: *The True History,* International Library of Famous Literature (ed. R. Garnett), Vol. II: issued by the *Standard,* London, 1900.

PAULSON, R.: *Theme and Structure in Swift's Tale of a Tub:* Yale University Press, 1960.

PLUMB, J. H.: *England in the Eighteenth Century:* Penguin Books Ltd., London, 1950.

PRICE, M.: *Swift's Rhetorical Art: A Study in Structure and Meaning:* Oxford University Press, 1953.

QUINTANA, Ricardo: *The Mind and Art of Jonathan Swift:* Oxford University Press (New York), 1936.

—— *Swift: An Introduction:* Oxford University Press, 1955.

STEPHEN, Leslie: *Swift:* English Men of Letters Series, Macmillan & Co., London, 1882.

SWIFT, Jonathan: *'Gulliver's Travels' and Selected Writings in Prose and Verse*, ed. John Hayward: Nonesuch Press, London, 1946.
—— *'A Tale of a Tub' &c.*, ed. A. Guthkelch and D. Nichol Smith: Oxford University Press, 1958 (2nd ed.).
—— *Irish Tracts 1720–1723*, ed. Herbert Davis; *And Sermons* ed. Louis Landa: Basil Blackwell, Oxford, 1963.
TAWNEY, R. H.: *Religion and the Rise of Capitalism* (1922): Mentor Books, ed. Harcourt, Brace & Co. Inc., New York, 1947.

CHAPTER 7 (COLERIDGE):

BAKER, James Volant: *The Sacred River: Coleridge's Theory of the Imagination:* Louisiana State University Press, 1957.
COLERIDGE, Samuel Taylor: *Letters, Conversations and Recollections of Samuel Taylor Coleridge*, ed. T. Allsop: Moxon & Co., London, 1936.
—— *Lectures and Notes on Shakespeare and Other English Poets*, ed. T. Ashe: Bell and Sons, London, 1888.
—— *Passages from the Prose and Table Talk of Coleridge*, ed. W. H. Dircks: Walter Scott Ltd., London, 1894.
—— *Facsimile Edition of 'Christabel'*, ed. Ernest Hartley Coleridge: Frowde, London, 1907.
—— *Biographia Literaria*, ed. J. Shawcross: Oxford University Press, 1907 (repr. 1958).
—— *Complete Poetical Works*, ed. Ernest Hartley Coleridge: Clarendon Press, Oxford, 1912.
—— *Poetry and Prose*, ed. H. W. Garrod: Oxford University Press, 1954.
CHAMBERS, E. K.: *Samuel Taylor Coleridge: A Biographical Study:* Oxford University Press, 1938.
DE QUINCEY, Thomas: *Reminiscences of the English Lake Poets:* Everyman's Library, Dent, London, 1907.
HOUSE, Humphry: *Coleridge; The Clark Lectures, 1951–52:* Rupert Hart-Davis Ltd., London, 1953.
JOHNSON, Samuel: *Johnson on Shakespeare: Essays and Notes*, selected and set forth with an Introduction by W. Raleigh: Oxford University Press, 1908 (repr. 1949).
JUNG, C. G.: *Modern Man in Search of a Soul:* Kegan Paul & Co. Ltd., London, 1936.
LOWES, John Livingstone: *The Road to Xanadu; A Study in the Ways of the Imagination:* Constable & Co Ltd., London, 1930.
SCHNEIDER, Elisabeth: *Coleridge, Opium and 'Kubla Khan':* University of Chicago Press, 1953.
(WARREN, Robert Penn): *'The Rime of the Ancient Mariner', by Samuel Taylor Coleridge*, with an Essay by Robert Penn Warren: Reynal & Hitchcock, New York, 1946.

CHAPTER 8 (DICKENS):

BUTT, John, and TILLOTSON, Kathleen: *Dickens at Work:* Methuen & Co., London, 1957.

CECIL, David: *Early Victorian Novelists* (1934): Penguin Books, 1948.

CHESTERTON, G. K.: Introduction to *Nicholas Nickleby:* Everyman's Library, Dent, London, 1907 (repr. 1909).

—— *Dickens:* Dodd Mead & Co., New York, 1906.

COCKSHUT, A. O. J.: *The Imagination of Charles Dickens:* Collins Ltd., London, 1961.

DICKENS, Charles: *The Works of Charles Dickens:* Special Authorized ed., Cassell & Co., London (no date).

ENGEL, Monroe: *The Maturity of Charles Dickens:* Oxford University Press, 1959.

FIELDING, K. J.: *Charles Dickens: A Critical Introduction:* Longmans, Green Ltd., London, 1958.

FORSTER, E. M.: *Aspects of the Novel:* Edward Arnold Ltd., London, 1927 (repr. 1958).

FORSTER, John: *The Life of Charles Dickens* (1892), ed. J. W. T. Ley: Cecil Palmer Ltd., London, 1928.

GISSING, George: *Charles Dickens: A Critical Study:* Blackie & Son, London, 1898.

HOUSE, Humphry: *The Dickens World:* Oxford University Press, 1941.

JOHNSON, Edgar: *Charles Dickens: His Tragedy and Triumph:* V. Gollancz Ltd., London, 1953.

KINGSMILL, Hugh: *The Sentimental Journey: A Life of Charles Dickens:* Wishart & Co., London, 1934.

LEAVIS, F. R.: *The Great Tradition: George Eliot - Henry James - Joseph Conrad,* ch. V: '*Hard Times:* An Analytic Note' (1948): Chatto & Windus Ltd., London, 1950.

LINDSAY, Jack: *Charles Dickens: A Biographical and Critical Study:* Andrew Dakers Ltd., London, 1950.

MEYNELL, Alice: 'Dickens as a Man of Letters' (1917), *English Critical Essays (Twentieth Century):* World's Classics Series, Oxford University Press, 1933 (repr. 1947).

POPE-HENNESSY, Una: *Charles Dickens,* 1812–1870: Chatto & Windus Ltd., London, 1946.

SAINTSBURY, George: Chapter on Dickens, Vol. XIII, *Camb. Hist. Eng. Lit.* (repr. 1953).

WARD, Adolphus W.: *Dickens:* English Men of Letters Series, Macmillan & Co. Ltd., London, 1908.

WATT, Ian: *The Rise of the Novel: Studies in Defoe, Richardson and Fielding:* Chatto & Windus Ltd., London, 1957.

INDEX

N.B. (quoted) indicates references where a quotation is given without further comment. Quotations which are accompanied by comment are included in the first section of each entry.

Meynell, Alice, 203–4; (quoted) 201, 218 n., 247; (mentioned) 205
Milne, A. A., (mentioned) 220 n.
Milton, John, 9, 40, 142; (quoted) 5; (mentioned) 49, 53, 143
Molière, Jean Baptiste, (mentioned) 2
Monet, Fr. Philibert, (mentioned) 9
Montaigne, Michel de, (quoted) 3–4
Montagu, Lady Mary Wortley, (quoted) 6
Moore, Henry, (mentioned) 61
More, St. Thomas, 142, 153 n.

Nero, (mentioned) 1
Nightingale, Florence, (mentioned) 218, 219

Orwell, George, (mentioned) 140, 141, 143, 220
Ovid, (quoted) 101
Owen, Robert, (mentioned) 229

Perét, Benjamin, 100
Picasso, Pablo, (mentioned) 61
Piccolomini, Cardinal Todeschini, 2
Pinturicchio, 2
Plato, 74; (quoted) 40, 79; (mentioned) 37, 161, 162
Poe, Edgar Allan, 14 n. (quoted) 23; (mentioned) 13, 14, 34, 80
Pollio, Marcus Vitruvius, (quoted) 19–20; (mentioned) 42
Pomey, Fr. François, (mentioned) 2
Pope, Alexander, 7; (quoted) 49 n., 87, 92, 150; (mentioned) 10, 138, 139, 216, 233
Price, M., (quoted) 153–4
Priestley, Joseph, 162; (mentioned) 163, 165, 170

Quintana, Ricardo (quoted) 135–6

Rabelais, François, (quoted) 3; (mentioned) 61
Radcliffe, Anne, (mentioned) 34, 73
Raphael, 2, 39
Richelet, César Pierre, (quoted) 4; (mentioned) 8
Richardson, Lady, (mentioned) 165
Richardson, Samuel, (mentioned) 237

Ruskin, John, 36–42, 44, 47, 48, 56; (quoted) 11, 14–15, 23, 206, 211; (mentioned) 18, 24, 43, 49, 214
Russell, Bertrand, (quoted) 24, 127–8, 161; (mentioned) 180

Saintsbury, George, (quoted) 205
Santayana, George, 16–17, 55–58; (quoted) 23, 82, 93, 182; (mentioned) 44, 92, 184
Schiller, Friedrich v., (mentioned) 82
Schneegans, H., (quoted) 24, 49 n.
Schneider, Elisabeth, 198, 199
Scott, Sir Walter, 32–36; (quoted) 12–13, 22–23, 85, 104; (mentioned) 236
Shaftesbury, Anthony Ashley Cooper, Earl of, (quoted) 6 n.; (mentioned) 7
Shakespeare, William, 193, 194; (quoted) 68; (mentioned) 53, 66, 232
Shaw, George Bernard, (quoted) 94, 205
Shelley, Percy Bysshe, (quoted) 89, 91, 110, 183 n.; (mentioned) 88, 187
Sheridan, Richard Brinsley, 217
Signorelli, Luca, 2
Snyder, Alice, (mentioned) 198 n.
Souriau, Maurice, (quoted) 23
Spenser, Edmund, 105; (mentioned) 106, 143
Steele, Sir Richard, (quoted) 6, 217
Stephen, Leslie, 125; (quoted) 87, 128, 132–3, 140
Stevenson, Robert Louis, 86; (mentioned) 34
Storm, Theodor, (quoted) 23
Swift, Jonathan, 104–5, 112–57; (mentioned) 100, 106, 232, 233, 247, 251
Symonds, John Addington, 51–55, 74, 99; (quoted) 15; (mentioned) 33, 49, 101

Taine, Hippolyte Adolphe, (quoted) 218
Theresa, St., 188; (mentioned) 189
Thomas, Dylan, (mentioned) 56
Tillotson, Kathleen, see Butt, John
Tillyard, E. M. W., (quoted) 56 n., 173
Titus, (mentioned) 2
Twain, Mark, (quoted) 45

Van Gogh, Vincent, (mentioned) 109
Verne, Jules, (mentioned) 147
Vitruvius, see Pollio, Marcus Vitruvius
Volkelt, J., (quoted) 21; (mentioned) 23